S0-AVJ-312

ACONCAGUA

The Stone Sentinel

◊▲◊

PERSPECTIVES OF AN EXPEDITION

Thomas E. Taplin

Eli Ely Publishers
Santa Monica, California

ACONCAGUA - The Stone Sentinel
Perspectives of an Expedition

Copyright © 1992 by Thomas E. Taplin

Printed in the United States of America.

All rights reserved under International and Pan-American Copyright Conventions. No part of this book may be reproduced or transmitted in any form or by any means, electronic or mechanical, including photocopying, recording or by any information storage system without the expressed written consent of the publisher, except for the inclusion of brief excerpts in a review.

All inquiries should be addressed to:
Eli Ely Publishers
P.O.Box 5245
Santa Monica, California 90409-5245

10 9 8 7 6 5 4 3 2 1

Library of Congress Catalog Card Number : 92-75052

Taplin, Thomas, 1953 -
  Aconcagua : the stone sentinel -
perspectives of an expedition /

  Non-fiction drama : p. 252
  Includes appendices.
  1. Mountaineering—South America—
Argentina—Cerro Aconcagua.
  2. Biography—American mountaineers.

ISBN 0-9634807-2-3 : $17.95 Softcover
ISBN 0-9634807-1-5 : $29.95 Hardcover

Cover design by Marika Van Adelsberg
Cover photograph by Tom Taplin

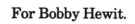

For Bobby Hewit.

CONTENTS

APPENDICES

Author's Note

◊△◊△◊△◊△◊△◊△◊△◊△◊△◊△◊

The events, places and people in this book, to the best of everyone's recollection, are all real. Only the names of the Argentine guides have been changed.

The frontispiece regional and topographic maps are designed for representational value only and are not intended to be substitutes for more accurate sources.

Comments attributed to each expedition member have been transcribed from personal interviews, diaries, correspondence and conversational notes. I am indebted to all of them for giving so generously of their time, for being honest, and for allowing me the vicarious opportunity to live days 4 to 12.

Edward FitzGerald's passages, including original punctuation and spelling, have been excerpted from the 1st American edition of his book, *The Highest Andes*, published in 1899 by Scribners.

Special thanks to everyone who provided criticisms of the early drafts.

Acknowledgements are also due Bob Bier, David and Linda Bujnicki, Debbie Dodds, Kathryn Engstrom, Pablo Fenjves, Jason Frank, Daren Henry, Victor Kotowitz, Kim McCloud, Kenny Mirman, Kirt Nakagawa, Sachi Parker, Rudy Parra, Winston Perez, Rick Ray, Mike Sanson, Marty Schmidt and Rob Wesson. This book would not have been possible without their assistance, advice and support.

I am especially grateful to Cory Freyer whose love and encouragement gave me the strength to heal and edit.

Preface

Cerra Aconcagua, rising nearly 23,000-feet, is the highest mountain outside of Asia. This book chronicles an expedition organized by an adventure-travel company whose Argentine guides would lead a summit bid via the standard route. While there are more challenging lines of ascent, such as the steep slopes of the Polish Glacier or the demanding South Face, Aconcagua's 'ruta normal' offers mountaineers the unusual chance to access a 7,000 meter peak without the technical expertise associated with other high-altitude behemoths.

By whichever route, Aconcagua is not a forgiving mountain. The perils of inadequate acclimatization, sudden storms, deficient nourishment and debilitating injuries often wreak havoc on those who gamble with this peak. The harsh reality is that there have been more than sixty reported climbing fatalities. Despite these tragedies the lure of Aconcagua persists.

Hundreds of years before European mountaineers arrived, the Incas, who venerated mountains as sacred sources of water, buried symbolic offerings to the sun and weather deities, sometimes at very high altitudes. Occasionally these rituals included human sacrifice, as was the case with a boy, seven years of age, whose mummy was discovered in 1985 at a 17,400-foot site on the southwestern ridge of Aconcagua. Such sacrifices are also thought to mark the death of an emperor, perhaps providing an escort for the journey into the after-life. Thus, Aconcagua—the name is derived from the Quechua words 'ackon cahuak' or 'sentinel of stone'—was but one in a series of high sanctuaries, important not only for their strategic proximity to a vast network of roads transversing various mountain passes, but also as spiritual passageways into a more divine world.

Edward A. FitzGerald, leader of the successful 1896-97 European team, and Matthias Zurbriggen, his Swiss guide who reached Aconcagua's summit, alone, and who claimed the first ascent, were both unaware that indigenous pre-Columbian people had already climbed fifty major peaks in the Andes, twelve of them over 20,000-feet. Altars, stonework, figurines and other artifacts have been found atop several of these peaks, and although such remains are absent from the summit of Aconcagua, presumably the Incas had already been there. Nevertheless, FitzGerald's was a bonafide expedition in the sense of mapping the region, taking photographs and triangulation measurements, as well as conducting geological and scientific studies. While FitzGerald himself never stood upon the summit, the inclusion of his 'voice' hopefully provides a historical perspective.

Today, mountaineering exploits are often interpreted as a metaphor for life's larger values. Seeking a change, defining an objective, and pushing one's physical and mental resources to the limit, all contrast nicely with our day-to-day routines. Granted, the metaphor is somewhat indulgent in the eyes of the uninitiated. Those not familiar with the spirit of such pursuits will wonder why we justify breaking from our seemingly normal lifestyles, professions and relationships to set foot on higher ground. On this expedition, everyone's desire to attain the summit only fulfilled part of a quest, for, at a certain point, Aconcagua became less a mountain than a defiant apparition; the fine line between challenge and struggle would dissolve, boundaries separating desire and obsession would blur, confidence in one's once strong body and clear mind would diminish. Those not prepared to deal with such idiosyncrasies were in for a rude and somewhat abrupt awakening.

In the course of editing these transcripts I began to fathom the diverse personalities of the expedition members in ways that probably would have been impossible while on the mountain. Those who signed up came from all walks of life, ranging from ages twenty-one to sixty-five. The participants represented the entire spectrum of mountaineering ability, from experienced climbers to absolute beginners. Half the group, interestingly, had had success on Kilimanjaro, the highest peak on the African continent. Five of us had been high-altitude trekking either in the Himalayas or Peru. One had climbed Mt. McKinley, while two others had made a previous attempt on Aconcagua. The remainder of the party had cut their teeth in the Italian Alps, Colorado Rockies or Appalachians. Yet the résumés, in the end, mattered little. Despite a shared wealth of past experience and intense commitment, we had each entered an unknown realm that was to defy every expectation.

Mountaineering, more than anything else, is a test of human nature within an inhospitable environment—'inhospitable' being a relative term coined when the going gets rough, when individual isolation impairs judgement, when poor communication between climbers (or climber and guide) breeds mistrust, when altitude sickness turns an innocent trek into a nightmare, when certain forces of nature howl vicious warnings of worn-out welcomes. Mountaineering also encompasses that murky zone of human temperament which forces one to dance along the fine line separating selfishness from self-sacrifice. Such elements, and the demands of defining and working as a harmonious team on a social and psychological level, conspire to insure nary a dull moment. Each day the bonds of solidarity either fragment or are reinforced.

The perspectives which follow reveal what beckons us to pinnacled glaciers, barren scree slopes, jumbled couloirs and rocky precipices in the first place; how well the inner journey—the motivation, movement and mindset of each individual—meshes with the overall collective effort; if the adventure (if one can call gasping for oxygen adventurous) is worthwhile and, if so, what is gained.

For many of these expedition members, the notion of scaling the 'Stone Sentinel' represented a dream in which both the longing for adventure and the hardships endured had an opportunity to be balanced by new found camaraderie and the discovery of previously untapped reserves of will-power. This is the story of some of their dreams—

dreams which became chastened and enriched; a weave of colorful, if sometimes contradictory, accounts while climbing a mountain that truly is a different genre. I hope both armchair and seasoned mountaineers alike will learn from our mistakes, as well as share in those precious moments of personal achievement.

Tom Taplin
Santa Monica, November, 1992

Cast of Characters

Thomas Borgel, born 1959 in Marietta, Georgia. Attended Kennesaw College. Vice-president of Mechadyne, a manufacturing and engineering firm in Marietta.

Previous hiking, camping and climbing experience in the Appalachian mountains {3,000-7,000-feet.} Previous best in terms of altitude: 11,000-feet while skiing.

Trevor Byles, born 1968 in Kennett Square, Pennsylvania. Attending the University of Colorado.

National Outdoor Leadership School (Wind River Range, Wyoming, 1985); high point on Kashmir Himalayan trek: 17,500-feet (1986); additional scrambles and winter mountaineering in the Colorado Rockies (Long's Peak, etc.)

Mark Cornwall, born 1950 in Bakersfield, California. B.A. in Philosophy from University of California, Santa Barbara; Juris Doctorate (1982) from the Santa Barbara School of Law. Attorney and land developer in Summerland, California. One daughter.

Camping and hiking in the Sierras; climbing in the Bavarian Alps (Mt. Watzman, 1969); Everest base camp trek (Nepal, 1983); Mt. McKinley {20,320-feet} (Alaska, 1988.)

Neil Delehey, born 1967 in Trenton, New Jersey. B.A. in English from the University of Colorado.

Rock scrambles and winter mountaineering on several 'fourteen-thousanders' in the Colorado Rockies with Trevor Byles (see above.)

Bill English, born 1944 in Wenatchee, Washington. Grew up in northern California. Attended Sacramento and Sonoma State Colleges. Owner of Riley Street Art Supplies in Santa Rosa, California.

Year-round backpacking and ski-mountaineering in the Sierras (Whitney and Shasta); high point on 1985 Peru trek: 16,000-feet.

Edward A. FitzGerald (1871-1931) Born in Litchfield, Connecticut (American mother, Canadian father.) Educated at St. Pauls School, New Hampshire and Cambridge University, England.

Early ascents (in his teens) of Piz Coruach and Piz Palu in the Engadine Valley (Swiss Alps.) Joined the Alpine Club in 1892. Accompanied Martin Conway on parts of Conway's 1894 traverse of the Alps, from Monte Viso to the Gross Glockner. First ascents of Mount Tasman, Mount Sefton, Mount Haidinger, Silberhorn and Mount Sealy, all in the New Zealand Alps (1895.) Saved from fall on Sefton by **Matthias Zurbriggen**.

FitzGerald launched his costly, well organized, and ultimately victorious expedition to Aconcagua in 1896. **Zurbriggen**, FitzGerald's Swiss guide, accomplished the first European ascent of Aconcagua, on January 14, 1897.

Dick Gordon, born 1957 in Jacksonville, Florida. Graduated from the University of Central Florida as an industrial engineer. Transferred to a defense contractor subsidiary in 1986 and resided for two years in Southern Italy. Currently the Vice President of High Mountain Land, a corporation involved with recreational leases. Resides in Virgina.
Trekking and skiing in the Alps along the Swiss/Italian border {14,000-feet.}

Mr. Kingdon Gould, Jr., born 1924 in New York City. B.A. in English from Yale (1945); L.L.D. from Yale Law School (1951.) Mr. Gould is an attorney and businessman.
Pleasure hiking in the Rocky Mountains, Andes and European Alps. Numerous adventures worldwide including Kilimanjaro (1971) and La Haute Route (ski mountaineering from Saas Fee to Chamonix; 1976), both with wife, Mary. High point with son, King, during first attempt on Aconcagua in 1986: 19,300-feet {Camp Berlin.}

Mary Gould, born 1925. Raised in New Hampshire and Connecticut. Attended Ms. Porters School in Farmington. Married to Kingdon Gould, Jr. (see above.)

Nunzie (Annunziata) Gould, born 1960 in Washington, D.C. B.A. in Humanistic Studies (1982) from John Hopkins.
Spent all her summers and vacation time while growing up in the mountains. Hiking in the Colorado Rockies; high point on Kilimanjaro: 16,500-feet (1971.)

Kingdon Gould, III, born 1948 in New Haven, Connecticut. Married with two children. Self-employed.
Basic camping in the Catskills', New Hampshire's White Mountains, and the Rocky Mountains. High point with father during first attempt on Aconcagua in 1986: 19,300-feet.

Gregg Lewis, born 1956 in Scranton, Pennsylvania. Graduate of Georgia Tech. Aeronautical engineer, living in Savannah, Georgia. Married.
Basic camping in the Appalachian mountains; also Kilimanjaro (1987.)

Mike Milford, born 1934 in Poznan, Poland. Graduated from School of Economics Marine Faculty in Sopot, Poland (1958.) Masters degree in Marine Economics (1963.) Moved to the United States in 1965. Supervisor at Micro Data USA, Inc. Married with one son.
Kilimanjaro, 1988 {Uhuru peak/19,340-feet.}

Dr. Anil Patel, born 1948 in Eldoret, Kenya. Educated in England; M.D. from University of Nairobi. Anesthesiologist based at the South Hampton Hospital on Long Island. Married with two daughters.
First climbed Kilimanjaro in 1967; also Mt. Kenya. Subsequent hiking and rock climbing with Outward Bound in the Cascade Range, Wenatchee Mountains in Washington State, and North Carolina.

Craig Roland, born 1935 in Lincoln, Nebraska. Bachelor of Architecture from the University of Washington. Married with one daughter. Architect, living in Santa Rosa, California.

Extensive backpacking throughout the United States (Mt. Rainier, Shasta, etc.), Canada and Alaska; also Kashmir trek, Himalayas, 1987 (high point: 17,500-feet.)

Greg Stasiak, born 1963 in New York. Attended Columbia University, School of General Studies. Cable television contractor in New York City.

Tom Taplin, born 1953 in Denver, Colorado. B.A. in English from Lake Forest College; BFA in Film / Video from California Institute of the Arts. Free-lance cinematographer and adventure / travel photographer.

Rock climbing in Colorado Rockies (Ashcrofters and Telluride Guide School, 1969-70); backpacking in Europe, the Sierras and Japan Alps; treks in the Annapurna Sanctuary and Everest region of Nepal, 1987 (high point: 18,300-feet.)

{Information at time of expedition}

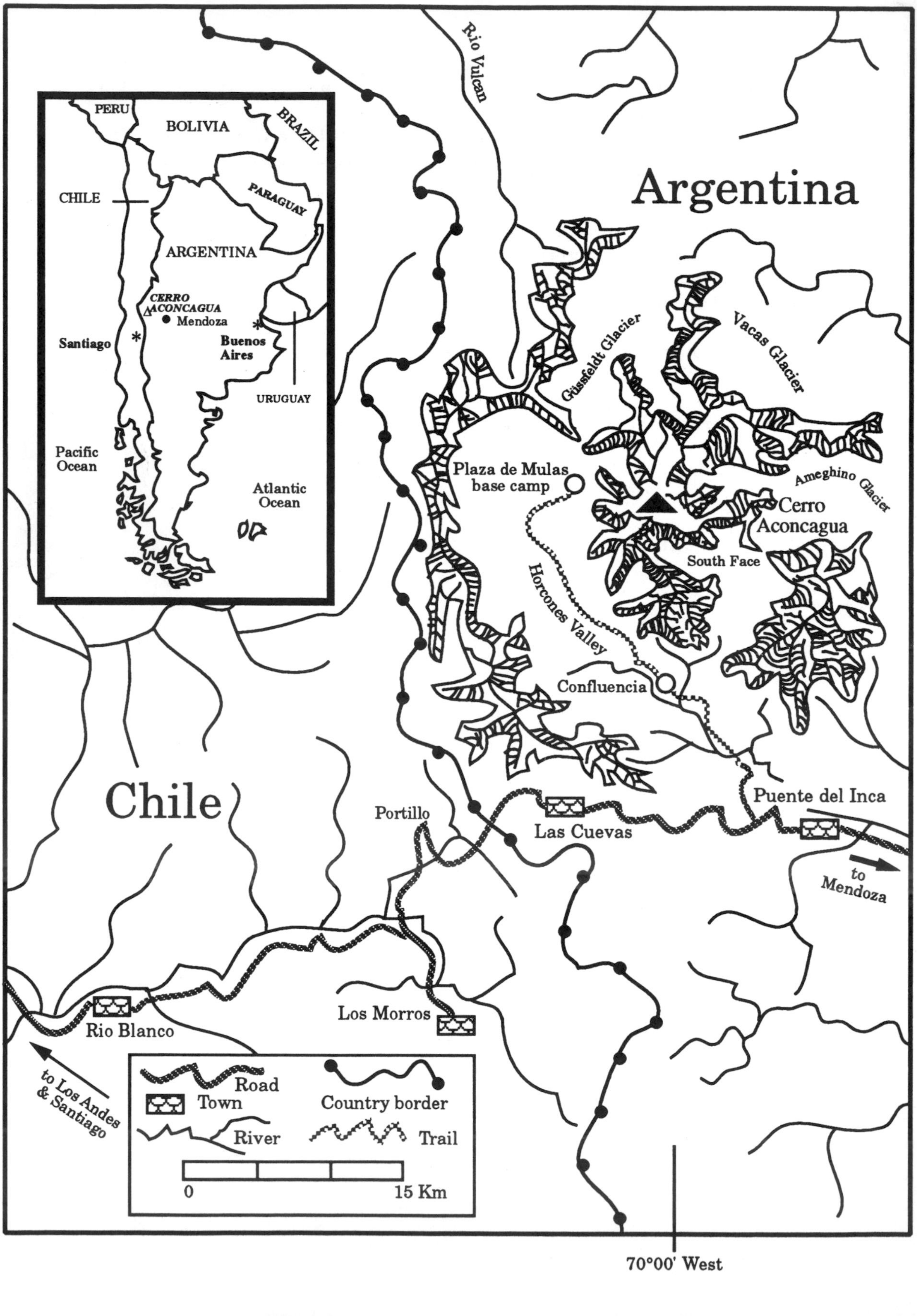

Rio Vulcan
Argentina
PERU
BOLIVIA
BRAZIL
CHILE
PARAGUAY
ARGENTINA
CERRO ACONCAGUA
Mendoza
Santiago
Buenos Aires
URUGUAY
Pacific Ocean
Atlantic Ocean
Güssfeldt Glacier
Vacas Glacier
Plaza de Mulas base camp
Ameghino Glacier
Cerro Aconcagua
South Face
Horcones Valley
Confluencia
Chile
Portillo
Las Cuevas
Puente del Inca
to Mendoza
Los Morros
Rio Blanco
to Los Andes & Santiago
Road
Town
Country border
River
Trail
0
15 Km
70°00' West

Camps along Aconcagua's ruta normal.

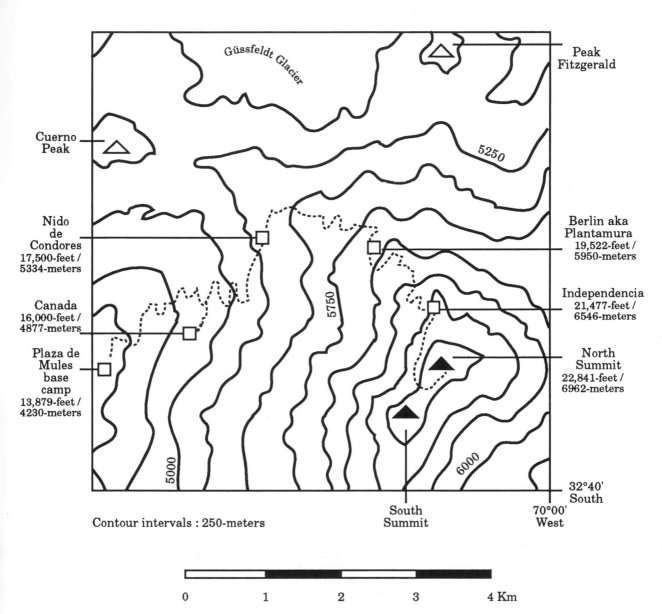

Güssfeldt Glacier

Peak Fitzgerald

Cuerno Peak

5250

Nido de Condores
17,500-feet / 5334-meters

Berlin aka Plantamura
19,522-feet / 5950-meters

Independencia
21,477-feet / 6546-meters

Canada
16,000-feet / 4877-meters

5750

Plaza de Mules base camp
13,879-feet / 4230-meters

North Summit
22,841-feet / 6962-meters

5000

6000

32°40' South

70°00' West

South Summit

Contour intervals : 250-meters

0   1   2   3   4 Km

Part 1

Other Time Zones

"There have been joys too great to be described in words, and there have been griefs upon which I have not dared to dwell; and with these in mind I say, Climb if you will, but remember that courage and strength are naught without prudence, and that a momentary negligence may destroy the happiness of a lifetime. Do nothing in haste; look well to each step; and from the beginning think what may be the end."

Edward Whymper
Scrambles Amongst the Alps

"Everything is sweetened by risk."

Alexander Smith
Dreamthorp. Of Death and the Fear of Dying

< 1 >

URBAN GAUCHOS

CRAIG ROLAND   My love affair with the mountains began when I was a little kid running around on the plains of Nebraska. I thought, If I ever see a mountain I'll be in heaven. Not long after that, my parents moved to Seattle which is located in a mountainous region.

Most of my previous experience has had do with backpacking, along with a few non-technical scrambles in the Sierras and Cascades. A couple of years ago I took a trek through Kashmir in the Himalayas and loved it.

For some time I'd been interested to see if I could get up a mountain that was 20,000-feet or over. I thought first of all about McKinley, did a little investigation, then decided there were too many 'iffy' conditions. My decision about McKinley was based not so much on the danger, but the high probability of not making the summit due to weather and extreme cold. So I started thinking about South America.

In some of the climbing and outdoor magazines I came across advertisements for Aconcagua. I knew it was the highest mountain in the Western Hemisphere, and darned if you couldn't walk right up it— at least according to all the articles I'd read. I did some research, contacted a number of companies that sponsor commercial trips to Aconcagua, and hit upon this particular company as the one to go with.

Commercial expeditions are big business. A lot of people pay their money to go off into the wilderness. Only in the last ten years can people go anywhere in the whole damn world by joining a commercial company; now you can go to the South Pole or Everest or wherever. What took explorers months or years to achieve before, is now being achieved fairly easily. What people encounter when they go on these trips—the contrast between expectations and reality—is a fascinating subject.

E.A. FITZGERALD   We sailed from Southampton in the R.M.S.S. Thames, on 15th October 1896, and on 29th November we left Buenos Aires, en route for Mendoza and the mountains. The director of the Great Western Railway had very kindly placed a small sleeping-carriage at our disposal. This had been coupled at the end of the train, but as it was not swung on bogey tracks, an absolute necessity in these countries, where the permanent way is not kept in the best of repair, we were nearly rattled to pieces. The journey takes about thirty-six hours, and when we drew up at the terminus in Mendoza we were so shaken and fatigued, that we could scarcely stand up.

TOM TAPLIN   What caught my eye, when I stepped off the plane and started walking across the tarmac, was a large banner decorating the one and only terminal building: "Welcome to Mendoza. Home of the

Fiesta de la Vendimia." Mendoza is the wine center of Argentina, and the Fiesta de la Vendimia—the wine festival—is an annual event which usually takes place at the beginning of March when the grapes are harvested. Certainly didn't want to miss that. At the time I thought, With a successful summit attempt we can get back here and have two celebrations rolled into one.

Arriving at the Mendoza airport was like that scene in *Butch Cassidy and the Sundance Kid* when they flee to South America and disembark in the middle of the Bolivian boondocks: a hot, dry wind was blowing; dust was swirling around; shacks on the outskirts of town. The beaches and lush hills of Rio de Janeiro, flown over a few hours earlier, were but a wistful memory. Once you cruise into town on one of the major boulevards, of course, the realization hits that Mendoza isn't a wild-west frontier outpost at all; it's one of Argentina's provincial capitals, and it has every modern convenience.

CRAIG ROLAND   Mendoza is a much larger city than what I had imagined. The trip material implied a city of 150,000, but the population is more like 600,000. I'm an architect and was immediately struck by the amenities of the streets. It was so much fun to be on the streets with those enormous, overhanging trees. Mendoza should really be a guide to all hot-weather cities; I'll bet those trees reduce the surface temperature 10-degrees. The mixture of high energy, color, and street life was very interesting.

E.A. FITZGERALD   One day we took the opportunity of visiting the old Mendoza that had been levelled by the great earthquake of 1861. It lies about a mile from the new town, and is one mass of ruins, not a single house remaining intact. There is something sad and depressing about these white, plastered walls, relics of the old Hispano-Moorish church architecture, invariably seen in all South American towns, and these heaps of fallen stones, broken arches, and sightless windows; and if you peer through the chinks you can see at the bottom of some cellar the bleached bones of the poor victims.

The old city covered some two hundred acres, and contained seven churches and three convents. The earthquake took place on 20th March 1861. It was an Ash Wednesday, after sunset, when the churches were crowded with the pious population who had thronged by the thousands to the solemn services of that impressive commemoration. The very first shocks levelled every building to the ground, and the greatest heap of the bones of the people lies under the ruins of the old abode of worship. Surely purgatory cannot long retain its hold upon the souls of the unprepared, overtaken as they were at their worship. The very traces of the streets were obliterated, some trees of the Alameda and a fragment of a church alone remaining erect, and 13,000 souls perished while only 1600 were spared. For a whole week fire raged among the ruins, and the robbers at their work of pillage paid no heed to the cries of the wretches buried in living graves.

TOM TAPLIN   Not much remains from Mendoza's colonial past. Possibly the only remnant from the original infrastructure are those deep, open water channels between some of the sidewalks and streets. That's part of an old, ingenious irrigation system which apparently is still functional; the downtown area is a wonderful oasis of foliage, gardens, parks and fountains. As a precaution against earthquakes there are not many tall buildings; the mulberry and sycamore trees are taller than most of the buildings. The city is laid out around a large central square, with a monument of San Martin rearing up on his horse, rallying his troops to cross the Andes to liberate Chile.

I checked into the Grand Balbi Hotel and was told my 'friends' were waiting in the room. Although I didn't know anyone else on the expedition, I had a general idea of who was coming from phone conversations with the commercial company—"This person lives here, this is their profession, they have this amount of mountaineering experience." I went upstairs, knocked on the door—no answer. I went in and found a human form sprawled sideways on one bed, totally oblivious to the world. So I quietly puttered around, did a little unpacking—all the time keeping a wary eye on the comatose one, wondering, If my 'friend' here regains consciousness, will he still want to climb Aconcagua?

This dead soul eventually stirred, rubbed his eyes, got his big, droopy moustache in order, and introduced himself as Mark Cornwall. Even though we both felt jet lagged, Mark suggested going for a beer at a nearby cafe. What better way to get into the rhythm of Mendoza and size each other up? After polishing off three large bottles of cerveza neither of us felt much of anything. We must have sat at that cafe for two hours, letting the world go by. The traditional afternoon siesta had just ended and the streets were bustling with tourists, shoppers and people heading back to work. It's so great to arrive in a new country, kick back, and watch everything unfold.

Mark and I regaled one another with travel stories, no doubt embellishing our daring youthful exploits past all bounds of credibility. We talked about mountaineers who had influenced us, especially Maurice Herzog, whose book, *Annapurna*, is such a classic.[1] And we reminisced about Nepal because Mark had also done the Everest trek.

Spending a month in Nepal was really the catalyst for me; it reawakened a dormant passion to get into high-altitude mountaineering. How can you trek through the Himalayas, viewing some of the most beautiful mountains in the world, and not want to climb them? One can have that desire at an early age, but sometimes life gets in the way.

---

[1] Maurice Herzog, French mountaineer, succeeded with Louis Lachenal in scaling the first 8,000-meter peak, Annapurna 1, in 1950.

MARK CORNWALL   There was once a notion in my mind, formulated in college, that I would be the first person to solo Everest. I found out later this is a delusion of grandeur a lot of men suffer from. I planned on climbing Everest when I was thirty-three years old because that is the age when Christ died on the cross. It had a symbolic significance as the death of one life and the rebirth of another. Remember, I was a philosophy major and these were the types of things I was constantly thinking about—how to make meaning out of existence. I'd been to 14,000-feet. Who cared if Everest was just another 14,000? It was a little ambitious but see, I had it all planned out. The problem was getting through the Khumbu ice-fall, so I was going to take a long aluminum pole to lay across the crevasses. That wasn't a bad idea!

On my way to Nepal, I met Dick Bass who co-wrote *Seven Summits*. Bass is a big aficionado of Richard Halliburton, an American explorer from the 1920s and 1930s who climbed the Matterhorn, Fuji and Mount Olympus, swam the Panama Canal and the Hellespont channel in Greece, flew an airplane around the world, and did a number of other things. Halliburton made a living by travelling, doing these physical feats, then writing about them in books like *New World's To Conquer* and *Seven League Boots*. That's the kind of person I wanted to be.

Bass had repeated some of Halliburton's adventures with his own kids. But the more interesting thing Bass laid out—the guy is a magnificent talker—was his 'seven summits' dream; his plan to climb the seven highest peaks on each continent.[2] Bass was open to me joining his Everest expedition in terms of being 'support personnel.' I went up to base camp, but going higher on the mountain was out of the question. I wasn't even aware that Reinhold Messner had already soloed Everest, without oxygen, a few years before.

Let's face it, Bass is legendary. He's a bullshitter, but part of his quest was to prove that he is more than bullshit, that he could go out and climb those seven mountains. And he did prove it.

Seven Summits has influenced a lot of people. It certainly influenced my decision about both Mt. McKinley and Aconcagua. With McKinley I was looking for something that would make me feel good about the achievement. The mountain climbing experiences from earlier in my life had given me the greatest pleasure and more reward than anything else I'd done. McKinley, which this particular commercial company had also organized, worked out just great, although it would have been

---

2 The highest mountains on each continent are: Asia—Mt. Everest {29, 028-feet / 8,848 meters}; South America—Cerro Aconcagua {22,841-feet / 6,962 meters}; North America—Mt. McKinley (aka Denali) {20,320-feet / 6,194 meters}; Africa—Kilimanjaro {19,340-feet / 5,894 meters}; Europe—Elbrus {18,481-feet / 5,633 meters}; Antarctica—Vinson Massif {16,067-feet / 4,897 meters.}

In Australia Dick Bass and Frank Wells chose Kosciusko {7,316-feet / 2,228 meters} while Canadian Patrick Morrow, who also completed a seven-summits venture, claims Carstensz Pyramid {16,023-feet / 4,884 meters} in Irian Jaya New Guinea as the highest peak on the Australasia continental shelf.

easier at twenty-seven than thirty-eight; on one carry my heart almost exploded.

Attempting to climb the highest mountain in South America after having just climbed the highest mountain in North America poetically sounded very good. I also knew Aconcagua would not be as dangerous as McKinley; there aren't the crevasses, and there is not constant ice and snow. I expected Aconcagua to be better because on McKinley you are always roped in, you have no freedom of motion, you cannot leave camp, and you have no privacy at all—everyone has to piss and defecate in front of everybody else. You're just like a pack of animals.

TOM TAPLIN   Back at the hotel Mark introduced me to our third roommate, Dr. Anil Patel. Anil looks more like a Yukon fur trapper than an anesthesiologist from the Hamptons.' Anil confirmed we were leaving the next morning for Puente del Inca, the starting point for our hike up Aconcagua.

As the three of us were organizing gear, Anil pulled out a pair of tattered leather boots. Those boots were just incredible relics; they looked like they'd been on a few mountaineering escapades. Even though I didn't want to impose my own finicky sense about equipment upon anyone, I knew the previous expedition up Aconcagua, organized by our company several weeks earlier, had endured 42° below zero on summit day. I assumed everyone had come prepared for horrendous conditions. I said, "Anil, don't you have double plastic boots? Are you going to the summit in those clunkers? Your toes will freeze with crampons on."

Anil, like most doctors, has a very polite, laconic disposition. He replied that his boots would be fine, that they worked well the last time he went to the top of Kilimanjaro, and that his feet would stay warm. Anil seemed self-assured, but I was glad when Mark showed concern as well.

We had a group meeting at 10:30 that evening in the hotel dining room. Everyone, except for Anil, Mark and myself, had come down with a friend or family member: Lewis and Borgel, the two Georgia crackers, were there; Craig Roland, a Shelby Foote look-alike; Bill English, Craig's sidekick; and two brothers from North Carolina. Buccaneers of the hills? I've seen more motley-looking crews.

CRAIG ROLAND   Only about three-quarters of the group were gathered for that meeting. The Gould family and Dick Gordon were already at Puente del Inca, and one or two others had not joined us yet.

My impressions were that the group was relatively young and, with one or two exceptions, strong and in good shape. I had expected older people partly because the trip cost a lot of money and I associate that with being a little more established in life—having the time to take off and pay for it. So I was a little surprised to see people in their twenties and thirties, but I wasn't concerned about age differences.

THOMAS BORGEL   Gregg Lewis and I planned this trip for a year and a half. The manager of the commercial company had told us, "You need to be in great shape. If you're not, we won't take you." Three times a week we would load seventy pound packs on our backs and climb 1200-feet up Mt. Kennesaw. Kennesaw is the sight of a famous Civil War battle—the battle for Atlanta. We were feeling pretty good. Lewis and I sweated the electrocardiograms and all that, thinking we'd be going with top-notch climbers. It turned out that the group was run-of-the-mill guys off the street. That was surprising.

TOM TAPLIN   Enrique, our Argentine head guide, introduced himself. The guy is balding—I could relate to that—probably in his late-thirties and built like an ox. According to his résumé, Enrique holds the first winter ascent of the Polish Glacier route, as well as an ascent of Aconcagua's South Face. In the winter he's an avalanche patrolman at the Las Lenas ski area. He also works for the commercial company as a guide on Denali.

Enrique may have thought the mood of the group a little too lackadaisical. Of course, Enrique comes across as a pretty intense guy; he has a very no-nonsense demeanor. Granted, this was not a 'get acquainted' scene for Enrique; he probably still had a lot of logistical details to iron out. He collected everyone's medical forms and EKG printouts, then briefly outlined our schedule for the next few days.

THOMAS BORGEL   I remember Neil Delehey and Trevor Byles staggering in. They'd been drinking since early afternoon. Enrique gave them that *look*. Oh Jesus, Enrique was hot! Enrique, as a guide, should have been prepared for this sort of behavior. I mean, these kids were in their early twenties, just out of school. I raised hell at that age too. If Neil and Trevor didn't want to make the summit of Aconcagua, that was their business. When you're that young, however, you're going to ward off the effects of drinking; you might wake up with a hangover, but it won't hang around long.

Some of the older people thought Neil and Trevor getting drunk was a piss-poor attitude—that the general attitude should be serious. I felt the opposite. I'd already decided I'd give the top of the mountain my best shot, but that I was going to have a good time and not be a 'stiff-neck.'

NEIL DELEHEY   To be honest, Trevor and I were out of our gourds. We drank three bottles of wine—really out of hand. Then we passed out and woke up when the meeting was going on. We came down and just kept a low profile.

I didn't expect Trevor and myself to be the youngest people on the trip. I expected the group to be our age or younger. About the only thing I remember was that I felt I'd definitely come prepared as far as conditioning and equipment.

TOM TAPLIN   Enrique informed us that unseasonably warm weather would prevail for our trek up the standard route, and therefore recommended leaving our ice axes and seat harnesses in Mendoza. I wasn't going to argue with Enrique, reputedly one of the top climbers in Argentina, but I honestly felt, and still feel, such advice to be presumptuous and unjustified. The reason is because Aconcagua, like most large mountains, creates its own weather. Fast-moving, unpredictable storms on Aconcagua are legendary, hence its reputation as a killer mountain. There are very good reasons that items such as ice axes and seat harnesses are listed on the equipment list in the company's pre-departure information packet. Who in their right mind wants to be stuck on a steep snow-field in a blizzard at 20,000-feet without an ice axe?

GREGG LEWIS   One impression I had was that Enrique showed little concern toward the other gear we had brought down. In fact he never checked our gear. I could have had L.L. Bean goof-ball shoes or a K-Mart windbreaker, and Enrique never would have noticed until we were on the mountain.

MARK CORNWALL   Enrique asked everyone, "Do you want me to check your gear?" No one took Enrique up on that, so he said, "Fine. Good." How were the people who had never been on an expedition supposed to know? On McKinley it was mandatory to check all equipment, and I'd found going through the gear piece by piece very enlightening.

Taplin and I had suggested to Dr. Patel that he try to get another pair of boots. His leather boots were very worn out and shabby. Patel had no concept for what the hell he was getting into by even contemplating using those boots he'd brought down. To me this indicated that, even though a person can talk as though they know what they are doing, sometimes they really don't. Dr. Patel, at the meeting, did arrange to borrow some bunny boots from Enrique. Bunny boots are very warm; they really make your feet sweat.

Patel left his old boots at the hotel when we left Mendoza, but actually I ended up with them. Somehow the maid found his boots and put them inside my pack.

◊∆◊∆◊∆◊∆◊∆◊∆◊

TOM TAPLIN   We left Mendoza the next afternoon, cruised through the affluent southern suburbs, then headed northwest on the trans-Andean highway. The first big peak we saw was Cerro de la Plata—the Silver Mountain—looming above the haze, attempting to disguise itself as a snow-capped cloud.

We took a brief rest stop halfway out a vast arid plain, at the small town of Uspallata, where Enrique presented some documents at a police check point. From there we followed the muddy Rio Mendoza, winding up through treeless valleys marking the start of the Andes' foothills.

One budget-minded guidebook stated that the cheapest mode of transportation from Mendoza to Puente del Inca would be in the back of an army truck. Instead we had a comfortable, air-conditioned bus, giving everyone a chance to spread out and relax.

The drive, for the most part, was quiet, introspective. It's 160 kilometers and took about three hours. Various topography maps were passed around, none of them all that great. Rumor has it that the U.S. Defense Mapping Agency produces the best topos. Good luck procuring one of those.

There were a few new faces on-board. Pépe, one of our assistant guides, had joined us. Enrique and Pépe are climbing partners and have made numerous ascents up various routes of Aconcagua. They sat in the front of the bus talking with Mike Milford and Greg Stasiak, two more clients fresh off the plane, that morning, from New York. Stasiak was wearing loafers. I'm usually not too judgmental, but for some reason that stood out.

THOMAS BORGEL   On the bus ride I started to focus on the expedition and worked on keeping my mental attitude right. Because this was the first mountaineering experience I was going to have in six years, I'd had a rough time deciding whether to put myself through the next sixteen days rather than go to some beach. All I'd heard were horror stories. Everybody I talked to said, "Aconcagua is going to kick your ass." I have four articles, and in each one the author is about to die. I never read an article about the mountain where someone made it up without a problem.

Reading all those articles is what drove me to do the trip. Aconcagua had become a big, big challenge. The people who wrote the articles had had a hard time, so I thought, Hey, I can do this, and I'm going to do it.

< 2 >

THE TRIBE GATHERS AT PUENTE DEL INCA

KINGDON GOULD III   My father and I attempted Aconcagua three years previous to this trip. That time we went with an American guide who had not been to Aconcagua before. Although he was a good climber, he was not a very good guide. We hiked to 19,000-feet on the Normal route, then a big storm hit. Everyone came down off the mountain, back to base camp. My father and I ran out of time and had to return home.

At Puente del Inca, on our way back, we met Enrique and the director of this commercial company. We talked to some of their clients and they'd had an enjoyable experience. When we had a chance to go back to Aconcagua we contacted this company. Knowing that Enrique was to be the guide gave us additional comfort because we felt he knew the mountain.

Picture my father, my sister, Nunzie, and myself running around before this trip, assembling our gear. You can spend an inordinate amount of time deciding which goddamn cup to take.

MR. GOULD   King, Nunzie and myself were testing different types of equipment: Does this fit?, does that fit?; Can you wear this over that?; If you have these kinds of socks on, will you get a blister?; How much do the shoe laces weigh?

At 5:30 the morning of our departure I woke up, then Mary, my wife, woke up. She said, "You know, I think I'll go with you after all." We'd been inviting Mary to come along and then, when she said she didn't want to about a month before, we just hadn't asked her anymore because we assumed she really didn't want to go.

I said, "It's 5:30 Sunday morning! You don't have any gear! You're not in shape and you haven't been training!" Then I asked, "Do you really want to go?"

"Yes, I really want to."

"Well, let's start in."

We got on the horn, made the plane reservation, and I wondered, What in the world will we do for clothing? Nunzie and King took Mary to REI {Recreational Equipment Inc.} They sat her down in a chair and started putting hats on her, sleeping bags, boots, crampons. They had Mary outfitted in an hour—what it had taken Nunzie, King and me three months to assemble!

MARY GOULD   Although I'd read my husband's diary and had heard things from his first trip that didn't really make me long to go to Aconcagua, I woke up that morning and thought, You know, when crumpets are passed, take crumpets.

We've done adventure trips for many years with the children, sometimes with our grand-children, and they have always been wonderful. It's great for a family to travel together to a mountain like Aconcagua and have an adventure with people you really care about.

NUNZIE GOULD   King and Dad's previous trip had been pretty raunchy in terms of a guide who was not responsible for the group, food which was inadequate, and sanitation problems which really disturbed both of them. Mom kept saying she could not believe Dad was going back to face all those conditions again. Her motivation was that if Dad was returning to try this adventure, then she wanted to be next to him. This is something she has done all her life. Mom is quite a person. She is very strong, both physically and mentally. I think she figured: 'If my husband is going to die on this mountain, I want to be there.'

When Dad and King decided to return to Aconcagua they invited me to come along. I'd been living overseas and had just returned to the United States. Leaving my friends and my job was quite a change. I probably should have gone somewhere other than my parents' home which has all its paddings and comforts. My folks realized I was at a crossroads and that perhaps the trip might help me get my life together.

Both King and I wanted to do a trip with Dad. That was our main motivation for going to Aconcagua. Dad always seeks a challenge. He can be kind of head strong. We really would like him to succeed without doing crazy things. His judgement is good—he was in reconnaissance during World War II—but you never know on one of these trips how well the group will take care of each individual member.

In general, our family doesn't seek out these large commercial groups. We'd rather go, not make a big deal about it, and just enjoy the outdoors. We are a big family; nine kids. King is the eldest boy—he's number two—and I'm number eight.

When our family arrived in Mendoza we got in touch with Enrique. The desk clerk at the Aconcagua Hotel arranged for Mom to get a doctor's appointment for a physical and an electrocardiogram. Supposedly these are required for climbing permission. I knew what my EKG said, but who gives a damn about that. It just means I would not die from a heart attack. That's how I interpret EKG. Enrique accompanied us to the permit office. When we presented our EKG's and our climbing histories, it was a joke. When does the permit office get around to using a climber's history? Do the guides read it, or is it just a statistic? I don't know. The Department of Permits was quite a farce.[3]

We didn't spend a lot of time in Mendoza. The following day our family hired a minibus and drove up to Puente del Inca.

KINGDON GOULD III   We had three days at Puente before everyone else arrived. I was pretty tuckered. You fly down from the States, don't

---

[3] The permit process has since been greatly facilitated. A simple form can be filled out at the Direccion Provincial de Tourismo office on Avda. San Martin. Medical statements and EKG's are not currently required, although this could change. The permit fee ($80 in 1991) is subject to yearly increases.

sleep much, and, if you're like me, you haven't slept much the week before because you're trying to wind up business matters and working late hours. Being at Puente del Inca a few days early gave us time to rest, as well as acclimate. My father and I had done this on our first trip as well.

We did some hiking in the hills behind the church. From up there you can see the South Face of Aconcagua and part of the Horcones Valley. You take pictures of the South Face, then wind around to the north, and walk up the easy side. For my sister and mother, who had not been there before, visualizing what we were going to do was very helpful.

It's fun to have quiet time with one's family. And it's nice to get away from the hassles I have to deal with—arguing with leasing brokers, government officials, and contractors. Sometimes I wonder why I do this type of work. There are good reasons to do it, but my work does not give me the same joy that I find in the mountains.

Aconcagua is awesome in the real sense of the word and I enjoy that feeling. I like to get out there and sleep under the stars. I like the powers of nature and feel it's good for mankind to come across greater powers than himself—powers he cannot control. This makes one humble and gives a perspective aside from the beauty involved.

NUNZIE GOULD   Spending several days in Puente del Inca puts you in tune with other hikers, the weather, the scenery, and the change in culture. The contrast between incomers and outgoers is great. The main lodge could be a ski chalet up in the Alps somewhere, with all those flags, pictures, pitons and ropes hanging on the walls. The waiters would bustle around when bus loads of tourists came in for lunch and then, in the afternoon, the scene would slow down.

There was definitely a climbers affinity in that place. In general, when people came off the mountain, other groups were interested in them—"How was it?; How far did you get?; What were the conditions?; Was it cold?; Did you summit?; How many days did you spend?; What did you eat?"

There was a Japanese guy at one meal who was eating by himself. I finally got up the guts to ask, "Do you want to come over and join us?" He looked so damn lonely. We talked with him about the fact that our family had been to Japan, and he talked of his plans to solo the mountain.

I chatted with Dick Gordon out on the grass outside the hosteria, where the pigs, donkeys and horses grazed the grass and walked through at night. I didn't talk with him too much. I hadn't realized, at that stage, he would be part of our group. Our family had several meals in the dining room, but Dick was usually sitting with another couple.

DICK GORDON   Originally I had signed up with another expedition through Fernando Grajales in Puente del Inca. That expedition started having problems when I arrived in Mendoza. The agency—the rendezvous contact—told me the trip had been postponed for five days. They were real sketchy about how many people were going to be there and this type of thing. I decided to head up to Puente del Inca before anybody else was due to arrive.

Fernando and I trekked around Puente del Inca for three days. We hiked on both the north and south sides of the valley, and also made a trek over the top of the Los Penitentes ski area. At the time I thought these treks would build up a little endurance and would help with the success of the venture. Fernando would say, "People are coming. It is looking good."

Fernando and I became friends. The guy is tough; he was a member of the first team to ascend the South-West ridge of Aconcagua, had climbed the Matterhorn, and also participated in a couple Himalayan expeditions. Fernando was a true mountaineer back in those days.

On the day everybody was supposed to arrive Fernando said, "I have some bad news. The expedition has been cancelled." Even now I'm really not sure what happened, except that the original group I intended to meet never left their place of origin.

Fernando and I sat down over lunch and tried to figure out what to do. Right after lunch Enrique's group rolled in. We decided to talk with Enrique to see if I could join his group. Enrique said he had a large group. Fernando felt comfortable and explained to Enrique that I would not be a liability. Enrique could have said that there was not enough room, or hesitated about me even coming along to base camp. But I'd come a long ways and had many more weeks to spend in South America, so I would have gone ahead and attempted to solo the mountain. Enrique was real good about it and was happy to have an addition. I piggy-backed on.

◊∆◊∆◊∆◊∆◊∆◊∆◊

TOM TAPLIN   Mendoza is 2,500-feet above sea level. Puente del Inca is nearly 9,000-feet. That's an invigorating change. You breathe in some of that fresh mountain air, scan the incredibly stark and beautiful Cuevas Valley, and think, Ah yes, the great outdoors. Across the road is a military compound with an armed sentry at the gate, nervously cradling a machine gun, and it's like—'At least the great outdoors is well protected.'

Besides the main lodge, there is a smattering of other small buildings: stores, houses, a post office, a school. Puente means 'bridge' and refers to a famous landmark behind the hosteria which, essentially, is a natural formation of mineral deposits spanning the Rio Mendoza. There's a dilapidated building—kind of a multi-roomed primitive spa—built into the cliff below the bridge. Pipes tap hot, sulfuric underground water into large wash-basins in each room. And there were several small dip holes scattered around the hillside, bubbling with lukewarm water.

Dick and the Gould's already had their own accommodations. Everyone who rode up on the bus settled into two dormitory-type rooms.

Oh god, those creaky bunk beds! No one could have slept well that night. We were all waiting for those flimsy bunks to collapse at any moment, not to mention a snore monster by the name of Bill English.

After arriving at Puente, we settled in, re-shuffled gear, then took our expedition packs to a storage area where Enrique and Pépe sorted the mule loads. The storage area also serves as a depository for saddles, stirrups and other riding paraphernalia, which was neatly stacked or hanging on the walls. A few of us deliberated in there for several minutes selecting ski poles with some character which would serve as walking sticks.

Enrique gave me 'snack' packets to be distributed to everyone for the hike to base camp. These packets consisted of candy drops, candy nuggets, hard candy, a couple candy bars, a few nuts, and an orange. Mark had already warned me about the need for the company to hire a nutritionist. After one gander at those candy bags it was obvious there was going to be a lot of black-market activity in the trading of supplemental food.

◊△◊△◊△◊△◊△◊

NUNZIE GOULD   Everyone could have been introduced to each other at our first group dinner at Puente del Inca. That should have been more important. Everyone was looking at everybody else, or feeling each other out on the previous experience of the person sitting across from them, but I felt kind of distant from the whole group. The group was so big there was no way for people at one end of the long table to converse with those at the other end.

We had been served a huge meal, then Stasiak got the waiter to bring another chicken leg with french fries. When he and Mike found out that it only cost $6 they were ecstatic. For anybody getting off the plane from New York and realizing you could get another dinner for $6 was great. Dad and King also ate as much as possible to stoke up their bodies.

TOM TAPLIN   All the members of the expedition were gathered together for the first time, and the mood was jovial. At least Anil Patel and I were enjoying ourselves; we complimented our entrees with a bottle of Carcassonne vino. Everyone seemed excited and confident. There was certainly an abundance of individual character.

The only thorn was that we had somehow grown to a group of eighteen people instead of fifteen. I'm sure the unspoken question on everyone's mind was: 'Will the masses gel?' It was difficult to comprehend how such a large contingent could move harmoniously up the mountain no matter how positive the collective disposition. The alternative, which Enrique implied would happen at our meeting in Mendoza, would be for everyone to travel together to base camp, then split into two groups. Even if there weren't two separate groups, there is an inherent 'dropout' factor of sickness, non-acclimation, or whatever.

One assumes that the strongest and more healthy members will forge ahead to the high camps, creating a smaller, more compatible summit team.

MARK CORNWALL   I'd seen large groups in the Himalayas and had felt sorry for them. I'd say to myself, "Look at that, a big old tour group moving up the valleys." To me it was embarrassing. So I was apprehensive about having a large group from the very beginning.

The most important element on these climbs is how well one interrelates with other people. I couldn't wait for the group to divide up so we could start doing our trip in a personal fashion. In a large group you just don't get any personal reward, or rapport, from anybody. A large group takes that intimacy away. And I think this is why Enrique did not check our gear; you can't give personal service to eighteen people.

But I laughed my ass off at that dinner—almost on the verge of being silly—because I was happy to be with the group and happy to be on the trip. One is looking forward, with a little anticipation, as to what is going to happen. That is the whole adventure.

< 3 >

WHERE RIVERS MEET
Expedition Day 1

CRAIG ROLAND   The building I particularly liked, and spent some time at, was the little chapel back on the hillside at Puente del Inca. I went there in the morning just as the sun was rising and took some great pictures. The facade faces directly east and the sun came pouring through that round window into the stone interior. It was just beautiful.

TOM TAPLIN   Roland had a gleam in his eyes—this was before breakfast—and he said to me, "Have you been up to the church? You've got to go up there right now! The light is amazing!" The early morning light was fantastic—everything was tinted gold—and the shadows along the hills ran deep and long.

The church stands at the bottom of a talus field on the other side of the bridge. It has a corrugated metal roof and big, heavy doors which swing open to reveal a simple altar and several small religious statues. There are some ruins of another hosteria near the church. The locals swear an avalanche came down, miraculously jumped over the church and razed this hosteria—which makes a great story, except that the damage was probably earthquake-related.

After breakfast everyone assembled in front of the hosteria. Borgel and Lewis were taking pictures of a small stuffed pig. They explained this pig is taken around the world by various people and photographed in outrageous adventure/travel situations. The idea would be to ultimately photograph little oinker on the summit of Aconcagua.

It was a clear day with occasional gusts from the west. Actually, we were extremely lucky because there was hardly any wind during our two-day approach to base camp. The dust storms, apparently, can be vicious. Most of the group left Puente at 10:30 AM. We shouldered our day-packs, hiked up the main highway past a hydro-electric project under construction, and came to the Aconcagua Park entrance. If you continue on that highway for fifteen kilometers you'll reach the Chilean border. Enrique and the others arrived in a pick-up truck, saving themselves a half-hour. Everyone continued up a dirt road, into the park, on foot. We took a brief rest stop at Horcones Lake. Up valley, rising like a Promethean mass, stood the upper half of Aconcagua.

If you fly over the Andes—sometimes flights from the States continue from Rio onto Santiago, then hop back to Mendoza on the Argentine side—it is possible to view the entire Aconcagua region. The cordillera resembles an interconnected root system, a vast labyrinth of formidable ridges, ice caps, cirques, and dead-end valleys.   That is really the power of the Andes.[4] Smack dab in the middle of all this stark geography is Aconcagua itself, and you can actually see a great aerial perspective of the standard route. Still, none of that quite prepares one when confronting the mountain for the first time from terra firma proper.

BILL ENGLISH   It was Craig Roland who stopped me at a Christmas party, a year before this trip, and said, "You're the one. You're the one who is crazy enough to do this mountain." Craig knew from my past experiences with Latin culture and the Andes, that I would probably be interested. Give me a choice and I'll head for the mountains any day. The ocean is fine, but I absolutely love the beauty and silence of the wilderness, the lack of mechanization and the absence of modern mankind. Sometimes a casual stroll or a casual backpack trip isn't enough, so I've got to push it.

I hadn't seen good pictures of the mountain, only poor quality Xeroxes in a packet sent by the South American Explorers Club.[5] I was amazed at the massive size of Aconcagua. From Horcones Lake onward, Aconcagua is just constantly on your mind. Even during the approach, when you can't see the mountain, you know it's up there.

Our goal for that day was to get to Confluencia. I didn't have any great fears, anxieties, or trepidations about the climb itself. I tend to take things as they come—'Things are cool so far. Just go along for the walk.' I was fascinated by what was going on around me, the other members of the group, and the trail. I tried to practice some Spanish with Enrique and the other guides. I could get by and function, but when the guides would talk amongst themselves I couldn't understand very much. Argentine Spanish is different from that in Peru, Bolivia and Mexico.

◊∆◊∆◊∆◊∆◊∆◊∆◊

TOM TAPLIN   The main reason Aconcagua appeals to mountaineers is because it's a litmus test, with the crucial factor being altitude. Having confidence in your stamina and metabolism isn't going to prove anything; the challenge is to ascertain how well your body and mind will adapt, and perform, in a cold, oxygen-starved environment.

---

[4] The Andes mountain system is the longest in the world—over 4,000 miles, three times longer than the Himalayas. The main chain, known as the Western Cordillera, begins in the Palmer Peninsula of Antarctica. The Eastern Cordillera forks off north of the Bolivian border.

[5] The South American Explorers Club is headquartered in Ithaca, New York. Regional offices are located in Lima, Peru and Quito, Ecuador. Informational packets, available for a nominal membership fee, include maps, historical notes, geological data and hand-written reports by people who have had on-site experiences in South America.

Aconcagua's summit is almost 23,000-feet. That's 5,000-feet higher than I'd ever been. Establishing a new personal best in terms of altitude would be a major stepping stone; if I could make 7,000-meters on Aconcagua, then I'd feel comfortable going back to the Himalayas to try 7500 or 8000-meters.

Frequently I'd just come right out and ask someone how high they'd been. This seemed like a good way to break the ice with other members of the team. The varying responses to this question, and the ensuing reaction, would always be interesting. Sometimes it was a disaster, such as when Mark casually mentioned he had climbed McKinley— 'Oh...*really?*'—my fear being that everybody else on the expedition was a high-altitude climbing ace, that they would convince the guides the standard route was a pansy route, and that we would end up on the South Face, hanging by the skin of our teeth.

That morning I walked for a few minutes with Dick Gordon, who was setting a fast and furious pace. If we kept up such a pace I would have been dead by lunch. To confirm my worst suspicions I popped the question. Dick said he had been to 14,000-feet in the European Alps, which probably brought a sigh of relief on my behalf. Dick had a bit of an insolent personality. I wondered if he was just a strong hiker, or if he had something he wanted to prove. When I asked why he was climbing Aconcagua, Dick replied, "Maybe this mountain will humble me."

My reaction was: "Well, guess you've picked the right mountain."

DICK GORDON   While residing in southern Italy my lifestyle had changed and I had become very non-energetic. I was looking for something which would test my mental and physical connections. I had questions about altitude and was curious if one could make rational decisions when the brain's effective ability to do so has been reduced. This particular ascent of Aconcagua would enable me to go higher and test that ability. I had to dig deep and see if I had what it took to do something that was difficult. It had to be something that was rated difficult, not just by me, but by experts. I was sure that no matter how good you are, unless you're Reinhold Messner, Aconcagua was going to be a humbling experience.

I wasn't sure how much time I was going to spend with the group. I felt like an outsider. Everybody on the expedition seemed to know each other—I found out later this wasn't the case—but it seemed that way to me. I was an outsider the previous week and I was going to be an outsider for the five weeks after getting off the mountain, so I took and self-inflicted that position.

Craig Roland had a good pace that seemed to fit my own. Actually Craig has a little faster pace, which didn't surprise me in the beginning because everyone was eager, but when I found out he could keep the pace, I was even more intrigued. During the first couple of days I explained to Craig that I was eager to push, that I wanted to go on long treks and walk a little harder. My feeling was that we could push each other. Considering our rest days at base camp, we'd have plenty of time to recuperate from any soreness, stiffness or fatigue.

TOM TAPLIN   The park road continues past Horcones Lake, so the trailhead is actually near the first river crossing. Most people were smart enough to take off their hiking boots. Absolutely frigid water, the kind that doesn't sting until you jump out on the other side. I would have slipped in if Anil Patel hadn't helped me with a ski pole. It was obvious that crossing any later in the day would have been even more difficult; when warm weather melts a glacier above, the rivers below can become impassable.

We entered a narrow valley strewn with geologic deformities: huge boulders, topsy-turvy slabs, and erosion gullies. Evidence of recent rock slides was everywhere. At first glance the valley seems a dismal, infertile wilderness. Just having a camera tends to make that type of landscape more surreal and enthralling, although Lewis remarked that black and white film would have captured the remoteness much better.

Lewis, Borgel, myself, and maybe one or two others decided to bring our ice-axes despite Enrique's suggestion to leave them in Mendoza. Whenever I crossed paths with Enrique, he would point to the axe strapped on my daypack, and give me grief—"You having fun with ice-axe? You use ice-axe to cut sleeping area in snow?" Enrique and I would josh back and forth concerning this matter. He stated that ice-axes and seat harnesses were useless, extra weight. I made some comment about chopping ice chips for cocktails at base camp and told Enrique that, if he was nice, he could borrow my ice-axe to level his own sleeping area.

It's important to establish a rapport with the guides early on. Despite the ice-axe issue, Enrique and I were finding some common ground. The problem was that Enrique's comprehension of English seemed wily. I was kicking myself for not learning more Spanish. Enrique didn't really get my sense of humor. Of course, some of Enrique's jokes went right over my head—'Sleeping in the snow? No one told me we would have to sleep in the snow!' I had visions of digging snow caves and bivouacking at 22,000-feet.

The trail gradually leveled out at Confluencia and we dropped down into a canyon, to the second river crossing. Confluencia is the junction of water run-off from the Superior and Inferior Horcones glaciers. We had to take our packs off and hand them to someone on the other side. There was a line of people waiting to jump across to a big rock. Everyone was being very careful about their balance and all, when these two dogs, which had followed us up from Puente, came along and just effortlessly hopped right over.

But that was a potentially hazardous place. You wouldn't want to slip and fall there, with or without a pack. There was a suspension cable down-river so that, if the water was really frenzied, you could clip on with carabiners and pull yourself across, or at least haul your gear over.[6]

---

6 Foot bridges across the river have since been installed at Confluencia and at the trailhead.

◊▲◊▲◊▲◊▲◊▲◊

<u>E.A. FITZGERALD</u>   The torrent was thundering down in immense volumes, and I could see that the passage was very dangerous. Our arriero was the first to cross, the water passing completely over the back of his horse. I followed next, and was fortunate enough to get across without an accident. Zurbriggen came next. He started well, mounted on one of our most powerful mules, but when he got to the middle of the river I was startled and horrified to see him turn his mule's head downstream. This was fatal: the animal at once lost its balance, and rolled over, precipitating him into the raging water. Poor Zurbriggen, the instant his mule rolled over with him, was swept rapidly down stream, turning over and over with the animal. He could not swim, but even had he been able to, I doubt whether it would have availed him much, the force of the water being so great.

In another moment they both struck on a great boulder, Zurbriggen underneath. The force of the water held the mule tightly jammed against the rock, effectually pinning his rider underneath. In a moment I was alongside of him, the arriero close behind invoking all the saints to our assistance. I noticed he was engrossed solely with the welfare of his animal; the fact that a man was rapidly drowning before his eyes was an unimportant detail to him.

It was necessary to move the mule first before we could help Zurbriggen; so we plunged into the torrent and tried to dislodge the unwieldy beast. I got my back against the stone, and pushed with all my strength; slowly the mule gave a few inches, and the water, rushing in between him and the rock with great violence, swept him out into midstream again. At once I grabbed Zurbriggen's arm and dragged him on to the bank; he was almost unconscious, and had swallowed considerably more water than was good for him. I laid him down on the grass, and with the help of a little brandy succeeded in restoring him to life.

◊▲◊▲◊▲◊▲◊▲◊

<u>KINGDON GOULD III</u>   Since I'd seen Aconcagua before, I was thinking I'd just kind of lolly-gag around. There was no point in going hard. There were people who wanted to make sure they were at the front of the pack. I knew the pack would only go as far as Confluencia. Being the first there was no big deal. My idea was to walk easy with my mother and sister and conserve energy. You get psyched from the anticipation, but once on the trail I could restrain myself as though I was in a line for a movie. You can't go faster than the line, so you try to enjoy what you're doing, try to get to know a few people, and watch other

people as to how they are holding up. You see who is running ahead and who is going slowly. Mike Milford was pushing hard. I walked with Dick some. He was self-sufficient and strong. He's a bit of a loner, but he could move right along.

It was a time of looking and remembering, as well as concentrating on what lay ahead. I tried to notice things I hadn't noticed before. I noticed more things coming down than going up.

The walk to Confluencia {11,000-feet} was a calm, easy day.

TOM TAPLIN   After crossing the river we doubled back through the canyon, then scrambled up a steep gully. At the top was our camp site, tucked away on a rolling plateau. It was a perfect place to stop and unwind, with a small, clear stream running down through tufts of soft grass—the last substantial vegetation anyone would see for some time. Most people relaxed or took naps while we waited for the mules. I hiked above our camp, got away from the crowd, reflected on the first day's hike, and took in the surroundings. The valley opens up onto these incredible, panoramic vistas. That was very, very peaceful.

We collected firewood and got some hot water brewing. The guides served up a dinner of vegematic potato salad mush and unidentifiable, practically rancid meat. Everyone was starved, so there wasn't much complaining. I did give a few tidbits to the canine mongrels, then washed down the remnants with waxy 'wine-in-a-box.' Enrique had a whole stash of these small wine cartons, complete with pop-in straws. I figured wine might help sterilize the meat.

KINGDON GOULD III   That first night's dinner was nice. Being on a trip like that you are expecting to eat off a petrol-fueled stove that hisses and smells bad. Making a fire where there were no trees by kicking up bush roots was mighty welcome. Having a barbecue was great.

I don't normally eat much red meat. Prior to going on the trip—knowing what the Argentine diet is—I went and bought steak to get my system adjusted. I figured we'd be eating steak up to the point of getting on the mountain. Eating fatty food leaves one a much slower burning energy source. If you look at what the Eskimos eat on their long travels, such as pemmican, which is fat with some meat, that provides a longer release of energy. Eating steak is probably good on a trip like Aconcagua.

THOMAS BORGEL   Lewis and I had steak in Mendoza that was very good, but that steak at Confluencia did not taste like any we'd had in town! We couldn't tell if it was horse meat or mule meat. It sure didn't taste like a four-legged steer! I said to Enrique, "Man, if you guys think this is a barbecue, what are you planning for meals higher up?" Enrique said his speciality was some sort of tomato concoction. I didn't really know what 'tomato concoction' meant. I asked, "Do we have any Lipton Cup-O-Soup mix?" Enrique replied they didn't bring stuff like that.

"Do you have fruit?"

"Yes. We have apples and oranges."

"Hell, that sounds good."

TOM TAPLIN   Our first night out was idyllic: no wind, relatively mild temperature, and a clear sky. We didn't bother setting up the tents. For a long time we just laid there in our sleeping bags, watching the stars flicker as a full moon arced from one end of the valley to the other.

NUNZIE GOULD   Dick was taking pictures of the moon and I wondered, Damn, how the hell does he get pictures like that? I've got the same camera. What am I doing wrong?

< 4 >

BLEACHED BONES AND BLOWING BUTTERFLIES
Expedition Day 2: To Mulas base camp

<u>E.A. FITZGERALD</u>   The giant cliffs and crags of Aconcagua towered above us, a great mass of rock rising like the battlements of some stupendous castle. Its vast proportions, bewildering to the pigmy onlooker, told infallibly of a mightier agency. More than once the thought passed through my mind, while amongst these mountains, that the masses of rock strata must have been actuated by living passions; must have fought and boiled, and torn one another in flame and lava, must have striven and writhed and crumbled along in frozen glacial majesty—true 'dragons of the prime'; that here, in such places as the amphitheater of peaks and valleys round Aconcagua, was one of the arenas of that early-world drama æons and æons ago,—here the scene of the tragedies and high moments of the great protagonists.

◊△◊△◊△◊△◊△◊△◊

<u>TOM TAPLIN</u>   Trevor kicked me awake at 7:30. There was an eerie scene of headlamps roaming around, flashing here and there, as everyone packed their gear. No one could figure out the mule loads, which pissed Enrique off to no end because he had specifically asked us to remember from which pile we had taken our individual packs.

One by one people drifted over to warm themselves by the cook fire and sip a hot brew. The leftover meat we had for breakfast tasted much better cold.

Dawn slowly broke. A group of us, impatient to hit the trail, started off. There are two ways to proceed from Confluencia. You can either recross the river and head northeast, toward a side valley where the Inferior Horcones glacier leads to the 10,000-foot South Face of Aconcagua, or you can hike to the northwest, left of the jagged peak Morro Promontorio, toward Plaza de Mulas base camp. The South Face is a monster wall—definitely not on our agenda—although going to see it would make an interesting day-excursion.

The dogs were yelping like mad. They'd sniffed out their breakfast and were chasing an enormous rabbit across some knolls. Despite the energy of their pursuit, those dogs were completely outrun—a little sad because they were nothing but skin and bones. Those mongrels couldn't possibly have been related to Blacky, a canine-climber who has been to the summit five times.

A short distance later the knolls petered out. We paused and looked into the dark shadows of the Horcones Valley. According to my map the valley was only about twenty kilometers long, yet it seemed ravenous and foreboding.

MARK CORNWALL   Was that landscape desolate or what? To me it was. The east side of the Peruvian Andes are pretty lush; the region around Machu Picchu is more lively, there are people around, there's a lot happening, it's colorful. And coming off the McKinley climb—well, it's just beautiful in Alaska; you have that pristine wilderness, all white, then beyond is Nature's green. The Horcones Valley is just somber by comparison. Everything is breathtaking in its own way, and the mountains along the Horcones are dramatic, no doubt about that, but it looked like a moonscape. The only thing missing were dust storms sweeping across that valley. Neil kept referring to the landscape as, "Lets go for a hike through Afghanistan." We were expecting mortar fire to come overhead anytime, with Mujahideen horsemen riding out from behind the boulders, strafing us.

CRAIG ROLAND   I like mountains for their wide open spaces and vistas, and found the landscape very photogenic. Probably for most people, who had not spent a lot of time in the mountains, the Horcones Valley seemed bleak and barren. The barrenness is there, but it is spectacular because of the array of rock forms and the way the light hits the shapes of the cliffs. It's metamorphic rock which takes on a lot of different hues and tones.

BILL ENGLISH   People were scattered all over the place. I don't know where the guides were, and I don't think half the people knew where they were themselves, yet everyone kept plodding along. Craig Roland is a much stronger hiker than I am, so we walked together on and off.

The way the Horcones Valley flowed down was just fascinating as hell. We'd come to places where the stream would be frozen, which was interesting because it didn't feel that cold, but in the shade I guess it was.

TOM TAPLIN   Roland pointed out these ice crystals in the stream bed. That was a little detail which, otherwise, I probably would have missed. I took several macro-focus shots of these abstract crystals and stared at them for about five minutes. What was striking were these tiny, delicate pieces of perfection in the middle of all this geological chaos.

The company itinerary stated: "Pine forests flank the base of the mountain, fed by splashing streams and punctuated by rocky outcroppings." Supposedly this company has been organizing trips to Aconcagua since the late seventies, but I'm not sure where they got their information about pine forests! The place is absolutely treeless!

While the Horcones Valley is very arid—most the precipitation generated in Chile is transformed into dry wind on the Argentinean side—the environment is not monotonous. The changes in landscape are very subtle: stream ice slowly melts; water trickles along the sandy river beds; banded rock strata moves in and out of shadow. There is one particular peak—Almacenes—jutting up from the valley east of Confluencia, which has the most amazing stratification layers exposed along half of its shaved dome.

MR. GOULD   The local name for Almacenes is the 'department store' because you can get any kind of stone from it's base. Geology, which I took as a college course, has been the greatest illumination for my life. You can't go through a road cut and not see all kinds of interesting evidence of times past. You have wonderful speculation of what the land used to be and what used to exist there.

The Argentine Andes are very stark—there is little vegetation and it can be quite windy—but there is a beauty in the coloration and in the scale of what you see. The Andes are mighty big and mighty austere, but that austerity has, in itself, a kind of grandeur beauty. I did look at the different strata and the different types of rock, which actually blew my mind because you never expect to find what you do find. In some instances you find sea shells on top of the mountains. You never expect that.

Aconcagua is not a volcano, but there is evidence of volcanic activity in the area—not so much as active volcanos, but intrusions by sedimentary deposits. These deposits have broken down over eons so that if you imagine a cross section of the earth from Buenos Aires to Santiago, took a slice and looked at it sideways, you'd see a gradual rise, intervening hills with some volcanic remnants, then the actual Andes which are pushed up, and which then run almost down to the ocean on the Chilean side. You can feel this great contortion and straining as the underlying mass—the tectonic plates—was driven up; the impact where the Andes have risen. You can see them twisted, deformed, flopped over and thrust up. Pretty exciting stuff.

◊▵◊▵◊▵◊▵◊▵◊

TOM TAPLIN   The phrase 'mountaineering expedition', in all its romantic, nationalist or fanatic connotations, conjures up images of a well-equipped team laying siege to some impossibly high peak for months on end. Aconcagua is definitely high, but there is no 'climbing' on the standard route in the pure sense of the word. You are hiking up the Horcones Valley toward base camp, however, look up where there is a breach in the ridge which affords a glimpse of the north and south summits of Aconcagua two vertical miles above, and you are thinking in expeditionary terms—acclimation, carries, camps—for the days ahead. 'Expedition' sounds good; 'expedition' formalizes the intrepid nature of the endeavor. So I was definitely in expedition mode, and was running all over the place trying to find unique photographic vantage points in order to capture the feeling of a large group marching toward this great unknown, dwarfed by their surroundings.

At a bend in the valley I met two young Argentine men coming off the mountain, stumbling across the river bed like shell-shocked zombies. They spoke a little English and said to me, "Where are your arrieros, your mule drivers? We need mules to bring our packs from base camp."

I told them our muleteers were down valley and asked if they had made the summit.

"Si, si."

"How was the weather?"

"Bueno, bueno."

I couldn't help staring at these two guys. Their faces were gaunt; they both looked completely dazed and depleted. They staggered off, waving their hands behind them, shouting, "Gracias. Buenos tardes. Buenos suerte!" I just couldn't imagine what their appearances would have been like if the weather had been bad.

The hours passed quickly. Everyone spread out into small groups of compatible pace, then we all congregated for lunch on a little rise at the end of the river bed. Someone had made a small, enclosed shelter there from a pile of rocks; it looked like a primitive mausoleum. I tried, without luck, to barter with Enrique for more bread and sausage by swapping candy from our 'snack packets.' Those candy bars had turned into science projects—three minutes till meltdown. You could either get that candy in your system and get it working for you, or throw it to the dogs.

BILL ENGLISH   Most people were pretty tired. We needed something to eat, we needed rest, and we needed water. That lunch was the first time I struck up a conversation with any of the Gould family, mostly just introductory conversation—"Where are you from? How is it you happen to be here?"

I tried to keep up with old man Gould that day. The Gould's and Dick had been acclimating at Puente del Inca for a few days which is a real advantage. I highly recommend that to anyone climbing Aconcagua. Spend a couple nights at Puente del Inca, instead of just one night.

◊∆◊∆◊∆◊∆◊∆◊∆◊

TOM TAPLIN   We followed the trail up through a glacial hollow, past boulders which had tumbled off side canyons, and came to the ruins of the refugio Columbia. There was a tall metal flagpole based in a large cement foundation, bent at a 30 degree angle, evidence of the vicious storms and avalanches which had laid waste to this refugio and several others in 1984.

The trail, just past the refugio Columbia, switchbacks up a cliff, which separates the low and high sections of the upper Horcones Valley. Below the switchbacks lay the bloated carcass of a dead mule. The previous expedition organized by our company had lost a mule, so that must have been the one. Bleached bones from other mules and horses, which had either fallen off the steep trail or cliff itself, lay scattered on the talus below. You couldn't have asked for a more Bunuel-like setting.

I waited at the top of the cliff as our mule team was coaxed and threatened up the zigzags; our mules saw the bones of their brethren and were having second doubts. Our muleteers passed by on horseback. Those guys had great smiles. One of them had perfect teeth and was wearing old-fashioned snow goggles which probably belonged to Zurbriggen.

At this point you see the lower portion of the Horcones Glacier, strewn with moraine rubble, and, above that, the glacier rumbling up, joining an ice cap stretched between Manso and Cuerno peaks. Flags marking base camp were visible a mile ahead. I followed Enrique, Pépe, Neil and Trevor into camp.

_____

NUNZIE GOULD   Everybody was pumping those first two days. We had all been cranking, and Enrique was shaking his head as if to say, "Why so fast?" I only realize now that there was absolutely no need to pump. Enrique walked behind everyone.

I spent most of the late afternoon walking with Mike. He was lagging back with Stasiak. I was trying to pace him out because he was pretty erratic. We would walk for awhile, then we'd break, chat, eat something and drink a little water.

Mike commented, in a positive way, about my condition, although I felt I was not in fantastic shape. Mike also commented about Dad. He felt Dad was in good shape and asked both Mom and Dad's age. Just from our discussions I inferred Mike was not in good shape. Apart from Mike's physique, this was apparent. Mike was aware that he was not in great shape, and he was aware that Stasiak, with whom King was walking, was in worse shape.

It did not help Mike and Stasiak to have tough days walking in to base camp. They weren't acclimated. That can only erode your strength. The first two days were relatively easy walks, considering the climb does not start until you hike above base camp.

_____

KINGDON GOULD III   I was carrying a fairly heavy load, and my mother's back was bothering her—her back is not strong, she's had a spinal fusion—so I carried some of her gear. That never weighed me down. My legs and wind are pretty good.

Stasiak had to stop every couple of minutes to rest. I finally got him to give me his day pack because I was worried he wouldn't make that last leg into base camp before dark. Stasiak and I were the last into camp.

_____

TOM TAPLIN   Plaza de Mulas is about 14,000-feet. Anyone not used to that kind of altitude always looks like hell warmed over. Borgel was hurting; he could barely pick up a rock to anchor his tent. Anil Patel was sitting cross-legged in front of a huge boulder, wearing a bright yellow poncho, looking incredibly zoned. Mike and Stasiak were basically still jet-lagged. Stasiak had a tremendous headache.

In the ensuing frenzy to find suitable sleeping space and level ground, I asked Neil and Trevor if they were amenable to having me as a tent mate, hinting I had some great music tapes.

Neil and Trevor were the young bloods. I'd played cards with them in the bar-lounge at Puente. They'd met at the University of Colorado, and have been hiking and climbing together for a couple of years. At Confluencia, Neil had given a rousing, very humorous lecture on the comparative qualities of synthetic fibres, down, pile, Capilene, polypro— you name it. Neil's condition at base camp, though, was anything but humorous. He was mortified about going another 9,000 vertical feet, and he kept asking Mark and me, "How will the altitude affect me? What if I do something really strange? Will you guys still talk to me?"

I gave Neil a Xeroxed copy of the *Climbing Aconcagua* article by William Broyles, figuring it would either help to inspire Neil, or send him screaming in terror back down to Puente del Inca.

NEIL DELEHEY   As we were setting up the tents I felt as though I had altitude sickness. I felt punch-drunk and my heart was palpitating. I was very freaked and thought I was having a heart attack at age twenty-two. I started deep breathing and told Trevor I had to lie down.

I'd never been on an expedition of this magnitude before, never experienced anything like it. Trevor had been to 17,000-feet in the Kashmir Himalayas. I'd only been on overnight trips to a few 14,000-footers in Colorado. What a rotten feeling to have just arrived at base camp and think, Jesus, this might be as far as I go.

TREVOR BYLES   I was concerned about Neil, but not that much. I figured he would get better and he did. Aside from being a little tired just from the up-and-down hike to base camp, I wasn't feeling bad. I didn't have a headache.

Neil and I both started taking Diamox at Puente del Inca, which Neil said was recommended by doctors. I think Diamox is a breathing stimulant and keeps your breathing regular, especially at night when it's important to have a constant breathing pattern. I don't know if Diamox was just a psychological factor, but I felt good the whole time.[7]

◊△◊△◊△◊△◊△◊△◊

CRAIG ROLAND   My impressions of base camp were plus and minus. I'd done some reading, so I had a pre-impression. What I hadn't expected was the spectacular outlook from camp across the pinnacled glacier, onto the cliffs and mountains beyond. You couldn't see much of

---

7   See discussion about Diamox in Chapter 15.

Aconcagua itself because we were too close to the base of the mountain. I expected to see hundreds of people and other expeditions, but it didn't seem particularly crowded, perhaps because of the time of year; we were nearing the end of the climbing season. There were a lot of empty camps.

The most negative aspect was that base camp was a pig sty, just one big garbage heap with blowing butterflies—streams of toilet paper shooting by—and camps abandoned, with food still sitting in the pots. It was outrageous, and very easy to control if the government entity wishes to do so. After a day or two I just blotted the toilet paper and garbage out of my mind. I just ignored it.

TOM TAPLIN   Everyone's attitude about the water situation was strangely nonchalant, considering the stream below camp was polluted with trash and probably contaminated with bacteria. Enrique mentioned there were pipes tapped into an underground source, upstream, which provided clean water. Several people looked in vain for those pipes.

Mark and I, somewhat naively, volunteered to go down to the stream and fill fifteen or so water bottles using a little filter I'd brought along. It took forever to fill two or three bottles since the intake valve immediately clogged with debris. I finally just told people to borrow my filter and fill their own bottles. If there is any question about water being unhealthy to drink, or to use for cooking, then it's a good idea to filter the water. In the Himalayas I boiled water, then filtered it.

The hygienic factors are important to understand because garbage was piled up haphazardly in every nook and cranny, and excrement was strewn everywhere. After our packs were unloaded, the mules, even though shackled on their front feet, headed for these huge trash piles and just wallowed through all the muck, scattering it everywhere. Attempts to burn these piles was evident, but there was so much rubbish the situation had clearly gotten out of hand. Dreadful. It's generally too cold for any of the shit to decompose. You didn't even want to put your pack on the ground for fear of setting it on a mound of turds. Thank god the chance of rain was remote; our tent would be spared from a torrent of human feces.

This was very depressing. Everyone expected an unspoiled Argentinean wilderness area, which basically it is, up until base camp. Nunzie said we should organize a clean-up party, but we hadn't really come as a restoration expedition or brought trash bags.

NUNZIE GOULD   There should be sanitation devices at base camp if people are going to live there. And people do live there. Dad and King had raised the issue of human excrement after their first trip. They had been very put off by that. And this was a point made by my sister, Melissa, who had told me, "You know, Aconcagua is just a dirty mountain. There is shit all over the place. Why do you want to go down there? If you want to climb a mountain, go to a fun mountain. Do a clean mountain." I guess the adventure, the fact that Dad was going down, the fact that I love a challenge—all of these overrode whatever was said.

There was a Bolivian team of women climbers who were appalled and had made an effort to clean up the base camp area. But Aconcagua, ecologically, is a disaster. Taplin expressed a real concern over sanitation at base camp and was troubled that no one else said anything. Taplin even expressed surprise about gathering heather bushes to burn for the cook fire at Confluencia. He said that he could not believe there was no control over burning the vegetation and that this practice would wreck the environment. He compared the situation to Nepal.

The real issue is how to provide controls which will preserve the environment. Whatever controls need to be made for the cleanliness of the mountain need to be enforced by a body that is concerned. And my feeling is that this administrative body was a joke. It was obvious that no government or park controls were being put into effect at all.[8]

KINGDON GOULD III   I never found those pipes, but I did study the water situation a bit. We consumed a fair amount of water at base camp and were able to get good water at various times depending on the place. I went and fetched water several times for Enrique. Further up stream, at mid-morning, I found a couple places with clear water. Early in the morning there was not much flow because the stream was frozen.

We had a water filter and tablets, but only used those when Enrique said to use them. I don't think Enrique used iodine at base camp since we had been able to get good water. Higher up some people wanted the water treated, so then Enrique would use iodine. I never had a problem with water—never got sick, or got the shits. Diarrhea is so debilitating. It dehydrates you, not to mention the interruption of sleep, getting up, getting dressed, trying not to wake anybody else, going outside and getting cold. I felt sorry as hell for my father.

◊△◊△◊△◊△◊△◊△◊

TOM TAPLIN   Base camp was surprisingly quiet. Occasionally a

---

[8] The Mendoza legislature established the "Parque Provincial Aconcagua" in 1983. Because the park is a provincial, rather than national, sanctuary, maintenance funds are severely limited. New policies have since been initiated, by which commercial companies are responsible for hauling out refuse by mules. The idea is to revoke operating licenses should the various companies fail to comply. Plans for the installation of solar toilets at base camp are also being considered.

Despite recent ecological expeditions, the higher camps, unfortunately, are still trashed to the point of disbelief. It's sad that commercial companies, private expeditions, as well as individual hikers and climbers, still treat the sanctity of mountains world-wide with such scornful negligence.

few hikers or climbers would drift through and we'd check them out. Someone would say, "Oh, here comes that Japanese solo climber we heard about in Mendoza. He sure got his permit fast."

Some Argentine guy wanted to borrow my ice axe and crampons to climb Cerro Cuerno, a rather ominous, crevasse-covered peak at the head of the valley. He and his girlfriend were loitering about. They looked like ordinary hikers—not very experienced—nor did I trust that I would get my ice axe back, so I declined.

Late in the afternoon a French climber straggled down the mountain from a high camp. He had that haunted look in his eyes, and was suffering from dehydration, exhaustion, and possibly acute altitude sickness. We talked with him for a few minutes, gave him water, then he crashed in his tent. Later I saw him rummaging through his old camp fire for food remnants. He explained his team had taken all their food up the mountain and asked if he could get a bite to eat with our group at dinner. I told him to talk with Enrique—that I was sure Enrique wouldn't mind. I saw him walk over and talk to the guides.

The various commercial companies customarily have their own eating/cook tents set up at Mulas for the entire summer season. Our group had two box tents, adjacent to one another. It makes a enormous difference having a warm place to serve meals, and to be able to sit on a little stool or whatever.

Fifteen or sixteen of us—some people weren't feeling well— crammed into the eating tent for our first dinner at base camp. I noticed the French climber was not present. Enrique passed out some bread, and bowls of soup of rather meager portions. Everybody was just starved, sucking down whatever was put in front of them. Enrique stood at the head of the table, near the zipper flap. He had a half-smile on his face, as though he was about to unveil the obviously fabulous, forthcoming entree course. Then he says, "I'd like to apologize because we only have enough food for twelve people." He qualified that by adding, "Don't eat too much bread now because we won't have enough for later on."

A majority of the group, judging from the moments of silence that followed, were pretty stunned. What could you say? I didn't really have a strong reaction, and I have a feeling it didn't bother Dick or the Gould's, because they had also brought supplemental food supplies. The company had issued a publication prior to the trip addressing issues such as food, equipment and safety relating to expeditions on Mt. McKinley. Everyone who had signed up for Aconcagua assumed, rightfully so, that the contents of this book applied to all of their expeditions. But I knew I would be crazy not to augment the company's equipment list with additional gear and personal supplies. The same goes for supplemental food. My experience with commercial companies has been that you shouldn't expect to be provided with anything other than the bare necessities. You always take more gear and food than you think you'll need, especially if mules are lugging everything up to base camp. For the people who had not brought supplemental food...well, all they could do was stare at the few remaining crumbs left in the bread basket.

< 5 >

CATS ON THE ROOF
Expedition Day 3: First rest day at base camp

GREGG LEWIS   It was apparent there wasn't enough room for everyone in the mess tent, so we decided to have meals in two shifts. At breakfast we were each allowed two slices of French toast. The only reason I got three slices is because Borgel was not in good shape; he was not acclimating well. He'd kept Mark and me up half the night, moaning and groaning. My stomach was never badly upset, but Borgel's gave him a hard time. He couldn't even eat his French toast. Borgel usually just gave his food to somebody else.

◊∆◊∆◊∆◊∆◊∆◊∆◊

DICK GORDON   Craig Roland and I decided to hike to the glacier. We viewed the panorama and picked out some points of interest. We talked about distances, but, perceptually, judging distances was quite difficult. We saw the pinnacle field and guessed the size of the pinnacles and how long it would take us to get there. We were off on all our estimates; we guessed the pinnacles as six feet tall and thought we could reach them in fifteen minutes when, in fact, it took an hour and a half to get close to the field, and the pinnacles were fifteen feet tall. I've skied glaciers, but that was a strange blend of moonscape and snowscape which I'd never witnessed.

We saw some glacial openings and, in places, could hear the water below. We looked at one opening and wondered, Wow, how deep is it? We threw some rocks in and, after losing sight of the rocks, they would travel some distance—twenty or thirty feet—to the bottom, judging by the sound.

CRAIG ROLAND   Dick and I crossed an area of glacial ravines. The moraine was clearly slippery and if you step on those rocks, which are just sitting on the surface, you could slide right down into a ravine. We could see more dangerous ravines at the upper end, so we bypassed those and came around to the pinnacled area which was on fairly flat ground.

We spent several hours wandering around the labyrinth that is created by the glacial pinnacles. It was absolutely fascinating. There were sluices of water running close to the surface, and rocks balanced on the top of pinnacles. The pinnacles were very solid—not huge seracs forty feet high that could fall over on you. The pinnacles were difficult to walk through; it was like walking through a forest of densely packed trees. One could get lost very quickly, very easily. Dick and I would shout to one another, but the ice would absorb the sound. We really had to keep our bearings. It was fun.[9]

We followed the glacier partway down to where a river materializes. We came to a little lake, washed off, then hiked over the gravely moraine back to base camp.

BILL ENGLISH   When Craig and Dick took off for the glacier I was writing my journal. I watched them for awhile and knew where they were heading—'No problem. I can hike over and catch up with them.' I went by myself but never did see Craig or Dick.

It was the first time I'd really been on a glacier like that. I remember thinking, What is all this damn gravel? I didn't realize there was a glacier underneath until I kicked into the gravel—the moraine— and saw the ice. I hiked up to the back end and there were places where the glacier was sheared off. Then I could see the blue ice, and I realized the *entire* area was a glacier and quite treacherous. I like to do a lot of crazy things, but in places such as that I have a healthy respect for situations I'm not real sure about. When I'm by myself I'm much more careful. I stayed away from the dangerous situations.

I was out there for a few hours. I went through the ice pinnacles and worked my way down to the lake, where I hung out for quite awhile and half-bathed. Then Trevor came out of nowhere. He was by himself. We sat and talked, then we both headed back. We'd done as much exercise as we wanted for that day.

TREVOR BYLES   That was the first time Bill and I talked one-on-one and really got to know each other a little bit. Bill seemed like a nice guy; nice enough—I mean he wasn't rubbing anybody the wrong way. He was alright. We talked about what he did for a living, and his daughter who was my age and attending school. I think he mentioned he was divorced and we talked about that because my parents are divorced.

My dad went through that whole mid-life crisis where he quit his job and travelled around the world for a year. He went up the Polish Glacier route of Aconcagua and made the summit. So I knew Aconcagua was going to be tough. I don't think Neil did.

It was definitely Neil's idea to go to Aconcagua. He conned me into it. Neil had graduated and wanted to do one great climb before he had to go out into the business world. He said he was going and that I was going. Aconcagua appealed to us because it's a high mountain, a good mountain, and a manageable mountain that didn't require a lot of experience. I decided to take fall and winter semesters off, go home and make some money to afford the trip. My father encouraged me to take

---

[9] Pinnacles initially formulate as sun cups, which further hollow an irregular glacial surface. Due to the intense solar radiation found at high altitudes, sun cups grow and intersect, eventually leaving portions of relief ridges. The greater the relief, the higher the pinnacle.

Rock debris, if thick enough, inhibits ablation, thus forming elevated glacial tables.

time off; he was in no hurry to pay for my education because my grades sucked.

Back at base camp Nunzie was near her tent and I was sitting nearby on a rock, reading a book. Everyone else was either hiking around or laying low. All the guides were hanging out and invited Nunzie over. Enrique goes, "Hey Nunzie, come have a drink."

Nunzie said, "No, no."

"Come on, come on. Here. Drink this."

"This is alcoholic, isn't it?"

"No, no, no. There is no alcohol in this."

It was funny because I think Enrique was trying to hit on her a little bit. Enrique either didn't see me watching, or he wasn't paying any attention; I was just sitting there laughing.

◊Δ◊Δ◊Δ◊Δ◊Δ◊

TOM TAPLIN   Word about the ice pinnacles was passed around by people who had already gone exploring. The pinnacles are called 'nieve penitentes'—snow penitents—because they resemble monks, or nuns, kneeling in prayer. I wanted to check out the ice pinnacles, as well as the ice falls below the Cuerno ice-cap. Craig Roland told me about some points of interest, but said he did not know what conditions were like near the ice falls. I tried to rustle up some volunteers. Everyone was noncommittal.

I didn't want to go out on the glacier by myself because I wanted to take pictures of people. I had to see another part of the mountain, a different view of the glacier—anything besides human excrement. I felt perfectly acclimated and considered hiking partway up to our next camp. The trail wraps around some cliffs, then switchbacks several thousand vertical feet up a wide scree slope, before disappearing at the edge of a plateau. It seemed possible to access the lower switchbacks by climbing a short buttress which, from base camp, obstructs the upper half of Aconcagua. Anil and Trevor were the only other people I knew, besides myself, who had any sort of rock climbing experience—Anil with Outward Bound, Trevor with the National Outdoor Leadership School—but they were both out on the glacier someplace.

So I headed toward the cliffs on a solo sortie. After scrambling to the top of a talus field I traversed a gully and edged onto a ledge. I only climbed ten feet up the cliff. It was the worst, most rotten rock I've ever been on; every hold crumbled. Without the protection of a belay there was no safe way to climb higher. Even with protection it would have been dicey with lots of rock fall hazard. That part of the west buttress was nothing but broken bands of tiered ledges and jagged towers. I retreated.[10]

10   A gully further to the right leads to the West Ridge route that Mason, Mackey and Hill pioneered in 1965. This line connects with the Normal route at 5800-meters.

Partway down the talus field I stopped to take a picture of the valley. It was an impressive vantage point: base camp stood in the foreground, with our yellow and blue tents; in the middle, like a white forked-tongue, was the pinnacled Horcones glacier, tumbling down from the Cuerno ice-cap onto the moraine; and a mile across the valley was Cathedral Peak. It was a perfect day without a cloud in the sky. Everything Enrique predicted about the weather had come true. The mountain spirits were being incredibly benevolent.

At the end of lunch Enrique introduced a grizzled ham radio operator, who lives at Mulas during the climbing season. Enrique explained that this guy could patch through international phone calls to the States. It was amazing that, from this completely isolated region, I could call my girlfriend in California, tell her I'd made it to base camp, and find out what she had for lunch.

I walked down to the radio tent. Even though someone had stuck a Master-Card decal on the sign out front, any phone calls were strictly a cash deal—$35 for the first three minutes. The radio operator told me it would take an hour to make the connection. I decided to place the call the next day because I was impatient to see the ice pinnacles.

After some cajoling Mark, Neil and Borgel expressed interest in going out on the glacier. I loaded a day pack with an ice-axe, crampons, munchies and film gear. I also packed a bundle of bamboo flag wands, scavenged from an abandoned camp site, so that we would not get lost in the pinnacles.

NUNZIE GOULD   My only glacier experiences were nature calls. I was basically sticking to my tent, pampering myself, and trying to get energy back from the flu. And I'd just gotten my period—if you can imagine of all times—so I was running on reserve.

I recall Pépe's expression when Mark, Neil, Borgel and Taplin took off, wearing their plastic boots and carrying some gear. Pépe and Gustavo, the other assistant guide, were between the cook tent and the dining tent, washing up or whatever. Pépe was shaking his head, almost smiling. He must have been thinking, What are these guys up to?

MARK CORNWALL   As we started off Taplin was in the lead. I was halfway into exploring the glacier because I was feeling pretty lazy. Neil and Borgel were a little less into it than I was; they felt like going for a short walk, nothing too strenuous. Borgel, especially, did not want to push it because his headache began to come back—he'd only recuperated about 80 percent—and because he knew we were going to Camp 1 after another days rest.

Taplin went out ahead to check the area. Neil and Borgel didn't know about going that far. Taplin made the comment about needing us for taking landscape pictures to get a human perspective. Neil's reaction was: "So that's it. I'm just reduced down to a standard of measurement."

We came to a ravine which Taplin had already gone down. Neil and Borgel were hovering back. Taplin kept saying, "Come on, come on."

Taplin would go ahead and I'd go as far as he had, while Neil and Borgel would wait for me. I'd say to Neil and Borgel, "I'll go take a look and if it's feasible, I'll call you down. If not, I'll just come back."

So I'd get to some point and find that the route wasn't feasible at all; the path might just drop off to a cliff or another ravine. But by this time Taplin would have worked his way one hundred yards further in another direction, and he'd be yelling back, "Come on, this is good down here."

Of course I'd be just out of view enough not to be able to see. I'd have to walk down in order to check it out. Then I'd say to Neil and Borgel, "Well, let's just go a little further."

KINGDON GOULD III   My dad, mother and I were out on the glacier. We stopped briefly with Taplin. We were all looking into this ravine. As my parents and I walked on to cross over the ravine up a little further Taplin said, "Gee, I don't like the look of that. I'd be pretty careful." It was obvious that somewhere under the ravine floor there was water, which you could hear.

My parents and I went up, gingerly, and came to two streams which merged. You could see a grotto with the water running out. We continued all the way up into these pinnacles which had big rocks on top of them. Bizarre formations.

I saw a lot of places on the glacier where we had to think about where we were going and how we would get back out. I hadn't really experienced that type of terrain; I had not been out on the moraine before. It was apparent to me the conditions were right dangerous and that some of that debris had gotten there by falling one way or another. During the course of the afternoon we noticed changes in the landscape as the glacier gradually melted.

When I'd been at base camp three years earlier, part of the glacier above Plaza de Mulas had melted and had clogged up one of the crevasses. Late one afternoon that wall broke loose; all at once water and debris came roaring out, sounding like a locomotive wreck, throwing large boulders down. I realized, in effect, that you could get flash floods and rock slides. You really did not want to stand in the bottom of gullies or stand near slide areas.

And you worry about ice pinnacles falling over. I was under a pinnacle with a big rock on it. My dad said, "Okay, stand there and I'll take a picture."

Well, I'm looking up at the boulder, thinking, The damn pinnacle has been here for I don't know how long. Will the boulder fall this time? If the boulder slides off, will it fall in my direction or the other direction?

"Look at the camera, son."

TOM TAPLIN   From the crest of one particular ravine, which was fifteen feet deep, you could tell by this fantastic, primeval sound that there was a large volume of meltwater flowing beneath the ravine floor.

There was also a enormous boulder the size of a Volkswagon bug perched on a thick pinnacle at the bottom of this ravine. I wanted to get a picture from a lower angle, but figured the ravine floor might only be a thin ice bridge. Some members of the Gould family were walking in the ravine further up. So the floor was safe, as least where they were. I slid down and poked around. The floor was solid. Mark, Neil and Borgel came to the crest. I snapped a picture of them posed against the blue sky with the ramparts of Aconcagua's west buttresses in the background. That was the last photograph I took.

On the other side of the Volkswagon boulder was a second ravine. The Volkswagon boulder was at the center of a Y, where both ravines merged. Sub-glacial streams gushed out of both ravines, down a six foot waterfall, and had sliced a huge, single gorge through the ice. These types of gorges, although they can be quite deep and have steep, icy walls, are not crevasses. Everyone thought it was a crevasse at the time. A crevasse is a fissure, or pressure crack, formed when a glacier undulates over erratic terrain. Gorges like this one are called 'moulins', and initially form as channels when meltwater runs down a glacier. Sometimes they are called 'glacier mills' because they swirl down vertically, creating a corkscrew effect through the ice. This moulin was basically an extension of the ravines. It curved around out of sight into a deep, dark corner and I didn't give it a second thought.

The two ravines and the gorge more or less ran parallel to the large pinnacle field we were trying to get to. If we scampered, perpendicular, up the embankment of the second ravine, we could head straight across the moraine toward the pinnacles. Partway up the embankment I saw another lone 'boulder tree' a hundred yards away, on a diagonal to the left. This was a landmark I recognized from earlier which was more in line with the lower part of the pinnacle field and the lakes.

Getting to the 'boulder tree' entailed a traverse. The traverse slope steepened to twenty-five or thirty degrees. The illusion of relative safety was enforced by the fact that the loose moraine would slide down a foot or two, bunch up and hold. My double plastic boots would then dig in and find some purchase. The traverse slope steepened a little more. That still didn't cause any warning lights to flash on. I was fixated on the 'boulder tree.' There was no cognizance at all of this dangerous chasm below the traverse.

Mark, Neil and Borgel were still standing on the crest. They seemed a little freaked out. After a few more steps I was going to tell them to go around and meet me at the lake. What's the saying?—'Three steps to heaven, but only two steps to hell.'

MARK CORNWALL   Taplin wanted us to keep going, so I said, "No. That doesn't look good."

Then Taplin would say, "Look, it's okay. Here's what we do. We cross and go here, we traverse across there, then we cut back. Everything is perfect."

Neil said, "You know Tom, you have a real confident tone of voice. Personally I think you are saying not to worry, but I don't believe you. It's not safe."

Borgel, Neil and I stood there while Taplin started up the left hand side of the slope, away from the ravine. The three of us were not going for it. There was no way were we going to follow him. The route up the opposite side was plainly too dangerous; that slope was just loose scree—a gravel topping. Forget our laziness. That earth, by nature being what it is, is not something you seek out to walk across.

I stated, in no uncertain terms at the time, that I thought Taplin was being reckless. I said to him, "That looks dangerous. You're only partway across and there's a lot further to go. Try it up that way."

And Taplin said, "Okay," moved on and continued, at a higher angle, across the slope. He only took a couple of steps and then his left foot slid right out from under him. He was coming down on his stomach. He looked like a cat falling off a roof; his arms and legs were going every which way trying to grab on. We just sat there watching him.

I said, "There he goes." The way I said it reflected something we'd all intuitively felt, which was that if Taplin went across there and fell, he was gone. So the appropriate statement was, "There he goes," and Neil said something to the effect of, "Yep, you're right."

We watched Taplin slide and by the time he came to the edge, where the slope dropped straight off into the crevasse, it was obvious there was no hope. Taplin realized he could not arrest himself. It seemed he began to prepare for his inevitable fall down into that deep abyss. He slipped, went boom, boom, boom...and then he just disappeared.

Neil and I immediately went down into the ravine and crossed over the traverse slope to a little ledge about ten feet from where Taplin fell in. That's as far as we would go. Borgel stayed on one side and yelled at us, "You all be careful! Don't get near that damn ledge because that surface is just slick!" We were all being very conscientious about ourselves not sliding in.

We started calling down to Taplin. The three of us were standing there with baited breath. We were astonished. Borgel, Neil and I didn't really talk to each other. We just hoped to get a response from Taplin.

One's mind goes into a state of suspension. I didn't think the worst. I thought, Well, he fell down in there and he's probably okay, if he's not knocked out or has broken his back.

THOMAS BORGEL   We yelled, "Tom, Tom, are you alright? Are you injured?" This went on for a few minutes and there wasn't an immediate response.

After calling and calling we finally got a little information. Taplin answered back, "I'm alright, but I'm hurt a little."

I yelled, "Are you hurt? What's hurt?" I'd have to yell twenty times.

Taplin's answers jibed somewhat with my questions. Taplin said his arm was hurt and that he was in water up to his chest. Not until later did I realize he said he was wet all the way up to his chest.

I told Mark and Neil I would get as close to the edge as possible to try to see and talk with Taplin. I followed the crest down-stream and had to descend the slopes of the ravine above the crevasse fifty feet in order to look over the edge. I dug a ski pole into the ice and made a hand hold with a piece of netting so that, if I slipped, I wouldn't slide off the edge. I could look straight down and see the water at the bottom. Once, I thought I caught a flash of Taplin, but I couldn't really tell. The crevasse was fifty feet deep from the point where I was standing. By combining his slide and fall, I figured Taplin had tumbled at least eighty feet.

MARK CORNWALL   At first, when we heard Taplin say he was okay, we thought, Well, he's fit. He's not hurt too bad. Then we realized what he really meant was: 'Thank god I'm alive.'

We were trying to evaluate the situation, wondering if Taplin could get out, or if there was something we could do. Neil and I said to each other, "What he's probably doing right now is adjusting himself. And what he'll do is walk his way to the end of the crevasse and come up the other side." It is amazing how optimistic you can be—that it might be possible for Taplin to walk out—but again, that was just hopeful thinking. Initially, when Taplin stopped responding, that's what we thought he was doing.

Borgel, on the other side, had a better view down into the crevasse. I shouted across and asked Borgel, "Do you think Taplin can walk his way out?" Borgel said no.

After we yelled again, and Taplin didn't answer, we asked ourselves, "If Taplin is really okay, and if he can hear us and we can hear him, why can't we carry on a dialogue?" We hadn't made the realization that the water was too loud. We yelled to him and asked if we should get help. Naturally, when there was still no response, we thought something was seriously wrong.

Neil turned to me and said, "We don't have a lot of time. Shit, this *is* a 'let's-get-going-for-help' situation!"

I said to Neil, "Why don't you get help. You should start back to base camp right now."

Neil started off. But I wondered, in the back of my mind, what would happen if Neil got on the wrong trail and got lost? Or what if any number of things happened? I got really scared. What if Neil fell into some crack? We had never expected Taplin to fall, yet when that reality came crashing in the possibility for a whole comedy of errors became apparent. It seemed better for two people to go back for help. I told Borgel, "Look, you need to stay here. Help Taplin out. Talk to him. Keep him alert. Monitor what's going on."

I left the accident site five minutes after Neil. I was sure I'd catch up to Neil, or see him ahead and yell to him. This is what made me pat myself on the back because, as I got further down the trail, I realized Neil was lost. He had vanished. Neil was caught in a maze of ravines—caught in the worst situation a guy could be in.

< 6 >

THE BIG KICKER

GREGG LEWIS   Not long after Borgel, Mark, Neil and Taplin left on their little day hike, I decided to head toward the glacier and stroll around. That's when I saw Mark staggering along, waving his arms. I could sense, by his pace, that something was wrong; Mark wasn't approaching as though he just wanted to talk. I walked fast toward him.

Mark said, "Oh man, Tom has fallen into a crevasse. We've got to go back and get Enrique."

I said, "I'll go get Enrique. You go back to the crevasse." Then I remembered I had no idea where this crevasse was located, so I told Mark, "Let's both go for help."

Now, I believed Mark was talking about my friend, Tommy Borgel— 'Shit! No, no! If Tommy drops dead what am I going to say to his parents? I'll choke the life out of him if I ever get to him! He better hope he dies down in there!'

It took us fifteen minutes to get back to base camp. Not until Mark said to Enrique, "Tom the photographer", did I realize Mark was not talking about Borgel.

MARK CORNWALL   As Lewis and I ran into camp I said, "Where's Enrique? I need to speak with Enrique. There has been an accident."

Enrique and Pépe heard me and came out of their tent. I was trying not to create a big, excitable scene. I knew we had a communication problem; I wanted to lay it out in pure, simple English. I told the guides that Taplin had fallen into a crevasse, that he needed help, and that we needed a rope to get him out. I asked Enrique, "Do you have a rope?"

Enrique goes, "We have no rope. No, we do not have rope."

"Oh, man! How can you tell me you don't have a rope?! Taplin is down in there. How can you not have a rope?" Rope was the key for the whole rescue.

Word passed through camp and everyone became aware of the situation.

CRAIG ROLAND   Enrique had a mini-tirade. All the sudden it was as if he realized he'd barely started this trip and had a catastrophe on his hands. Enrique rushed around and got Pépe.

The most shocking thing was that Enrique did not have a rope. Everyone ran around to some of the adjoining tent sites trying to find rope, but there was no climbing rope in camp.

MARK CORNWALL   The guides said they'd have to take sash cords, these 100-pound anchor lines, from the tents. I thought, Off the tents?! Oh no, no.

People jumped right in, unhooked as many tent lines as possible, and tied them together in knots. That's what the hell they had to do. The sash cords were stuffed into a day pack Pépe was fixing, along with an ice-axe and crampons. The guides didn't have a harness. Stasiak gave his harness, which he'd brought to base camp by mistake, to Enrique.

Enrique asked me, "How far down is Taplin? How deep is the crevasse?"

"He's down forty or fifty feet."

"Do you think Taplin's life is in danger?"

"I don't know. He's alive. He yelled that he was hurt. He might have a broken arm. He cannot climb out. He is down there at the bottom, in the water. I don't know how the hell we're going to get him out without a rope."

I really didn't think we had enough cord to reach Taplin. Also, Borgel had seen the water and his impression was that Taplin might be waist or chest-deep which, of course, would be very, very serious.

NUNZIE GOULD   Enrique was really pissed. You could tell from his facial expressions he was very upset that Taplin had had a problem and that something fairly major had gone wrong. Enrique seemed to internalize his frustrations; I never heard him swear or become irate. The first thing Enrique did, after speaking with Pépe and Gustavo, was to find the medical kit.

When rope was asked for, I went to King's tent. On their previous trip King and Dad experienced mean weather—wind and whiteouts—so King had brought extra cord which he planned on taking up to the high camps. He had one hundred feet of 300-pound test line with which to tie down our tents. King and I had been repacking our gear at base camp and had color coordinated our stuff sacks for easy access. I knew which bag the cord was in.

It seemed dumb to use tent ties; what could you do with those short little pieces? I gave King's cord to Enrique. That was about the last item Enrique packed.

MARK CORNWALL   The general attitude was to let Enrique and the other guides handle the rescue. I tried to explain to them where the crevasse was located. The big kicker was when Enrique said to me, "You must lead us back."

"Okay, but don't you know where I'm talking about? The crevasse is down there. I have to lead you? Oh, man." I was completely exhausted.

And I kept asking, "Where the hell is Neil? Neil left before me. He should be here. Where is he?"

◊▲◊▲◊▲◊▲◊▲◊▲◊

<u>NEIL DELEHEY</u>   That was a shitty time for me. Even though I still had not completely recovered from the day before, I was running as fast as I could, with double plastic boots which is not an easy thing to do. I took several face plants. I thought, I don't care what happens...I might get really sick, but I have to hurry.

I knew for a fact that Taplin was having a rough time. There was this image of him in my mind—a 'freeze memory'—before he dropped over the edge and free-fell into the crevasse; I could see him going down and I could see the color of his ice-axe.

I saw the trail leading up to Camp 1 from base camp and decided to head for that reference point, thinking it would be quicker to take a straight route across the moraine instead of following the path—which did not turn out to be true at all. At one point I had to descend a gully and cross a stream which blocked my view of the Camp 1 trail—'Way to go, Neil. It's not my fault Taplin's had an accident. Now I've really blown everything.'

It's a little self-centered I guess, but Jesus Christ, I felt I'd really screwed up.

I ran into a girl near another stream who, just randomly, was out on the moraine. I don't know who she was, or who she was climbing with, but she was Spanish speaking. I tried to speak my pig Spanish to her. I asked her, "Which direction is base camp? My friend fell in a cold river. It is necessary to get a rope." But I was nervous because I felt pretty bad for both Taplin and myself. I couldn't remember how to say 'rope.' I said 'ropa' which means 'clothes.' She kept pulling on her sweater, and I said, "No, no, no."

I was losing my gourd—'Oh shit, she's no help either.' Finally I asked, in Spanish, "Base camp is in this direction?"

She said, "Si, si," so I started running again.

< 7 >

THE LEDGE

THOMAS BORGEL   If I hadn't felt so bad I probably would have followed Taplin on the traverse. I hadn't seen him do anything ignorant, and I never thought he was being reckless. Taplin had no idea the slope was that slippery.

When he started to slide, I thought he would stop any second. Taplin slid maybe thirty feet to the edge, then I heard this 'boink' as he hit the opposite side.

TOM TAPLIN   The slide only took a few seconds, just enough time to grab some rocks and to realize, with horror, that not even the bottom layer of moraine on the traverse slope was bonded to the ice. There certainly wasn't enough time to reach for my ice-axe. When I saw the ice underneath, I knew it was all over. That mixture of panic and helplessness is such a sickening feeling.

I slid off the edge, slammed into the opposite wall and momentarily blacked out. That was just as well, if you can imagine a human pinball bouncing from side to side all the way down to the bottom. Somehow I landed crouched on my hands and feet, in a foot of water. Jesus, that water was cold—that water perked me right up.

The first pisser was my wet camera, still hanging around my neck. Trashing a good camera is pretty depressing. I stood up and started to slip my daypack off to put the camera away. My right arm caught in the shoulder strap, sending out a bolt of searing pain. Fuzzy stars exploded in my eyes. I held my breath and fought hard not to pass out. Something in the forearm was obviously fractured; I couldn't put any pressure on it or twist it without a wince. That lucky streak had come to an end. You really had to hand it to me, I thought: when I wipe out it's a bonafide garage sale. I screamed expletives until my throat hurt. It's amazing how much better you feel after throwing a little tantrum and berating yourself for being a wank-head. Then I collected myself and checked for other injuries. There was no other critical pain, probably attributed to being totally numb from the cold water. I was drenched from head to toe.

Realizing my predicament, I started looking around. The sides of the moulin narrowed at the bottom to less than four feet. Five yards downstream the channel curved out of sight. Because of overhangs there was no sky, no direct sunlight. The most amazing aspect were the walls which were subtle shades of blue ice, smooth as glass. I'd fallen god knows how far and was standing in a foot of freezing cold water with a smashed arm. The outlook was pretty grim, yet the place was so damn alluring. I had never seen ice like that before. I was mesmerized by those blue walls, totally spellbound.

The rushing water made it impossible to communicate with Mark, Neil or Borgel. It was only possible to make out a few distinct words. After awhile I just stopped shouting; trying to communicate was too frustrating. At least they knew I was conscious. Then the shouting from above stopped, or maybe I just tuned it out. I don't remember hearing anything after that.

My brain was switching back and forth. On one level all senses were compressed. There was so much heightened reality. The fabric and colors of the clothes I was wearing—blue Capilene longjohns under a pair of hiking shorts—were incredibly vivid. And it was almost as though the sound of the water was a color. The folds in my glove liners matched the movement of the water as it rushed down the channel. Everything happening on this level was like being seduced. You're enthralled by all these textural nuances that you normally take for granted.

On another level I'd made the decision that I couldn't wait to be rescued. There was no way Mark, Neil and Borgel could help. Who could envision those guys initiating a rescue? They didn't have any gear. I had all the gear! It was absurdly ironic.

I started talking with myself about how to get out. It was more comforting to have a conversation with someone. Who knows how long that lasted? Maybe that type of behavior is a way for the brain to deal with traumatic circumstances; you know you've gotten yourself into a jam, but you're trying to convince yourself everything is going to be alright.

Going up-stream seemed a poor option because of the waterfall pouring off the ravines. I couldn't bear the thought of getting even more drenched. I decided to investigate downstream and walked around the curve. The moulin only got deeper and darker. The bottom of the channel was incredibly slippery—pure ice. The force of the water suddenly threw me off balance, swept me off my feet and carried me along some distance. I finally stopped by pressing my hands against the walls. My arm didn't like that too much. I was even more miserable and chilled to the bone. Now the water came up to my knees.

Out of nowhere, I remembered the lake near the bottom of the ice pinnacles—'Yeah, the lake! I'll just sit down, surf out on my ass and end up in the lake. It'll be like popping out of one those Wet and Wild theme park rides. Splash down. Brilliant! Everything will be fine.'

That was when I knew I was going to die. There was a realization that the water flowing along the bottom of the moulin probably went underground before surfacing again, if it ever resurfaced. Had I surfed down the channel and the water went beneath the glacier, then I'd be trapped—wedged against some underwater obstacle—and would drown.

I stood there, stunned, my mind filled with horrible thoughts: 'I'll be dead and the big mystery will be what really happened. My family and friends will blame these guys even though it was my own stupid fault. They'll never find any trace of my body. No one will ever know if anyone could have done anything about it.' Very excruciating thoughts. I could not answer to them at all. There was too much anguish. It was the beginning of a madness, and my mind knew it. My mind began to shut down from the shock, to protect itself from dealing with so many negative thoughts.

There was gradual acceptance—'So, this is how the end will be; numb and quiet, all alone, then no consciousness.' I just stood there, held my throbbing arm, tried not to slip again, listened to the rushing water, and stared into that blue translucent ice. It was a beautiful place to die. That's when I tranced out.

THOMAS BORGEL   Once Mark and Neil left for help I kept yelling to Taplin the whole time. At first I just tried to get him to say something because I hadn't heard from him in awhile. I'd seen Mark and Neil heading off and could tell they were having a rough time. I yelled to Taplin, "It's going to take awhile for Mark and Neil to get back with a rescue party. You need to do whatever you can to get your ass out of there!"—even though I didn't think he could. Taplin finally shouted that he could not get out.

I was getting paranoid staying in one spot. I walked around to a couple of places and could tell, by Taplin's voice, where he was. I tried to figure out every which way how to get down into the crevasse. The thing that bothers me most is that I could not come up with an answer; I never once came up with a way to get down to Taplin. Do you know what it's like when you *have* to do something, but you can't figure out a way to do it?

As we talked to each other, I could tell Taplin was cold. I was cold because the sun was not hitting me where I was standing, so I knew that if Taplin was wet he would be having a hard time. His voice started getting very weak. The last thing he said was, "Someone has got to help me now."

Then he just stopped talking. I didn't think he was dead. I thought he had gone into shock.

TOM TAPLIN   Once the specter of death became a tangible reality, there was a big debate going on, subconsciously, about just how peaceful death was going to be. As the day progressed and more of the glacier melted, the water level would only get higher and the current stronger. Slowly losing consciousness, then being flushed down the channel was not going to be as peaceful as, say, walking through some beautiful valley, laying down in the snow and going to sleep. So although the notion of dying was comprehensible, dying beneath a glacier was completely unacceptable. If both my legs were shattered there would have been no debate.

Basically you know when your time has come, and deep down something or someone said, "Don't give up. This isn't the time." And that realization won the debate. It was either a spiritual epiphany or a very practical revelation, and it caused a huge mental jolt—I came out of the trance. But I also became truly gripped; dying was so senseless, so idiotic, so scary. To be all alone was even more terrifying. Those guys were up above, just out of reach. And how long would it take for a hypothermic stupor to set in? Two hours? Less? I didn't much fancy drowning or freezing to death. I made up my mind not to succumb without a struggle. There wasn't a whole lot of meaning in dying without at least looking for another way out. I've seen people on the event horizon, starting that slide into oblivion. Been in a few situations myself, climbing or otherwise. But in this case the fear of dying instigated the will to live to a level I've never before experienced. Never. When you scrape the bottom of the barrel the only thing left is that primordial urge to survive.

From that moment on, all thoughts were directed toward extricating myself from the moulin. My adrenaline and noradrenaline hormones were having a wild party; everything was crystal clear. I was also pissed as hell at myself for being careless, and that anger had a lot to do with finding a solution. But I had to act fast.

I pressed my hands against each side of the narrow walls and walked back up the channel to where I'd landed. One side of the moulin arched into an overhang halfway up. The other side was an eighty-five degree pitch which rose about 25 feet until just below the overhang, then tapered off. I couldn't see above that point. The answer was absurdly simple: if I wanted to live I had to get up this ice wall. The only way to get up would be by front-pointing with crampons. Well, this was ridiculous because I'd never done any technical ice climbing. I said out loud, "Forget about not knowing how. This is as good a time as any to learn. Just do it."

I took off my day pack again to unlash the crampons. I don't know why they hadn't been ripped from the pack during the fall. Luckily my ice axe had stayed attached as well. There was a tiny shelf above the water on which I could rest each foot to fasten the crampons. They're hinged, step-in crampons which I'd modified with extra, wrap-around straps. Weeks earlier I'd adjusted them to fit my plastic boots perfectly by walking up very steep, hard-packed ski slopes. But now I was on the verge of tears because my fingers could only fumble with the straps. My feet were still alright, but I couldn't bear to take my glove liners off and look at my hands. My fingers were gone; they had no feeling whatsoever. It took a long time to get both crampons on.

I debated leaving the pack, then decided against it. That was part of the game; I wasn't going to leave anything, not even the willow wands. The moulin would have to be satisfied with all or nothing.

Have you heard the story of the leopard who has been shot and wounded? Before dragging itself off into the bush, the leopard runs around and maims as many people as possible in the hunting party. That's how I felt—like a trapped animal. I went berserk and attacked that blue ice. I'd chop out a hole and anchor the axe as high as possible, bend-kick a crampon in, hold onto the axe with both arms, pull my body up, place a free foot on the opposite wall, lean out with my good arm, rest, whack out a higher niche with the axe, then repeat the sequence. It was a good pattern that had a flow. The moves were similar to bridging a chimney crack in rock climbing. The crampons held beautifully, even when only penetrating the ice a quarter-inch.

The ice was incredibly hard and just chipped off in glassy flakes. It took half-a-dozen blows before each axe hold was secure. Every time I swung the axe or put weight on my right arm there was a searing pain. I didn't care that it was broken. I was solely obsessed with surviving. Each step was a little further away from death, and a little bit closer to sunlight. Every so often glacial debris, loosened by the warm weather, poured down. I'd have to kiss the ice and wait for these little avalanches to stop bouncing off my head.

The sides of the moulin widened. It was no longer possible to place a foot or hand against the opposite wall, which curved away and then formed the overhang. Just above, on my side, was a small, sloping ledge. The crux of the ordeal came down to one desperate move. I could feel the last reserves of strength ebbing out of my body, bit by bit, minute by minute. I knew if I fell that I would not have the energy to climb up again. I reached up with my free hand, found a small hold on an ice knob, quickly swung the axe into the ledge, where it fortuitously held a grip, put all my weight on the axe, then shimmied up on my belly.

The ledge brought me into another world, a world two feet wide of blinding sunlight, dank smells, and the dull roar of water echoing through the gorge below. I stayed crouched on my knees for a few moments, totally exhausted, trying to absorb every ounce of warmth from the sun.

Borgel was on the crest, slightly higher up to the right, on the same side as me. Climbing above the ledge crossed my mind. I really wanted to get closer to Borgel. An exit ramp sloped 30 feet up to the left. The ramp wasn't very steep—fifty or sixty degrees. The snow, however, was not consolidated. Everything was melting and there was a possibility the whole slope might slide. It didn't matter because when I stood up, I couldn't control my limbs; my arms and legs were like sewing machines. This kind of violent shivering is an involuntary way of producing heat; it's a vicious metabolic battle as heat flows from your shell—your extremities—to your body core.

When I first got to the ledge I knew I'd cheated death and had won that round. I looked down into the moulin and tried to figure out how many lives I had left. But it was stupid to think I was home-free; I was only halfway out and the beast was still there, waiting with open jaws. I was still trapped and could barely prowl around the sloping ledge, not daring to move more than a few inches. All my effort seemed pointless; all that focus and adrenaline which had allowed me to get to the ledge seemed to dissolve into a kind of wasted, hypothermic numbness. I tranced again for a long time.

THOMAS BORGEL   I was so damn relieved to see Taplin climb up to the ledge and get out of that crack. Once he reached the ledge I started talking to him. He was thirty feet away. He said his arm might be broken. His arm looked broken; it just dangled there. I could see he was soaking wet and offered to throw him my sweater. He couldn't pull his wet shirt off. He tried to pull his shirt off a couple of times.

Then Taplin went into convulsions. He started to shake like something I've never seen. He was shaking so bad I expected him to shimmy right off that ledge. I yelled, "Tom, you get up against the wall and stay there!"

Even after Taplin made it to the ledge I was real scared because I knew I still could not get to him. I felt so helpless because I could not do a damn thing to help him get out. I've never been in a situation like that. It was the first time I've felt somebody was going to die when I was the only person right there.

< 8 >

RESCUE ETIQUETTE

NUNZIE GOULD   Enrique's last words before leaving camp were to Dick. He said, "Keep an eye on me. I will signal if I want you to come."

By then we had prepared an extra backpack with food, water, and an extra set of warm clothes for Taplin, which Trevor had gotten from their tent. The arrangement was that if Enrique needed additional help he would signal Dick to come out with this backpack.

GREGG LEWIS   Mark was absolutely exhausted, barely standing. He was like a marathon runner who had hit the 'wall.' Now the poor bastard had to lead the way back. Thinking the rescue team would need all the help they could get, I decided to accompany them.

Before we got to the moraine we saw Neil. He had fallen down an embankment and was several hundred yards away. Enrique yelled to him, but Neil was so tired he couldn't talk. Neil had been staggering around in circles. Enrique said, "Forget him. Let's go."

TREVOR BYLES   The guides didn't want anybody else to leave camp. Enrique, and even the Gould's, had told everybody to stay put. Enrique was worried about another accident. Everyone was curious enough to want to go help, or to see what happened, but too many people might have caused more problems.

I was worried because Mark had said Neil left the accident site first. As the rescue party headed out I packed some gear and was ready to search for him. Nunzie told me not to go on the glacier, but I wasn't listening to her; I wanted to find Neil. I was just about ready to leave when I finally saw him come over the top of a crest, on the other side of the creek.

I went out to meet him. Neil was just about dead with exhaustion. He said, "Taplin's fallen. Taplin's fallen."

"It's okay. Mark has already reached base camp. The rescue party has left. Are you alright?"

"I don't know. I guess, but I feel like shit. Trev, I've never been on a trip like this. Is there some kind of etiquette that says you have to go on the rescue, even if you think you'll just be in the way?"

"If you don't feel good, you shouldn't go."

BILL ENGLISH   Enrique had the rescue covered about as well as he could—judging by the fact he had no rope—but he had it covered. The rest of us hung back and made sure we were there for anything to be done when Taplin came back to base camp.

A group of us sat on some rocks overlooking the glacier. Dick had some Zeiss pocket binoculars which we would swap off to follow the progress of the rescue party. They would disappear in a ravine, we'd lose track, then we'd pick them up again. Dick would say, "They're over by that next mound. Keep looking. You'll see them,"—in other words indicating how vast the glaciated area was, and how small Enrique and the others appeared, even through binoculars. They were a long ways out there, weaving up and down ravines.

GREGG LEWIS   Mark started off in a daze, kind of a half-jog. Even Mark didn't know, once we got on the moraine, exactly which way to go; he couldn't remember. The rescue party was pressuring him, saying, "Think Mark, think. Which way? Where is he?"

Mark would say, "Goddamn, I'm not sure. I know the crevasse is not down there, and not up there, but I don't see anything here. Maybe it's this way."

Mark realized that every second we screwed around something could be happening to Taplin.

MARK CORNWALL   Enrique expected me to head like an arrow toward the accident site. We came to a juncture and I couldn't tell which path to take. There were paths going everywhere!

Pépe took off like crazy and I appreciated that, because at least here was someone taking charge with some energy and not waiting for me. I sat there huffing and puffing, trying to collect myself. Finally I saw a path I recognized and shouted after Pépe, Enrique and Lewis. When we converged we saw Borgel yelling, "Over here!"

One of the most beautiful sights we saw was Borgel standing on that ridge. He was about two hundred yards away. We would have had a hell of time finding the exact site if Borgel hadn't instinctively come up to that crest. When the guides saw Borgel they sped off in that direction.

I caught my breath, then joined the rescue party at the crevasse. The Gould's, who had been exploring the ravine further up, arrived on the scene just before I got there. Enrique and Pépe were at the edge, looking down, telling everyone to stand away because of all the loose rock. All eyes were fixed on that abyss.

THOMAS BORGEL   From the time Taplin fell until the rescue party returned, exactly ninety minutes had passed; Taplin was in the crevasse, in the water, for forty-five minutes, then he climbed out and stood on the ledge for another forty-five minutes.

When Enrique pulled out the cords I said, "Holy shit, what the hell are these?" Only some of the cords had been tied. I had to tie three or four knots.

We used ten or twelve tent lines. Lewis, being an engineer, asked, "What test is that?" The tent cords were hundred-pound test lines. Enrique and Pépe's big concern was how much Taplin weighed. Mark knew that Taplin weighed about one hundred-seventy pounds because they both went into a pharmacy in Mendoza and stood on a weight scale. The guides had no concept of 'pound', so we had to convert the measurement to kilos.

There was another long piece of cord which was Kingdon's. Enrique and Pépe wanted to send down a single cord. I said, "You better double that up because if Taplin leans back, that will be all she wrote." Kingdon's cord is the one we doubled up. Enrique and Pépe attached a harness to the cords and lowered it down.

We never could have rescued Taplin if he hadn't put his crampons on and climbed to the ledge. He would have frozen to death. We only had about eighty feet of cord; not enough to reach the bottom of the crevasse—no way, especially not doubled up. There was just barely enough cord to reach him on the ledge. The common practice is to have thirty extra feet for safety precautions, for people to hold onto or to anchor someplace.

Enrique realized Pépe and himself might not have enough strength to pull Taplin out. He asked me to come down and help. I'd stayed with Taplin the whole time, so I wanted to help.

Enrique and Pépe started to pull. Taplin slipped once or twice. Enrique and Pépe began sliding toward the edge. I grabbed hold of the cord, wrapped it around my ice axe, which Lewis had brought from base camp, and walked up as they pulled.

KINGDON GOULD III   Taplin came over the edge, Enrique grabbed him and walked him to the top of the slope. Taplin was blue with cold and almost in shock. We could see he was pretty shaken. He was a little incoherent. I imagined his adrenaline was going strong.

Enrique said to him, "Now sit down."

Taplin kept saying, "Oh, I'm alright, I'm alright." He wanted to start walking and warm up.

MARK CORNWALL   Taplin said he wanted to get his crampons off. That made sense. But although Taplin was saying lucid things, he might well have been a little more out of it than he realized.

Enrique certainly thought Taplin was gone—"Why don't you do what I say? Why don't you listen to me. This is my job. I deal with injuries all the time." Enrique could not understand why Taplin would not completely submit himself to his care, so Enrique just picked him up and forced him to sit on the ground. Then Enrique checked him for injuries.

Taplin had blood on his mouth, was sopping wet, and his arm was swollen. Everyone was hoping he didn't have a compound fracture.

TOM TAPLIN   I was zoned enough not to recognize anyone else standing there. Someone was taking photographs—'Yeah, let's document this disaster.'

Enrique made sure not let go of me as we headed back to base camp. He had me by the harness and every time I slipped, he pulled me up. There was no conversation. The only sound was that horrible crunching noise crampons make when you walk over rocks. It was good to be moving, good to get the circulation going again.

My head was not on this earth. I felt outside my body. Moving across the glacier—across that expanse of undulating moraine and ravines—was like floating over an alien landscape in a very bad science fiction movie. Unreal.

Pépe ran ahead to find the trail, but we still took the wrong path once or twice.

CRAIG ROLAND   A lot of people, in their minds, had expected Taplin to be carried back to base camp. The thought was of him down in this water with hypothermia and all that. Hypothermia is an extremely dangerous situation. Everyone was very relieved to see him walking and in reasonably good spirits.

TOM TAPLIN   I was led directly to the cook tent. All the stoves had been turned on and Gustavo was boiling up a big pot of hot water. Gustavo made me drink a cup of tea, then brewed another and insisted I drink that as well. If I put the cup down he would hand it back and say, "Drink, drink."

Gustavo's English consisted primarily of swear words. So we started swearing—not at each other, but at my pitiful condition and the absurdity of the whole situation. My mind wanted to shut down and go into deeper shock. I didn't want that to happen, not that it's possible to control that type of thing. Having Gustavo there and cussing away with him was a diversion. Gustavo was trying to keep me alert.

The strange thing was that the tent fabric was blue and was back-lit from the sun. The color of the fabric looked just like the blue ice in the crevasse. There was a little window flap through which I could see sky and hear people. Then someone closed the flap, probably so no one would look in.

Pépe and Gustavo peeled off my wet clothes. I sat there stark naked for a few moments, shaking like a leaf. My knees and arms were covered with minor abrasions. My hands were not too badly cut up, but there was no feeling at all in the fingers. There were dozens of tiny red dots covering the fingertips where the blood vessels had burst. My feet were fine, a little moldy but fine.

NEIL DELEHEY   Pépe said, "Neil, we need his clothes. We need to keep him warm."

Trevor and I found Taplin's extra Capilene underwear, pile pants and a down parka, which we handed in to Dr. Patel.

ANIL PATEL   It was obvious Taplin had broken his arm, which was swollen and painful. He was hypothermic as well. I knew he would go to the hospital in Mendoza and find his radius bone, ulna bone, or possibly both to be broken. I told him to look at the X-rays and determine how bad the break was. I also told him his broken arm could be reduced—fixed with a plate—but I imagined this operation could only be done in North America.

<u>TOM TAPLIN</u>   The combination of warm, dry clothes, sweet hot tea and shivering brought my core body temperature back to normal; the hypothermic convulsions stopped. Enrique and Anil utilized several pieces of flat wood to set a temporary splint.

Anil ran to his tent, grabbed his camera, and managed to snap a couple of shots before Enrique shooed him away. Then Enrique gave me two pain pills.

<u>NEIL DELEHEY</u>   Mark and I were standing there talking when Taplin called to me from inside the cook tent. He said, "Neil! Neil! You would have loved it! It was cool! I should have taken pictures!"

He joked about the traverse he slid down being a 'good route.' I laughed nervously—'That's great. Taplin's alive and everything, but he's not quite with it. He's freezing his ass off and he's out of his mind.'

Dick came over to Mark and me and said, "Good job, gentlemen. Way to go." We thought, Who is this guy? Is Dick in the Marines? We knew we'd done a good job—Taplin was safe—but several times we heard "Good job, gentlemen." Mark donned Dick 'The Sergeant.' Dick was very analytical and seemed very confident.

<u>DICK GORDON</u>   With all due respect, the incident induced a bit of excitement. Neil, Mark and Lewis were pretty excited. Conversation helped to relieve some of the anxiety—not from participation or guilt—but there was a sudden surge of naturally produced chemicals, adrenaline being one of them, which taper off after a lag time. There was a long duration of excitement; twenty minutes getting over to the crevasse; time spent on the rescue; twenty minutes getting back to camp; time spent getting Taplin's temperature back to normal. So while physically calm, Neil, Mark and Lewis' minds were still racing. And everybody was talking. People were also concerned and worried. Conversation was certainly in order.

<u>GREGG LEWIS</u>   The amount of good luck Taplin had in one day, no one deserves to have in a lifetime. Yeah, he was unlucky to fall in the crevasse and unlucky that Enrique did not have rope, but boy, he was lucky that he'd been able to climb out of the crevasse as far as he did, and that a horse just happened to be at base camp to take him out. He probably could have walked down, but god-almighty, that would have been brutal.

<u>TOM TAPLIN</u>   When Enrique came back into the cook tent I told him, probably only half-jokingly, that I wanted to stay in base camp and try for the summit. I told him I could hold a ski pole in my good hand. Enrique got completely livid—"No, no, no! This expedition over for you! Over! You leave now!"

I came out of the cook tent and was amazed to see a horse standing there. No one had said anything about riding out. I walked over to my day-pack because, for some bizarre reason, I remembered that my passport was tucked away in the inside pocket. Luckily it hadn't gotten too wet. Neil and Trevor zipped up my down parka with my slinged arm on the inside, then handed me my gloves and a wool hat. Everyone tried to put on their best face.

NEIL DELEHEY   Those of us who had been able to get to know Taplin a little were glad he was alive and had survived. The others agreed no doubt, but thought the evacuation scene was exciting. They wanted to take pictures. I felt weird—'God, I watched someone almost buy the farm today.'

Pépe thought Taplin's gear would be evacuated with him and said to pack Taplin's bag—"Pone su ropa y suplemento." That's a key Spanish phrase in every seventh-grade book which translates: 'Pack his bags and supplies.' Trevor and I separated the clothes Taplin needed for the ride, then packed everything else.

MARK CORNWALL   The decision was made not to load Taplin's gear onto the horse. There really wasn't any room for his big expedition pack, not if both he and the gaucho rode together. We put an ensolite pad behind the saddle for Taplin to sit on. He was amazingly alert and cognizant. He climbed on the horse and said, "I'll have to come back and do this climb next year, but right now I'm going down to Rio and bask in the sun for a few days."

TOM TAPLIN   The gaucho steered the horse through camp, down to the radio tent. Enrique was standing there. I thanked him for rescuing me. Enrique shrugged his shoulders. He didn't say much, except that his brother, Willy, would drive from Mendoza and pick me up at the trailhead near Horcones Lake. Enrique wasn't pissed off or anything, he just seemed spent from dealing with the whole scene. He waved the gaucho off and we started down the trail.

< 9 >

DEAD MAN'S BOOTS

MIKE MILFORD   The big question in a situation like that is, What a helicopter rescue? I knew Taplin was a strong fellow, but what about someone in worse condition? Enrique said, "A helicopter will take three hours. The Argentine army will send not one, but two helicopters, and each helicopter will cost $800 an hour."

So a helicopter rescue might cost $5,000. What is that compared to a human life?

MARK CORNWALL   The incident was hashed and rehashed in detail a thousand times that night. Borgel explained how Taplin had put on his crampons and miraculously climbed part way up the face of that ice wall—basically, to everyone's astonishment, saving his own life.

THOMAS BORGEL   Taplin was being adventurous and I still believe he just had bad luck, but we really should have had guidance before we went off to explore the glacier. Hell, Taplin doesn't guide for a living. Our guides should have known that 90 percent of the group had no experience with high-altitude climbing. People, by nature, are going to want to explore, but you need to guide them through it. When you negotiate a glacier every group should take a rope, a harness and an ice-axe. It was unbelievable that Enrique had said to leave our ice-axes and harnesses behind. I thought, Piss on that, man...I'm taking my ice-axe and harness to the top because anybody can have an accident.

I really began to get worried about Enrique—worried about him being able to get us up the mountain without anybody else getting hurt. I told Mark and Lewis, "If we're going to make it up Aconcagua, we're going to have to do it on our own."

BILL ENGLISH   There were three issues. The first was: Why the hell did Taplin try to get so close to the crevasse? He should have known better, or at least should have been more careful.

The second dynamic was that flares were sent up regarding the guiding. Enrique's reaction when he heard that Taplin had fallen into the crevasse was very negative. His attitude was: 'Don't these people know that it is a glacier and that it is dangerous out there? Why can't they be careful?' But nobody had said a word about the glacier. Not one word. There should have been some counseling on that. As for the rope issue, Enrique had cursed and said, "This is not the Polish Glacier route. We don't have any ropes for our climb. This is not a technical climb. You never need rope unless someone does something stupid like this."

So there was a lot of talk about Taplin falling in, how lucky he was to have gotten out, what kind of shape he was in, there being no rope and how unprofessional that was, and Enrique's reaction.

The third issue, or concern, was: Why does Taplin have to be evacuated this evening? Taplin was pretty much out of it; he was either really closed in, trying to deal with the pain and the shock, or he was making good sense-of-humor comments. I didn't think it was delirium, but I had a really dim view of his success in getting down to Puente on the back of a horse in the middle of the night. I'm usually an optimist, but I saw him get on that horse with hardly any way to hold on, his arm in a sling, and a horseman who hopefully was skilled. There was no way the horseman could hold Taplin on. It had to be up to Taplin to stay on the horse. I figured Taplin was only so far from going into deeper shock. I didn't agree that he should ride out that night, and brought this up with both Dr. Patel and Enrique. Enrique wanted Taplin out of base camp. He told me, "Taplin has to get to a hospital to receive care since there is no care to be given on the mountain."

Although I was very concerned for Taplin's safety there was nothing I could do about the situation. I said to Craig, "I have a horrible feeling about Taplin's ride down the mountain." I didn't sleep well that night; I was sure we'd get a report Taplin had fallen off that damn horse.

◊△◊△◊△◊△◊△◊

TOM TAPLIN   The horseman's name was Victor. We rode for five agonizing hours from base camp to the trailhead. Victor spoke practically no English, not that I was in the mood for a whole lot of conversation. When we came to a gully we'd both lean way back and then, as the horse scrambled up, we'd both lean forward, I'd lock my good arm around Victor's waist and hang on for dear life. The switchbacks just below base camp were too steep to ride down. That was the only place I saw Victor's horse stumble. Otherwise that horse was very strong, with an excellent trail sense.

The pain pills wore off before we reached the river bed in the Horcones Valley. My whole body ached beyond belief. The throbbing in my arm got worse and worse. At the upper end of the river bed we came to a camp of three Argentineans. I assumed they were the climbers whose gear Victor and his gaucho partner were ferrying down in two mule loads. The Argentines paid Victor in U.S. dollars, apparently getting a better rate.

We trotted off to catch up with the second gaucho who was a least a mile down trail. I asked Victor not to trot because it was unbearable; the slightest jolt was excruciating. When I requested water Victor's partner pulled out a thermos which contained the strongest coffee I've ever tasted. That coffee didn't quench my thirst, but at least it was liquid.

At first all I felt was emptiness and weariness. Then all these emotions from the ordeal began to surface—'Can this be happening? I was walking up this valley only yesterday.' I'd travelled thousands of miles for the chance to stand on the summit of Aconcagua and, in a matter of seconds, that hope was shattered. I felt lucky to be alive, but fate had really dealt a cruel hand. Thank god Mark, Lewis or Borgel hadn't fallen into the moulin. If one of them had been injured or died I never could have forgiven myself for leading them onto the glacier. The physical trauma meant nothing. Having a dream snatched away like that destroys part of your spirit. Containing my emotions was impossible; there came a point where I had to let everything go.

Darkness crept over the valley, while twilight lingered on the surrounding peaks. The wind picked up and chilled the night as we ambled down the river bed. Victor gave me his sweater to wrap around my neck. For a long time the moon remained hidden behind the Promontorio ridge. Victor would say, "Where's the moon? We need the light of the moon." He sang a song about the moon. That song was so damn melancholy.

By the time we came to Confluencia I'd had enough of riding the horse. My ass was killing me; nasty saddle sores. Victor and his partner were having a difficult time keeping their mules in line. One mule had already rushed down the trail and was out of sight, while the other one had strayed off course and was in an obstinate mood. I told Victor I wanted to walk for awhile, somehow communicating this would give him a chance to round up the mule behind us, and stumbled down the rocky trail in the darkness. My hand was soon covered with tiny thorns from tripping over prickly bushes.

I was totally dehydrated and crazed with thirst. Thirst obliterated any other thoughts; all I wanted was get to our old camping site and plunge my face into the stream. But we'd taken a different route and I didn't recognize any familiar landmarks. Victor caught up and talked me into riding with him again. I was so weak Victor had to help me get back on the horse. We forged the river and began meandering off the trail to find the first mule. Victor took a flashlight and checked the dirt for hoof prints, but that lead mule had vanished.

There were places along the trail above the river where I could not bear to look down; one slight misstep by the horse and we would have plummeted hundreds of feet into oblivion. Victor took me across the last river crossing at the trailhead, then said that I would have to walk out the rest of the way. He had no choice but to go back up to try and find his lost mule. I honestly felt lucky to have survived the horse ride, which was almost more of an ordeal than falling into the moulin. I thanked Victor, gave him my ensolite pad, and told him I'd buy him a whiskey at the hosteria if he made it down at a reasonable hour. Victor flashed one of those gaucho smiles, turned his horse around, and headed off.

Aconcagua loomed, up valley, in the moonlight. I couldn't look at the mountain for long—didn't want to dwell on the fact that I had blown months of planning and training. It was awfully hard not to feel totally humiliated. The mountain spirits were mocking me, laughing at my back, as I limped down the road towards Horcones Lake.

My mind began playing tricks: rock formations became strange animals, while the wind accentuated every spooky sound. After wandering along in this semi-delirious state for thirty minutes, praying for car headlights, Willy and his father finally pulled up. They had sandwiches and water, which was such a blessing. We stopped briefly at the hosteria in Puente—this was well after midnight—for a quick soft drink. I'd forgotten to give back Victor's sweater, so I left it at the front desk. Then we took off for Mendoza.

◊△◊△◊△◊△◊△◊△◊

GREGG LEWIS   I shouldn't say this. This is like taking the dead man's boots. You don't really want to, but...

First you think, Oh, what a bad experience for Taplin, a real tragedy. Then after a couple hours someone would say, "Well, Taplin's not here. He won't be needing that piece of gear. Do you think he'd mind if I borrowed this or that?"

One by one everyone eyed his gear, wondering what Taplin had that they didn't have. Mike used his air mattress, and Trevor used his sleeping bag because it was warmer and bigger than his own. Trevor said, "Hell, I guess Taplin wouldn't mind if I used his bag, would he?"

Neil and Trevor remembered Taplin had some Fig Newtons—"We're sure Taplin wouldn't mind if we eat these sons of bitches."

TREVOR BYLES   Taplin had energy drink mixes, beef jerky, granola bars, white chocolate and Fig Newtons. Neil and I were psyched about the Fig Newtons. We were joking with Borgel, Lewis and Mark that we'd go off and eat Taplin's stash. I thought we gave them a little, but maybe we didn't.

MARK CORNWALL   Neil and Trevor had a running gag about 'searching for Elvis'—"See that footprint in the snow? That must be Elvis. Look at this piece of meat. Just like the mutton chops Elvis used to eat."

Neil and Trevor were in good shape, always had a good attitude, and now they had a tent to themselves. They ate all of Taplin's supplemental food—the works—and we're talking no sharing with anybody. Everyone got down on their asses about that.

I can't believe how screwed up my mind was. I was so paranoid. In fact, on the day of Taplin's accident, my major concern was that my girlfriend, with whom I'd just split up, might break into my house. I wanted to use the radio at base camp, make an international phone call, and have someone check my house. That's horrible. How far do you have to go to get away from it all?

< 10 >

SHOP SIGNS

TOM TAPLIN   Willy was a banshee, screaming down the highway through the night, like a deranged ambulance driver; we were at the Mendoza General Hospital less than two hours after leaving Puente del Inca. Willy eventually found and roused an X-ray technician. The X-rays were too murky to tell exactly what was broken in my forearm.

There was a brief conference, conducted in Spanish, between a doctor, Willy and a policeman. That was at 4:30 in the morning. The doctor said to return to the hospital at 7:30. We procured some prescription pain killer at an all-night pharmacy, I grabbed two hours of sleep at the Hotel Balbi, then Willy drove me back to the hospital where my arm was cast with a 'South American Special'—about twenty pounds of plaster. I thanked the doctor for not amputating.

There was no point in staying in Mendoza. The best plan was to fly home to obtain proper medical care. I hobbled down the streets toward the Aerolineas ticket office feeling like a battered old man. Mendoza seemed dreary and unexciting. Five days earlier I hadn't noticed the shop signs for the Aconcagua Pizza Parlor, the Aconcagua Leather Shop, or the Aconcagua Record Store. All those shop signs were constant reminders of the mountain which had spit me out like an annoying fish bone. Very depressing.

That evening Willy and his girlfriend took me to an outdoor cafe and helped cheer me up. Willy's compassion and generosity were way beyond the call of duty. We went to an Italian restaurant, Estancia La Marchigiana, had a fabulous lasagna dinner, drank a couple bottles of wine and talked for hours. There was actually a life-size statue of San Martin on his horse, inside the restaurant. Willy and I gave a couple of toasts in honor of San Martin. It's ridiculous to be angry at a mountain, so we toasted Aconcagua. We were toasted. The proprietor, a sweet old woman by the name of Mama Teresa, finally kicked us out.

The next morning I caught a flight to Buenos Aires, briefly strolled around Florida Street in a catatonic state, continued on to Los Angeles, and immediately started getting referrals for orthopedic surgeons.

Troubled dreams of falling into the moulin, water roaring through the gorge, and that cold, blue ice were replaced by the sterile simplicity of an operating room, the gleam of overhead lamps, and the noiseless movements of nurses attired in ghost-like gowns and masks as the surgical team prepared for their theater, their ritual.

An anonymous voice said, "You will begin to feel drowsy." That doesn't quite prepare you for a descent into the netherworld; three hours lost forever in the locked chambers of general anesthesia.

Part 2

─────────

The Invisible Barrier

"From a certain point onward there is no longer any turning back. That is the point that must be reached."

Kafka

< 11 >

MONSIEUR SPEEDY
Expedition Day 4: Second rest day, Base Camp

KINGDON GOULD III   People take chances. One stands on the edge to look over. Why the hell else does anyone go on adventures? You have to be as careful as possible, but sometimes you are unlucky.

Taplin's accident was sobering for a lot of people. Folks figured Taplin had done as much mountaineering as anybody else in the group. He had been walking well, had good equipment, and had been in the Himalayas. Some of the younger people had a party attitude. For them Taplin's accident meant: 'Well shit, guess we can get hurt here.'

NUNZIE GOULD   Enrique wanted people to relax, stay in camp, and not go off to explore the glacier. I respected his being the head guide and his many successful ascents, so I was heeding his words. I don't know how much of the information Enrique conveyed to the group with whom I ate was repeated to those at the other meal shifts.

MARY GOULD   Enrique suggested that we take hikes. My husband, son and I made a point of taking a hike each day at base camp. It was good to go on those hikes and continue to acclimate. We walked up partially toward Camp 1, and we walked out to the ice pinnacles one other time. Enrique probably told people to be careful about the glacier. It wasn't really necessary to warn anyone at that stage; people were aware of the problem firsthand by then.

TREVOR BYLES   Enrique never said not to go back to the glacier. Out of boredom and curiosity I wanted to see exactly where Taplin had fallen. I found the crevasse, took a picture, and was surprised Taplin had not been killed. I didn't go to the edge and look down, but I did throw some rocks in and wait for the splash.

The place is what you make of it. Glacial landscapes are great—I've also been on glaciers in Switzerland and in the Himalayas—but I was by myself. I wasn't going to get too close, or get into any dangerous situations to the point where, if I fell or slipped, no one would have known where I was located.

◊△◊△◊△◊△◊△◊△◊

THOMAS BORGEL   After breakfast Mark, Lewis, and I went down to the creek just below camp to wash up a bit. Mark and Lewis took their britches off and sat right down in that creek. Unbelievable. Their butts were purple when they got out. It was the funniest thing you ever saw. They said taking that bath felt so good that it was worth it. I scrubbed down with a wash cloth. Afterwards we threw cologne under our armpits, which reeked like rotting carcasses.

KINGDON GOULD III   There were a few climbers from different expeditions at base camp, a couple of whom we'd already met. We saw the Japanese guy we'd had dinner with at Puente del Inca and chatted with him. He was soloing. There was a New Zealand group of five or six climbers who were disappointed in their guide. They were within sight of the summit when, at 5 PM on the day of their attempt, their guide told them there was not enough time and that they had to go down. They told us about conditions higher up on the mountain. They were feeling good and looked like rugged fellows, but they were upset and wanted another shot at the summit.

CRAIG ROLAND   The guide of the New Zealand team was telling me about leadership, and some of the 'do's and don't's' about tackling the upper parts of the mountain. There were also some other Americans.
  And there was a French group, including a journalist and a television crew, with a guy trying to break the summit speed record. They'd been acclimatizing for a week or so on the mountain. In fact, this Frenchman broke the record. When he tackled Aconcagua he set off in running clothes with two ski poles. This was fascinating for me as a marathoner. What happened was that he got to the upper mountain and it was cold—below zero—and he got frostbite. You can't exercise hard enough to overcome that kind of cold. He walked down the mountain in a lot of pain and arrived in base camp while we were there. Dr. Patel looked at his feet and said this fellow might lose some skin from his toes due to frostbite.

NUNZIE GOULD   When I asked about Pépe's and Gustavo's mountaineering experience, Enrique was a little offended; he reacted with a 'how dare you' look. Enrique explained Pépe had climbed all the routes on Aconcagua and had even pioneered a route. Enrique really respected Pépe's climbing abilities. And Pépe recently held the speed record on Aconcagua. Pépe was very interested to see the Frenchman pass that morning. When the Frenchman came down with his crew, both Enrique and Pépe wanted to know his time, look at his feet, and find out about conditions. The Frenchman's record time was around six hours. Pépe's old record, I believe from several years before, was six-and-a-half hours. So the difference was very close.[11]

---

[11] According to Luis Alberto Parra, who is affiliated with the Club Andinista Mendoza, established speed records by the normal route (Plaza de Mules base to summit) are as follows: German Michel Dacher: 6 hours 15 minutes (1988); American Marty Schmidt: 6 hours 13 minutes (January, 1989); Argentine Daniel Alessio: 6 hours 7 minutes (1990.)
  The French record is apparently unofficial, or was negated by Alessio's time in 1990.

<u>MR. GOULD</u>   The French speed-climber had frostbitten feet and hands. Nunzie lent him down booties. Of course, I could never figure out how they knew when the guy arrived on the top. Was somebody up there waiting for him? Who presses the stop watch when you leave? Maybe they have binoculars and he signalled from the summit. Is there some International Commission controlling it, or do you just take your partner's word? It has to be verified somehow.

We also saw a mountain biker. He was riding down that last steep spot above camp, where you could get water from a pipe stuck out of the ground. I don't know his name or if he had gone all the way to the top on his bike, but other people have. He rode down, fell in a heap, and just lay there for awhile. Then he pulled himself together—we were all watching from a distance—and he hopped on his bike and continued, wobbly, down the trail into base camp. He wasn't hurt. I imagine he had fallen about two hundred times.

< 12 >

SUCKING WIND
Expedition Day 5: First carry to Camp I

NUNZIE GOULD   As a result of his first trip, Dad, come hell or high water, wanted us to be able to go up Aconcagua by ourselves if no guides turned up, if there was mis-communication, or if there was no group. Since Dad wanted to be completely self-sufficient we'd brought a foot locker of cooking equipment, pots, pans, utensils, and a whole duffel bag full of food, including freeze-dried items, soups, snack food such as unsalted nuts, dried fruit, chocolate and granola bars. Enrique was quite surprised—a little taken aback—when he first saw our extra gear in Mendoza. Perhaps he felt we were questioning his ability to supply the expedition, which wasn't our intent at all.

Our family weeded out some gear and food stuffs at Puente del Inca. Everything else was packed into our big Army duffel bag which had been brought to base camp with a mule load. At base camp we selected supplies that we would take higher. Enrique also selected from some of our cereals, soups and freeze-dried food which he did take up to our next camp. Some freeze-dried food and granola bars were left in the duffel bag at base camp, for when we would come off the mountain.

Enrique asked certain people to pack more weight for the first carry to Camp 1.[12] Some carried fuel. Some carried food. Enrique had been watching everyone from day one, and was very aware of people's physique and their conditioning. When Mom came down the stairs of the hotel in Mendoza and was introduced to Enrique, she was wearing a skirt above her knees and had on a pair of sandals. I distinctly remember Enrique staring at her thin legs. That was funny. And I remember the look Enrique gave me when King introduced me as his sister. I'm not a very big person and I think that is what stuck in Enrique's mind. When we were pairing up gear for the first carry I felt that Enrique underestimated my abilities. I said to him, "Hey, I'm on this expedition. I'm a strong person and I can carry."

But twice Enrique said, "No. You don't carry."

That was Enrique's decision and I accepted that decision. He was the group leader. I basically carried nothing. King carried mostly all our family's extra food; his pack was damn heavy. And Dick was carting around one hell of a heavy pack.

---

[12] In non-alpine styled ascents, the ferrying of supplies upwards in multiple carries divides gear and food into manageable weight loads. High camps thus remain stocked with vital supplies, enabling the team to move up or down the mountain. Carries also aid in the acclimatization process.

CRAIG ROLAND   We left at 11 AM. The sun was just coming into base camp. We had thirty-pound packs—not much weight—filled with all the gear and food we didn't need at Plaza de Mulas. One comes up a series of switchbacks on the western slope of the mountain, and over the edge. We were supposed to stay at Camp Canada which is at 16,000-feet, or Camp Alaska at 17,000-feet. Alaska is at the base of an ice field. We continued on to Nido de Condores—Nest of the Condors—which is about 17,700-feet. Nido is on a big, flat plateau and it is surprising to find a camp there. I got up to Nido way ahead of the others. It took me three hours from base camp. I don't know if they started late or what, but people straggled way out and were hours apart.

People were wondering why we had ascended 3700 vertical feet when the itinerary has us going 1500 feet. Enrique said, "I know this mountain. The best way is to go up as fast as possible." Enrique wanted the expedition to return to base camp that afternoon, bring the second loads up to Nido the next day, spend the night at Nido, go to Camp 2, spend the night there, go to the summit, then come down and leave. For the first time we realized we were going to have just three additional nights higher on the mountain. Then the trip would come to an end.

Our communication with Enrique began to break down quite seriously at this point. Enrique was very defensive about passing those intermediate camps. He said, "Look. This is the best way to climb this mountain. I've been on this mountain dozens of times and I know the best way to climb it." No one was really challenging him exactly, but he answered in that way.

I dumped my load at Nido, scouted around a little, then went back to base camp.

DICK GORDON   Enrique elected to put some community gear in a tent I'd set up at Nido. We knew theft existed and, while theft perhaps was not a problem that high on the mountain, leaving our gear in a tent would be more secure. For the first time I started to feel the effects of altitude. One of the most severe headaches I've ever had was when I was putting up that tent.

NEIL DELEHEY   Dick and Craig Roland were well ahead of everyone. It was strange passing Camp Canada and continuing on to Nido. Enrique would say, "Didn't you look at your itinerary?" But we never followed the itinerary one bit! We came to a point of blind faith as Enrique would tell us how many hours the hike would take.

I'd just spent three days at the highest altitude I'd ever been and now I was going higher. I didn't know what to expect—'What's around this corner?'

Trevor and I were a team the whole way. If he wanted to lead, that was fine. I was content to let him lead, but if he got going too fast, or was screwing up our pace, I'd tap him with my ski pole and say, "Hey, Trev. Slow down." And he would. We kept a slow, steady pace and hardly ever stopped. Neither one of us was stronger than the other in any way.

Trevor had been to NOLS {the National Outdoor Leadership School} and perhaps had more confidence than myself.

Sometimes we discussed the condition of other people. There were some, more than others, I was betting on. But if we saw someone who did not look good I'd say to Trevor, "I don't want to talk about their condition. It might happen to me. My condition might change in an hour." I felt much better from acclimating a day and a half at base camp, but I didn't want to get cocky.

At base camp part of my problem, besides being altitude weary, was dehydration. On our rest days I started drinking water like crazy and ate well. No one checked to see if we were drinking sufficient amounts of water. Trevor and I just knew enough to do that.

TREVOR BYLES   Neil and I made Nido without too much fatigue. Coming down was when you got tired. We dropped our loads and Enrique said to spend some time. We were at Nido for half-an-hour and walked around a little. A few people came in and we'd greet each other.

As we were coming down most of the group was still on their way up. We passed Mark, Borgel and Lewis. They didn't look too bad. Both Mark and Borgel said they had headaches.

That was a big day and a long hike. Neil and I got back down to base camp before the sun set.

BILL ENGLISH   Part of the reason I never went back to the glacier during our previous rest day was because I felt I'd seen it. The other part was because I wanted to save my energy for what I knew was coming. What was coming was that hike to Nido.

I'd been to Peru, on a trek which went over a 16,000-foot pass. That was a fairly good test of how my body was going to react to altitude: on and off headaches; on and off nausea; on and off appetite. The altitude in Peru never stopped me—I was never unable to function. That first carry to Nido, however, was nasty.

Halfway up I became very concerned. Then, on the descent, there were times when I seriously questioned my ability to control my bowels and my bladder—'Everything is going to let loose!' It sure as hell would have if I hadn't really fought it. I guess this is sometimes common. I remember watching the Ironman marathon in Hawaii and some woman literally shit in her pants at the very end on the last push. She could not control herself. I knew that was what was happening to me. My muscles, including my sphincter, were quitting. It was scary and uncomfortable.

I staggered back to camp, but didn't want such an ignoble occurrence right there. I felt sheer exhaustion. I've downhill skied for seven hours straight and been exhausted but this, somehow, was different. If someone had told me I had to go another mile, I couldn't have done it. I was wiped out.

After catching my breath and drinking some water, my mood improved considerably. I remember sitting down in the tent, unlacing my boots and kicking them off. The smell of my hot, sweaty feet emanating from those boots made me damn near throw up. I had to stick my head out the tent flap and practically hold my mouth shut.

So, besides the altitude and exhaustion, I was nauseous as well. That smell was a trigger—like sticking your finger down your throat. If I'd been by myself I might have thrown up, but Roland was sitting right outside the tent. He felt fine of course. Nothing effected him. I couldn't show I was in that bad a shape. I fought it all back.

All I could manage that night was soup and a little tea. I had to eat something. That was the toughest day of the whole trip for me. There was no way I could have made it back to Nido the next day. I would not have been the only one; Roland and maybe a few of the others could have made it back up, but everyone else was hurting.

GREGG LEWIS   There were people like Mike, and especially Stasiak, sucking wind on that first carry. When I returned to base camp Enrique asked about Stasiak. I told him that I'd seen Stasiak struggling up the ice patch as I was descending, that Stasiak was not a happy camper, that he should have stopped then and there, and that Stasiak had two or three hours before he would even get to Nido. Then Stasiak would have to drop his stuff off and come all the way back down.

◊△◊△◊△◊△◊△◊

MIKE MILFORD   During the first two days at base camp Stasiak and I were content to rest most of the time. We did go out on the moraine and walk around the small lake. That was the first time Stasiak had been on a glacier. There were noises coming from the ice pinnacles which scared him a little bit. Other than that we stayed in camp. It was difficult for us to sleep properly because we were so tired. Even reading was quite a task. On the second night at base camp, I gave Stasiak a Halcion sleeping pill. He slept a few hours that night.

GREG STASIAK   Four hours into the first carry I became surprised at how far Mike and I had gone. Enrique caught up with us and we had lunch. Enrique asked how I felt. In all honesty I felt okay, although it struck me as odd that we were going to return to base camp that night. Enrique said we had one-and-a-half hours to go, so I was confident I could make it to Nido. After lunch Enrique left us, then passed us on his way down.

Three hours later we reached a long ice field. I was exhausted. I strapped my crampons onto a pair of boots lent to me by Enrique. The crampons needed some adjustment. Mike left me and continued up. I got through the ice field and saw other members of the group coming down. They told me I had one more hour to go. Trevor said, "Keep on trudging. You'll make it. You'll get there."

MIKE MILFORD   I went ahead of Stasiak because I knew there were people behind him. I arrived at Nido at 7 PM—seven hours after leaving base camp—and left my load in the cache.

Gustavo said not to rest too long because it would be difficult to get back down after dark. I waited for Stasiak and rested for about half-an-hour. Stasiak was the last person to make it to Nido.

GREG STASIAK   Pépe, Mike, Dick and Gustavo were at Nido when I arrived. I'd only carried a small amount of food and community gear, maybe fifteen pounds. I was totally dizzy. My head was pounding and I couldn't get enough air—much more out of it than I wanted to be.

I wanted to stay in Dick's tent rather than descend to base camp. Gustavo said, "No. We have to go down. There are no stoves here."

I said, "That really doesn't matter. I don't feel like eating anything anyway."

Staying at Nido was definitely out of the plan. I tried to catch my breath and rested for about ten minutes, although it only seemed like a few seconds. Mike finished resting and was ready to head down. I told Mike, "See you at base camp." Mike was off like a shot; he had a second wind and was gone.

Gustavo said we had to descend because it was getting dark. It wasn't really getting dark; a few clouds had blown in. We had a couple hours of daylight left.

MIKE MILFORD   Partway down I looked back and saw that Stasiak had begun his descent. He was in the middle of the ice field, five-hundred feet below Nido.

Lower down, near the bottom of the switchbacks, the trail forked. No one told me which trail to take, so I went to the left and soon I could see base camp. I stopped to look which way to descend and before I made a move someone from base camp saw me and screamed, "No! No! Go to the right!"

I was at the edge of a 100-foot vertical cliff. In daylight it is possible for experienced climbers to go down near the cliffs, but you still have to be careful. In the darkness, if no one had noticed me, I could have walked right off that precipice.

DICK GORDON   I wanted to spend more time at Nido than what Enrique recommended, which was to go up, stow, turn around and come right back down. I spent three or four hours, resting both inside and outside my tent.

Gustavo was stowing gear when I told him I was heading down. He said he was still waiting for two more people, which surprised me because I thought everyone had come and gone. Gustavo said, "They have community gear and I have to wait."

I descended and, halfway through the ice field, saw Stasiak. Stasiak did not make it to Nido. I'm quite positive. He was two-hundred feet below me, on the ridge below the ice field. I stopped and watched him a bit. He looked weak; his motor skills had deteriorated substantially. He took a few steps, then he sat down.

When I got to Stasiak his face was pale, his breathing was shallow and fast, and his legs were shaking. His pulse was up to 150 plus. The temperature wasn't that cold. Stasiak was dressed well, so his shivering seemed to come from fatigue. I don't want to over dramatize this, but I was concerned. I dug through his pack and he still had most of his water which did not taste good because it had been treated with iodine. I guessed that he hadn't eaten or hadn't had enough fluid intake, so I started him on some Gatorade and energy bars. I put him behind a rock and ferried his equipment up to Nido, which took about forty minutes. Then I came down with Gustavo.

Stasiak was in better shape when we got to him, but still not with the program. We got him on his feet and asked if he could make it down. Stasiak wasn't sure, then he was sure, then he wasn't. This went on and on. We started him down the hill and his steps were very slow. We took frequent rests—not every hundred yards, but every twenty feet. Stasiak would breath for awhile and then say, "Okay, I can go, I can go."

We just tried to get a pace on the trail where Stasiak could keep up. The frequent stops began to concern Gustavo and me because it was 7:30 and we figured another two hours till dark. We were nowhere near base camp. We dug into Gustavo's pack, took a harness and a small lead rope, and put these on Stasiak like a leash, to where he could really lean down the mountain. We could resist his forward motion. That really helped a lot. We got off the trail and went straight down.

GREG STASIAK   The desire to take ten steps, or even one step, and then rest was incredible. Dick and Gustavo ignored me after a bit. They tied a cord around me about halfway down. I needed someone to pull me along. They encouraged me, then their tones of encouragement became increasingly nasty. They were impatient because it was getting dark, and they did not want to listen to me saying 'stop' every few feet. Dick and Gustavo kept me going and, in this respect, did a great job. I owe them a lot.

DICK GORDON   Gustavo had such a hard time communicating that I took over in back while Gustavo led the way. It was beneficial having a front person to give direction without communication. Gustavo could just walk down the most direct route. If Gustavo was having a problem with the way Stasiak walked—the size of his steps for instance—he could tell me and I would work with Stasiak on it. We worked out a pattern pretty fast for the way which worked best.

We only got Stasiak halfway to base camp before total exhaustion set in. His breathing became extremely sporadic. His steps and movements were almost out of control. If we were on relatively level ground—on the trail—Stasiak would take a step and it looked like his legs were broken—as though they were rubber—because they would swing and wobble under him. I have never seen anybody as completely fatigued as

Stasiak. I've run several marathons and seen exhaustion, but nothing like that.

When we sat down for rest periods we'd make a point to ask Stasiak questions: "Where are we? Why are we here? What are your parents names? How many brothers do you have? How old are you?" There were times when Gustavo and I became worried because Stasiak did not know his mother's name or his own date of birth. Obviously there is a close connection between mental and physical fatigue.

Stasiak didn't care anymore. He said, "Why don't you all go ahead? I'll be down later." That didn't make a lot of sense! So we knew he was not in a logical or rational state of mind. He did not get overly emotional about anything. Of course, that is Stasiak's personality; he has a very passive personality.

Three-quarters of the way down to base camp Gustavo said to me, "Okay, stay with him. It is getting so dark that I'm going to get help. I'm going for Enrique or Pépe."

Gustavo took off. Boy, did he take off!

MIKE MILFORD   Most people at base camp were sleeping. I sat alone in our tent, waiting and waiting—'Oh shit, if Stasiak dies on the mountain, what am I going to tell his girlfriend and his parents?'

KINGDON GOULD III   By the time it got dark, Dick and Stasiak still were not down. Gustavo went back up with Enrique to meet them above the cliffs. They took a lantern to help get Stasiak through that section. There are several couloirs below the scree field you don't want to come down. It is important to know which path to take.

DICK GORDON   Gustavo and I arrived at base camp around midnight. Stasiak showed up with Enrique forty-five minutes later.

I was so hungry I could have eaten a horse! Gustavo started cooking everything that was left on the table. I chowed down. Then I went to sleep. That was the best sleep I had on the entire expedition.

GREG STASIAK   When we got into base camp I was put in the mess tent. Mike was waiting. He was tired and said he had been worried about me. Enrique asked me questions to determine if I had altitude sickness. I wasn't in any shape to hold a conversation. Enrique told me that I could have any kind of food I wanted and that he was going to have a steak. I agreed to eat. I didn't feel like eating, although I knew I had to get some strength back.

As we ate, Gustavo and Enrique were having a conversation in Spanish. Gustavo, referring to me, said to Enrique, "He is twenty-five or twenty-six years old and he is out of shape."

Enrique said, "Well, he is probably screwing his secretary." Enrique was really annoyed and was venting steam.

MIKE MILFORD   Stasiak was suffering. He was half-dead and incoherent. He was not up to his normal mental capacity. We did not talk to each other. There was nothing to talk about. After Stasiak was given something to eat he just crawled into our tent. I helped him get into his sleeping bag and that was it. The guy was totally exhausted. He was shivering and his teeth were chattering.

Stasiak is a friend of mine, but I made a mistake because I talked him into coming on the expedition. He had been impressed by my trip to Kilimanjaro last year and had said, "Maybe I'll try to go with you next time." He'd signed up in late December, and the commercial company, although they said their trips have a limited number of participants, agreed to take him as an exception.

The general consensus was that Stasiak should not be on the expedition. He was not prepared at all. He tried to condition himself, but that was zero. He ran a little, but it takes four or five months of hard training to prepare for a mountain like Aconcagua. Stasiak had never even been in the mountains, only on a 3500-foot ski hill! He is not the mountaineering type. That was my fault for talking Stasiak into the adventure.

13

APPLES & MARBLES
Expedition Day 6: Third rest day, Base Camp

GREGG LEWIS   On Kilimanjaro the guides would never, never let a client be the last person. If someone crawled, the guides crawled. That's just the way it was. Those Tanzanian guides always gave us a massive head start and would then pick up the trail. I could not believe our guides left Stasiak alone on that damn mountain. As bad a shape as Stasiak was in, he could have easily died.

I suspected, from looking at both Stasiak and Dr. Patel's equipment, that they lacked experience in the mountains. These guys were into big, baggy wool pants and goofy gloves—as if they'd gone to K-Mart and asked for the cheapest clothes. Not that you have to be Mr. GQ up on the mountain, or that everything has to be North Face and color coordinated, but you can look at people's clothes and equipment and get a feel for what their experience has been.

DICK GORDON   In a small fact log dealing with weather, strange occurrences and personal information, I wrote a somewhat detailed description about helping Stasiak down and his fatigue. In the morning Stasiak and I discussed what had happened and what we had done. He showed relatively good signs of remembrance, foggy in some cases, and total non-recollection in other areas.

My opinion is that the commercial company would have ended up with a large number of complaints if Enrique was asked, or told, to make judgements as to which people might not understand what it took to move up the mountain. To tell Stasiak, before the first carry to Nido, that he was not going to be able to go up—even if Enrique knew he was not in shape, and I personally think Enrique did know—would have caused Stasiak to argue. Enrique would have had to say to Stasiak, "You are here at base camp. Getting here was hard for you. You cannot make the first carry. Turn around and go home." If Enrique said that to me, I probably would have argued, "What right do you have?" Enrique, having climbed Aconcagua thirty or forty times, is in a good position to make that judgement, but it would not have been easy for him to do so. That would have caused difficulties and friction within the expedition.

The first carry to Nido was a test trip, so afterwards was a good time to discuss the issue and ask Stasiak what he thought. This gave Stasiak the opportunity to say, "Gosh, I don't think I can make the second carry." Then the situation was to make arrangements for him to go down to Puente del Inca.

◊△◊△◊△◊△◊△◊

MIKE MILFORD   Enrique told us, "Since everyone looks tired we will have another rest day at base camp." Enrique probably knew if he said we had to go directly up to Nido again, there would have been open mutiny. Having another rest day helped everybody a lot.

Despite my age—I'm fifty-five—I anticipated that Aconcagua would be just a slightly higher degree of difficulty than Kilimanjaro. I was expecting to follow the itinerary. Knowing how difficult it is to climb mountains, every stage is important. Enrique, however, had eliminated the intermediate Canada camp and pressed on to Nido.

I also thought the food situation was a disaster. This commercial company collected $30,000 from eighteen people. The food in Argentina is so cheap and so good, but, as far as quality and quantity, the meals Enrique served were very inadequate—nowhere near normal caloric requirements.

Enrique warned us that anyone hiking at a slow pace on the second carry would have to turn back and return to Puente del Inca. I started complaining because we were being deprived of proper acclimatization, decent portions of food, and now, with this warning, Enrique had introduced a new factor of competition amongst the expedition members. Expedition mountaineering is not competitive. One can only make progress and eventually reach the summit by adapting to one's own pace.

It was not only I who complained. I only complained openly and loudly.

CRAIG ROLAND   Mike said to me, "You know, I've climbed Kilimanjaro, but for some reason Aconcagua is not the same. This mountain is much more difficult and I am not in condition." He just said, flat out, that he could not climb Aconcagua. Then Mike had a discussion with Anil Patel, and Patel talked Mike into going up to Nido again.

Between the time Mike told me that he was not in condition and his second carry, Mike decided that the expedition wasn't being run correctly. Mike decided that had the expedition been better operated, his chances of getting higher might have improved. But my view is that Mike had not been in good condition from day one.

I was concerned about the size of the group. The trip was advertised at sixteen people maximum and we ended up with eighteen. That's too large; the group becomes unwieldy. We were also told that the group would be split into a couple of teams, so I expected the guides to match up people of similar condition in well-fitting groups. That did not materialize. We essentially remained one large group.

THOMAS BORGEL   When Enrique picked us up at the Mendoza airport he immediately mentioned, "Oh, I want to leave tomorrow, but we have to wait for all these other people that the manager of the commercial company is sending down. I'm not supposed to have all these people." He was upset.

I did know that if you have sixteen, seventeen or eighteen people, there should be five or six guides. At base camp this doesn't matter; no one is moving anywhere. The commercial company told Lewis and me to expect three guides per eight people. I'd asked Enrique, at Confluencia, "Where are the six guides?" Enrique told me, "Two other guides meet us at base camp. Then two more we pick up at Camp 1." But, besides Enrique and Pépe, the only other guide we would have was Gustavo.

I wasn't freaked about the size of the group or the lack of guides...yet. I was becoming more concerned about the food situation. I still had a queasy stomach, but could eat a little more. I asked for a damn apple. Enrique had a whole case of apples. Before the trip the company manager told me, "Listen, that food is yours. If you want to eat, you go eat." When I tried explaining this to Enrique and Pépe, they got all bent out of shape. I figured I had better not rock the boat. But I was going to get that apple. I ended up swiping an apple when no one was looking.

DICK GORDON   Before the first carry to Nido it became apparent that several individuals were having difficulties such as headaches, or not being able to eat. Stasiak was one of those individuals. Someone not being able to eat was a very real concern. We were at 14,000-feet. What was going to happen to them higher up at 18,000-feet?

There was still concern with a couple of individuals after the first carry. I'd take a minute and ask them, "Is it the food? Is it the quality of the food? Can you not keep the food down?" I'd mention alternatives—"How about trying some energy bars? How about something to sweeten that water up?" Gatorade was real high on my priority list because it helps maintain electrolytes.[13]

Thomas Borgel had not been able to consume dinner one night either due to a headache or taste. He expressed to me that he wasn't eating well. I asked, "Could you get some liquid down, or some soup?" He said, "Yeah. Well, probably." So I said, "Let me get some Lipton soup for you." It was easy to be hospitable because I had such an abundance of supplemental food, as did the Gould's, that we were certainly sharing with anybody that wanted. I'd brought quite a bit of freeze-dried food, candy bars, sweets and soups—boxes of soup.

Other individuals, for whatever reason, could not eat the expedition food. There were complaints. I don't know that the quantity was so insufficient that we went hungry. We all could have eaten more. The altitude may have caused the complaints; when you've been at sea level for a long time, then whip up to 14,000-feet, it is easy to get agitated. There were times when you might say, "I don't want to eat this," or,

---

[13] Water and 'athletic' drinks help combat dehydration, when loss of body fluids inhibits blood circulation and affects body temperature. A sugar content between 2.5 percent and 5 percent is recommended for re-hydration. Specialty drinks help replace vital electrolytes (salt, potassium and bicarbonate.) At high altitude glucose, rather than electrolyte, replacement is a priority.

"This isn't enough," but you make the adjustments you need to make, then move on.

What it gets down to is that there were some people, even at the higher camps, who did not understand the importance of eating when they could. There was some extra-curricular reading that should have been done on that particular subject. If I had put the trip schedule together I would have stressed the need to eat like horses at Puente del Inca and gain weight because everyday thereafter your appetite would progressively get worse. That's a fact. If you are not eating well at base camp, you can't expect to eat any better at the next higher camp. It just is not going to happen. This raised some questions in my mind about whether I had my marbles off, or somebody had their marbles off— 'This is an organized group. They should know more about the mountain than I do. Don't they know you can not ascend the mountain without eating?'

I was eating most of the expedition food that was edible, and supplementing meals with high-energy bars, nuts, and particular types of sunflower or sesame seeds which contain helpful vitamins. I'd keep that food around and pump it. Prior to the trip I tried to be consistent and ate what I thought I'd be eating on the mountain. Every once in awhile, because of guests or business, I'd go out and have a nice meal, but I tried to keep my eating habits simple; I didn't want any major changes in my body once I got on the mountain. Although I'm a wino from those years in Italy, I had stopped drinking all alcohol three or four months prior to the trip. I wanted a successful trip and a good, clear mind.

NUNZIE GOULD   When everyone split up at meal time our family would either decide to be ready for the first serving, or we would say, "Let the chow hounds go for it, and we'll all meet for second serving."

At one particular dinner, when we were handed a bowl of stew containing a piece of meat and one potato, Lewis, and perhaps Mark, commented on how tasty that Big Mac would be when they got back home. I felt we had very decent meals and that our diets on the mountain had been planned. On a couple of mornings, when we needed energy to get up to Camp 1 for instance, we had very salty, fried salami with eggs, or were given hot cereal with raisins and nuts. We were not at a five-star gourmet restaurant. We were out in the middle of nowhere and this wasn't an 'all-you-can-eat' scene.

The meals at base camp were feeding frenzies. It was like—"Here's the food," and all these pigs came grunting in. We realized the expedition was not going to work that way, and this is when a group of people disbanded. Those not caught up with the 'plunge-in' scene— those who had better self-control and more of a sharing attitude— became more aware of collective needs. This was a group that was more communal, a group that would ask, "Is there something extra we can do?" If you were thirsty and wanted water, well, were you going to ask Enrique to get water? Or would you realize you needed to walk to the stream with a ten gallon jug to get water for the group, as well as fill up your own water bottle? I do recall some people not being aware of group needs and not picking up on collective responsibilities. Other individuals were more self-centered, but when called upon would perform community chores. Of course, certain individuals at that stage were not physically comfortable. Those individuals needed to take care of themselves.

GREGG LEWIS   Enrique really vacillated. At times I thought, Well, Enrique is trying his best. He seems like a decent guy. Then I'd see him get pissed off at someone if they asked him a question, and I'd have to shake my head. He would get mad at people's jokes. A rock has more sense of humor than Enrique. He took everything so personal which, as a guide, you just can't do. Strange guy.

DICK GORDON   Enrique has a good sense of humor, and he has all the physical requirements and mental reasoning to deal with the fluctuations, lags and surges which occur with climbing. Having a large group made it difficult for him.

One weakness was a breakdown in communication. Several times words would not be taken as they were meant. Someone might say something in text, but in connotation—because of English—what they said might be different and Enrique would take it wrong. Or vice versa. He might say something in English with a certain inflection that others would misinterpret. I'm sure there were hard feelings, misunderstandings, or indecisions based on poor communication.

BILL ENGLISH   Better communication would have accomplished four things: it would have made the trip educational, enjoyable, safe, and would have developed better camaraderie between the guides and the group as a whole. There should have been staff meetings. This is the problem with me and my work; it's hard to get together and communicate with everybody. But on Aconcagua you had a captive audience. We could have had two meetings a day and people would have been there with rapt attention. Enrique didn't talk about the mountain much at all.

NUNZIE GOULD   Enrique is not the kind of guy that just spills his guts and tells everybody how to do everything. He did consult individual people to get a feeling for how they were doing at the end of a hard day or the following morning. There was no point in being dishonest with him—even for your macho image. I mean, it was obvious that just walking up to Nido and coming back down took some effort, so to pretend that hike was just a piece of cake did yourself no justice. And did Enrique no justice as group leader.

For some people it was not necessary to ask. You could look and tell if another climber was having a hard day. You see changes in their character: how much are they talking at meal time?; are they going out to get extra water like they've been doing for the past few nights?; are they helping somebody else take off their pack?, or did they simply beeline for their tent and we haven't seen them since they've come down? These are the clues one looks for.

The guides generally did not eat with us. They also had their own little group. They could have intermingled more. I don't think the guides felt terrifically comfortable around all of us because we were pretty raucous.

MR. GOULD   I didn't think our group was raucous. The raucous crowd were the Brazilians who had been at base camp during my first trip, and who had celebrated Carnival for three days in a row. One never got to sleep.

◊▲◊▲◊▲◊▲◊▲◊▲◊

NUNZIE GOULD   Dad and I chatted at base camp about who we thought would make the summit. There was the physical scrutiny and then we even came to verbalize who we thought would be successful— 'Trevor, Neil and Mike will not summit. Stasiak and Taplin, of course, are out of the picture. Craig Roland, Dick, and all of our group will probably make it.' This conversation with Dad was part of evaluating everyone's progress. It was all too apparent that people were scrutinizing each other.

Playing cards in base camp was an evening activity. King, Dick, Bill, Craig, and sometimes Mom, Dad and I, were usually the participants in those mad sessions of "Hearts." We definitely had major giggles playing "I Doubt It." The world's worst "I Doubt It" player has got to be Bill. He can't cheat without laughing. He does not have a poker face. We had to teach Craig how to play and then he always won. Craig was very smooth.

Craig and Dad got along in an interesting way. Craig did not have a macho front at all. Dad could relate to Craig on this intellectual level instead of just having to talk about day-to-day events or people's individual history.

MR. GOULD   Craig is an architect, a marathon runner and an amateur astronomer. He had a book on the southern constellations. I don't really know much about the field of astronomy, other than what one learns about the stars to get around, and the wonder they create. I found Craig a contemplative man and enjoyed him very much. If we were neighbors we would probably become good friends. Bill was a very nice fellow. He was suffering from bad health—some stomach disorder or mountain sickness—but he was very uncomplaining.

Dick was an interesting man and a good athlete. I think he had had personal misfortunes in his family fairly recently. Dick liked his privacy and I respected that. I was with three other family members, so I really wasn't trying to intrude or probe the nature of anybody else's personality. As chance had it, sometimes you found yourself with someone during meals or hiking. There was a wide spectrum of abilities and personalities. Each person acted out what he wanted people to consider him to be.

I was reading a wonderful biography of Abraham Lincoln, which has just been re-published. This biography was written by a contemporary of Lincoln's, a man who had been his law partner. That was my primary reading. I hadn't been able to find a great deal of reading material about Aconcagua.

KINGDON GOULD III   I was reading *Even Cowgirls Get the Blues* by Tom Robbins. A smart-alecky book, kind of outrageous—pretty far from what we were doing, but I wasn't trying to read anything that related to what we were doing. I was looking for material that moved right along.

I was trying to rest and not push myself. But I didn't just want to sit around since base camp could get a little boring. I walked on the glacier some more and hiked to Rabbit Ears, a particular rock formation partway back up the hill toward Nido.

TREVOR BYLES   *Lonesome Dove* was a good book; better than the mini-series. I like the western genre. I finished four or five books, including a couple by Sidney Sheldon. We kept switching books around. *Lonesome Dove* was Mark's book, but he couldn't get into it. Neil was reading *Road to Gandolfo*.

Neil, Borgel, Lewis, Mark and I sat around after meals and talked about getting laid and getting drunk. That's mostly what we talked about every night—girls, the mountain and drinking. It was funny. Mark would tell us stories about Bangkok. And Neil would talk about clothing for mountaineering.

BILL ENGLISH   Mark, Lewis and Borgel's tent was near ours and I got really tired of listening to them. They sounded like high school kids most of the time. A lot of their conversation was immature, sexual stuff. I had the feeling all three of them were live-for-today yuppie yahoos who had the money for this trip and did it. They didn't have a real social consciousness, and they didn't have a real appreciation for what was at hand. Every time something went wrong they had a negativity toward Enrique and the total effort. I tended to wander away when they were gathered somewhere; I tended to gather somewhere else.

MARK CORNWALL   Some of us were sitting in the eating tent, cussing up a storm, when Nunzie came over and said, "I just want to tell you that I'm beginning to find your language very offensive. If you continue we'll have to separate the camp."

Then Borgel or someone said, "Well fuck, what do you mean?"

It was just bizarre, as though we now could not cuss on the mountain.

NUNZIE GOULD   Hearing this coarseness was one of the things that put a lot of other people off. If that is what people want to talk about, well great—when they are at a distance, or in their own tents. But to talk like that in a public meeting area, where we gathered to chat, drink tea or play cards, was not necessary.

I came right out and said something to the effect of: "Hey, why are you guys being so offensive? You can talk clean. Why do you have to talk dirty here?" The result was quite stunning. It almost shocked me too because usually I can sit through a lot of discomfort before I say anything. This is true of our whole family, in terms of sitting through physical or mental difficulties without saying anything until you're really hurting, even though you've actually been irked the whole time. Whatever I said had an effect and they stopped saying foul language in front of me. Whether it was only in front of me I don't know, but they made a concerted effort and leveled out.

TREVOR BYLES   That's just manners. That was a fine request to make. Nunzie made that request, although I think she made it with her mother in mind. The other guys probably thought Nunzie was a bitch, but it didn't bother me. I could live without cussing in front of an older lady.

< 14 >

A FRAME OF MIND
Expedition Day 7: Second carry to Camp 1

TREVOR BYLES   Dr. Patel and Mike were the first out of base camp for the second carry to Nido. They left very early, at 7 AM. Neil and I headed up at noon, just ahead of everybody else. The hike to Nido is steep, long, and everyone was carrying heavy packs; not unreasonably heavy—mostly personal gear and the tents. The second carry was only easier in the sense that there was no anticipation of wondering whether you could make 17,500-feet. It was just a matter of getting there.

Neil was a good pacer. He and I walked at a constant flow. Nunzie and the rest of the Gould's were on our heels the whole way up. The Gould's were very nice, but I didn't really talk with Mr. Gould or Mumsy. They were from another generation and a different background. While climbing the mountain I wanted to reach the summit, so, for my own reasons, was hoping these older people were not going to hold us back. But Mr. and Mrs. Gould were tough. I couldn't believe them. The entire Gould family was tough, especially Nunzie. She hiked the drawers off me.

The Gould's would take a rest, we'd pass them, then they would catch up to us because they had a faster pace. They came in right behind us. Dr. Patel and Mike were already at Nido when we arrived.

GREGG LEWIS   The second carry was much easier—my pack was lighter—and I felt good. Borgel had a tough time again. Anytime he changed altitude 3,000-feet he would be in agony, moaning and groaning. Mark and I were trying to get him through day by day. We were not thinking summit; we were telling Borgel that he looked good and that he could make it to Camp 2. Borgel told us, "This is it. I've had enough. This is too fucked up."

As usual, Mark and I talked him into waiting another day. Mark showed a lot of concern for Borgel. Mark was always in a good mood and helped keep spirits up. He's a perennial jokester.

MARK CORNWALL   Both carries to Nido, for me, were horrible. It was the toughest hiking I've ever done. I got blisters coming down after the first carry. Those blisters, though not a factor walking uphill, burned me for the rest of the trip.

The lack of oxygen played a role, but going all the way to Nido was too high. Camp Canada would have been just right at 16,000-feet. That extra 1,500-feet to Nido is a tough little hump. Above 16,000-feet there was a demonstrative slow down; my body hit a wall and did not want to press on. I was a bit taken aback because I expected to be fresher and in better shape.

I was one of the last persons into Nido after the second carry. Once I sat down and rested, I stabilized.

<u>NUNZIE GOULD</u>   Invariably the guides would start behind us, pass us, and arrive at camp first. When they passed us they would always be singing. King made the comment that the singing was just put on for us so the guides could show they were bombing along and that it was no big deal.

Mark really suffered from his blisters and was near the end of the line. I walked and chatted with him a little bit at rest stops. His whole attitude had changed and he was acting more mature. The fact that Mark had climbed McKinley did not impress me. A lot of people thought Aconcagua would not be a problem because of their previous accomplishments or training. There was this cocky attitude—'We're going to conquer this mountain'—yet, as people began to be effected by altitude, food, or lack of sleep, their personalities came down to earth. As we progressed their attitudes changed to: 'Maybe I'm not so great after all.'

I was glad to be back at Nido; frankly I felt I was starting to get somewhere. But I lost some focus and started to have character problems with the people in our own little network. Specifically, when we arrived after the second carry, Dad was quite particular about where he wanted to place our tent. Enrique had told us to pitch our tent near his, mostly for convenience of food. Dad had not heeded this advice because he wanted his own camp. Nido is just rock on top of rock, yet Dad was determined to level a nice place for our tent and have a flat place for Mom to sleep. Well, after a certain stage it was dark, a storm came in, the wind was blowing like mad, we were tired, and I wanted to just lie down on my bag—'Hey guys, we're not at home. We're camping. Just pitch the tent and take away the obvious rocks. Let's not try to excavate Aconcagua.' King, who was tenting with Dick, was getting frustrated trying to help. He was hollering at Dad, "If you want me to help you, do it this way."

We had this big family squabble. You know how it is when too many people try to put up a tent. Dad was getting on both my nerves and King's nerves. The altitude had effected Dad more than us. He'd had difficulties on both carries to Nido. It wasn't a time to be fussy but this, for us, was Dad's expedition and he was going to do it the way he wanted. I was pretty hot, so I just walked away to let Dad and King finish with the tent. I knew that if I stayed around I'd blow up. There is a time when you need to be by yourself. It was pointless to be picky about where to put the tent because we could move it the next day. I was pretty bitchy that night.

◊△◊△◊△◊△◊△◊△◊

<u>ANIL PATEL</u>   Mike and I left base camp, without breakfast, and arrived at Nido around 3 PM. I tried to be good to Mike because he was older and slower. He had done poorly two days before on the first carry, and had wanted to give up. When we were going up on the second carry we encouraged each other. I told Mike he could make it to the top.

<u>MIKE MILFORD</u>   We met a German climber about three-quarters of the way up to Nido. We stopped and chatted with him. He told us he was a teacher from Hamburg who gave up his work for one year because he had been asked to go on an Everest expedition. Using his own money, he was training by spending several weeks in the Aconcagua region. He was really in good shape; he had hiked to the summit three times in three weeks. This German climber told us, "About half-an-hour from now you will find a Japanese fellow. He took a fall. Something is wrong with his head."

When we saw the Japanese climber he said hello—"Banzai" or whatever—and told us he was from Tokyo. He was alone. As I was putting my crampons on to get across the ice field, he said to me, "Excuse me sir. Do you know how far it is to the beach?" Then he said, "Tomorrow we attack the summit."

Maybe he had fallen and hurt his head. All I know is that rushing up a mountain by accelerating one's own pace is an invitation to high-altitude sickness.

I felt very good on the second carry; still no headache and no problem with the altitude. I was completely acclimated from resting at base camp. Since Stasiak decided to stay at Mulas, I didn't have a tent. When I arrived at Nido the weather was getting bad; it was windy and had started to snow. Everybody was preparing their camp sites. I waited for Enrique to arrive and assign me to a tent. I started to feel chilled from not moving, so I pulled out my sleeping bag and crawled in, wearing everything, including my parka.

When Enrique came into camp he thought I was exhausted. He said, "Mike, I suggest you go down. If you continue higher and have to walk alone, I will have to give you some assistance, and I cannot spare anybody in case someone else needs assistance."

When someone comes to you after you've been hiking all day and says you look like shit and should not go any further, you just lose all motivation. Maybe I shouldn't have, but I lost all desire to continue. I didn't want to impose on anyone and ask, "Can I sleep in your tent?" Enrique was the leader and should have said, "You will sleep with so-and-so tonight in their tent." This was what I was waiting to hear from him, not how shitty I looked.

I told Enrique, "I can still continue up."

He said, "You better go down."

There was no argument. Enrique thought it would not be fair to the others because I might be a liability higher on the mountain. If the head guide says, "You are exhausted and are not thinking normally," what can you do? I was totally disappointed at how the expedition was being handled, my confidence was undermined, my mental ability was weakened, and my heart was just not there. I decided to descend to base camp.

GREGG LEWIS   After arriving at Nido, we asked Mike how he felt. Mike said he felt fine. Mike had a nice personality. He looked good and didn't seem exhausted, so we all assumed that he would stay at Nido. Two or three hours later I saw Mike packing his gear and asked what he was doing. Mike said, "I'm going down."

"What's the beef?"

"Well, I don't get any damn encouragement from Enrique. Enrique thinks I should go down."

"Mike, you look great to me! You can make it."

"No. I don't need this shit. This trip is nothing like I expected it to be. I just don't want to go on anymore."

Mike packed his gear and that's all we said. He headed down. We'd already worked it out so that he had a place to sleep. There were plenty of tents. When Mike left we were shocked; everyone was surprised. What was scary was that people were peeling off and going solo. I felt bad for Mike, I really did. I thought he could have made it to Camp 2.

TREVOR BYLES   Mike asked Neil and me if he could tent with us. We said, "Yeah, sure. No problem. That's fine."

Mike put his stuff by our tent, then went and lay in his sleeping bag. When Mike came back around to our tent he said he was going down. We asked why and Mike said, "I want to make sure Stasiak is okay."

Later, when I heard Enrique had asked Mike to descend, I thought it was a reasonable request because Mike was dead tired. He would not have made it any higher. I wrote in my journal: "Mike has decided to descend. Dr. Patel should probably go down also. The doctor will die if he goes any higher." Dr. Patel was sick—he had diarrhea—and was walking around in a daze. Both Mike and Dr. Patel had an eight hour day on that second carry from base camp to Nido. It had taken Neil and I five hours to hike up.

After Mike quit, Neil and I decided we were hexed because all our tent mates were dropping out.

KINGDON GOULD III   Enrique was concerned about Mike and tried to convince him, at base camp, not to make a second carry. Mike talked with several people, including myself, about whether to go up again or not. He felt maybe he would go, then felt maybe he wouldn't. People have to make their own decisions with these types of matters. I didn't particularly advise Mike one way or another. If I'd had to say should he continue or not, I would have said no. I passed Mike toward the end of the second carry and he seemed to have gotten as far as he could go. He was whipped and he was having a hard time. When people get beyond their limits, continuing upward is dangerous for them and dangerous for others.

I know Mike felt the expedition was not being run the way he would have liked, but we were at an altitude that is tiring for people. The altitude effects your mind, and you are bound to be discouraged if you are unable to live up to expectations. Also, it was clear Stasiak would not come up to Nido again. I think Mike felt some obligation to stick with Stasiak, since Mike had talked Stasiak into coming along on the trip. Stasiak was a nice guy, but he didn't know squat about the outdoors.

Acclimatizing doesn't happen on a particular schedule. A lot of it is if you are a little sick, or get very tired at some point, or don't sleep well—these can all set you back. Not getting proper rest can have a heck of an effect. However, if you are able to maintain your composure and relax, you can get back into it. Bill English suffered going up to Nido, especially on the first carry. Bill had headaches at base camp and felt pretty rough for a couple of days, but he did not get excited about what was happening. A lot of people had headaches of one sort or another. Craig Roland was in good aerobic shape and also quite experienced with the outdoors. He had run a marathon in under three hours, so he knows about the effects of good breathing. Deep breathing helps a lot against headaches. A lot. As I walked to Nido I made a very conscious effort to breathe as deeply and regularly as possible. I had a slight headache when I arrived at Nido, but not too bad. I was not suffering like I had on my last trip.

It's a frame of mind. You don't conquer a mountain but rather get in sync with the mountain. You have to accommodate yourself to the mountain. Knowing what to expect, drinking more liquids on a regular basis, and being conscious of breathing all become second nature to someone who is at altitude a lot. I don't know if they were second nature for me, but it was my second trip to Aconcagua.

◊∆◊∆◊∆◊∆◊∆◊∆◊

GREG STASIAK   Base camp had become the in-spot on Aconcagua. There were horseman ferrying loads for all kinds of people trying to get in their last shot at the mountain. There was a young kid who was soloing. He had about as much equipment as I did, which was frightening. There were two Australians, Max and Milton. Max was an eighty-year old guy who had made the summit. Milton was his guide. I was able to socialize with these people, but I also wondered what the hell I was doing there.

Enrique had told both Mike and Dr. Patel, on the morning of the second carry, that they should not continue on the expedition. I'd said to Mike, "Look, you should continue if the altitude is not bothering you. You have all this gear, you've spent all this money. Try the second carry and see how you feel. If you think you will not continue above Nido, return to base camp." So, although I didn't expect it, there was this possibility Mike might come back down.

I knew it would get dark soon, so I walked up the trail for about half-an-hour, and was surprised to see Mike. He was exhausted and out of breath. He was going down for the count and was not talkative. It was good to see him in one piece. I helped carry his pack and we made it back to camp before dark, around 8 PM.

We had the most disgusting meal in the world that night. Milton mentioned he had been saving something. I said, "God, anything you have would be good. Mike needs some food. He could use a warm meal."

Milton pulled out this industrial, twenty-eight ounce can of tuna fish. We mixed the tuna with wet rice and ketchup. We flavored that with salt and pepper. It tasted great at the time. I would never make it again.

Most of the expedition food Mike and I found at base camp was not well kept; it was not stored in the containers. We didn't bother to look at the containers. This food was all sitting in a box in the food tent, exposed to the air and temperature. There was five or ten pounds of meat, fruit, cheese—some of which was either rotten or rancid. We also found some beer. There was enough food for our group to finish their expedition, but when Mike and I left base camp the next day, a lot of people, at least five other groups, had come down off the mountain. I think these people were starving and attacked whatever expedition food was left over.

MIKE MILFORD   There was no point in staying on the mountain. Stasiak and I trekked to Puente del Inca with Max and two Californians. Milton, who had lived in the Andes for many years, called the mule drivers on the short-wave radio to arrange for our gear to be taken out. The mules did not arrive with our gear for two days because Milton tried to bargain the mule drivers down to ten dollars. Sometimes you can out-smart yourself.

< 15 >

THE FROZEN PLATEAU
Expedition Day 8: Rest day at Nido

<u>CRAIG ROLAND</u>   The rest of us spent a lay-over day at Nido de Condores. There were a few other campers and Nido was the usual garbage pit, but not as bad as Plaza de Mules. People laid around, or went hiking and took pictures. Everyone was breathing hard. No one was running around at top speed.

It was a gorgeous day. While Nido has some little ponds with scattered snow and rock, it's mostly a bleak, wild, barren, wind-swept plateau which runs up against the mountain on one side. One can see the summit from Nido—not a dominate view, but you can just barely make out the top of Aconcagua almost 6,000-feet above. There is a huge buttress below the summit, and the wind blows snow off that face everywhere it's not protected.

The other side of the Nido plateau drops off onto the Güssfeldt Glacier. There were vast views a hundred miles to the north and east. We could not see base camp, but there were views of mountains almost as big as Aconcagua, such as Mercedario.

<u>BILL ENGLISH</u>   The plateau is only about three football fields large; there wasn't too far we could go if we wanted to hike around. Then again, you don't have much energy. There is all this grandeur surrounding Nido, but no oxygen to speak of. Any distance one traveled, one worked for harder than at base camp.

Just going to get water was quite a trek in itself. We got water from one of the frozen ponds, which only thawed in the late afternoon. There were problems finding water, determining if the water was clean, and confusion—just as there had been at base camp—about Enrique's directions. The water source was a couple hundred yards from the tents. We carried open buckets over frozen, icy, somewhat pinnacled snow. The water was sloshing out, so you were either losing water or getting water all over you and freezing to death.

Nido is beautiful but I don't know how you could be any more exposed. The tents were the biggest objects on that plateau; the rocks were not any larger than chairs. There was one little out-cropping of rocks where Enrique pitched the guide tent. The guides were tucked back into this shelter where they were able to cook. At meal time it was windy; you'd have to huddle behind anything you could find, sit there and eat. There was always soup and a ladle full of something. You could stand around outside for a little while and talk, but often-times people would just retreat back into their tents. We just did things to occupy time because it was too cold and uncomfortable to sit outside.

Nido wasn't nearly as laid back, casual or as social as base camp had been.

I was damn glad I was there and functioning. I didn't have serious crash-out problems like I'd had two days before. And my sphincter was holding firm.

KINGDON GOULD III   The expedition was now smaller by three people. The group was less expansive and more focused. People knew each other a little better. And we were getting closer to the moment of truth. On the other hand, you are less likely to eat or sleep well. Sleeping at that altitude is not resting because you are not getting any more oxygen in your system. You are actually draining your system. At this point you are working against time. You want to spend a little time at Nido to acclimate, but not so much time as to begin to deteriorate.

And I imagined Enrique didn't want to spend more than two nights above Nido because it would be harder to get water, harder to feed people, and considerably colder. Obviously your ability to cook decreases the higher you go. At base camp we had better food because it was easier to cook—we could cook on Coleman stoves—whereas at Nido we were cooking off a WhisperLite MSR which feeds off a pump bottle.

E.A. FITZGERALD   In the afternoon we had a fine view of the Pacific Ocean, the clouds which so often hung to the west of us having been dispelled by a heavy gale of wind.

Another of our great difficulties (as we discovered later), was that the food that we were eating at this time was not of the right sort. The digestion is so weak at these altitudes that the ordinary kind of camp food is quite unsuitable; afterwards, when we brought up eggs and port wine and condensed beef-teas, we suffered less than we did in these first attempts. We also found that the tinned foods did not agree with us, and it was not till we had fresh meat, and plenty of wood to cook it with (as spirits would not burn), that we were able to fortify ourselves sufficiently to fight against the combined effects of cold and physical depression.

CRAIG ROLAND   At this point we were on freeze-dried food, and the quality of it deteriorated a lot. The quality was much more inferior to what we had been having at base camp. You can't cook freeze-dried food properly when you're that high; nothing quite congeals or becomes reconstituted the right way. It always tastes as though you're eating sand. I knew, from previous backpacking experience, that freeze-dried food was not going to be particularly appetizing. That's just the way it was, but it may have been a shock to some people.

The initial meal we had at Nido, the night after the second carry, was fine. There was plenty of freeze-dried food. It wasn't until later that I thought we had a serious problem in quantity of food. I lost a lot of weight, most of it in a few days, higher on the mountain.

GREGG LEWIS   For breakfast we had some granola bars and hot tea. My appetite was fine, but I was never full on the whole trip except when we had freeze-dried pasta-noodles in clam sauce. That was the only meal I walked away from full.

MARK CORNWALL   The worst dinner we had was noodles in clam sauce. At that altitude noodles in clam sauce was not gourmet. The grub tasted like hell.

Enrique, Pépe and Gustavo served food right from their tent, which is understandable, but the guides never came out of that tent. They'd sit in there and they'd be rapping away in Spanish. Ridiculous. We never saw the guides above base camp except at meals.

NUNZIE GOULD   Enrique again told us to take it easy and rest. The guides never left their tent unless necessary. They too were conserving energy. Occasionally Pépe would come out, sing romantic songs, and beat on a pot as though it were a drum. He was always pretty shy about his singing, but I would clap and encourage him from our tent.

Pépe and Gustavo were both very friendly. I took a picture of them and Enrique looking out of their tent. They have three big smiles and there is a cooking pot out front. That's how I remember them: huddled in their tent, but still with smiles.

Our family never cooked our own food at base camp or at Nido. We contributed freeze-dried food, along with white gas, into the communal pot. At mealtime everyone would walk over with their cups and spoons. Each person drank and ate out of one cup because putting anything down just got cold. If someone felt sick they would not come out to eat. A few people like Dad and Bill were not feeling well.

Once at Nido it was a major effort to drink more fluids. The trade off was you would drink more fluids, but then you would have to pee—'I don't want to go outside the tent again! I was just out there five minutes ago.' Yet you realized that you needed to restore fluids lost at altitude through perspiration and breathing.

NEIL DELEHEY   I felt more confidant, more acclimated. I wasn't doing calisthenics, but I was comfortable. Nights at Nido, though, were frigid; we had to sleep with our cameras, boots and water bottles. Trevor's camera was the worst because the shutter kept freezing.

Trevor and I weren't complaining about food. We didn't expect great food. We never went hungry going up Aconcagua. If someone was sick, or didn't feel like eating, we ate their food. We were eating whatever was available—we ate dehydrated food right out of the bag.

The group mostly had a liquid diet: soups, hot chocolate, tea and coffee. I couldn't believe we were being served coffee. I'm no brain child, but coffee is a diuretic and makes you pee. Why pack diuretics if you want to retain liquids? That didn't make sense, so I didn't drink any coffee at all.

We all talked about what we were shitting. That was a source of entertainment. Everyone just shit their brains out.

NUNZIE GOULD   Enrique gave us these apricot bars made in New Zealand. A lot of the pre-packaged food was either from New Zealand or Australia. Dad just could not stomach anything. When you have major trots even something like a dried fruit bar is enough to make anyone think twice. Dad was super sensitive and did not even want to talk about it. Enrique got diarrhea and Dad gave him some Lomotil. Enrique was impressed by the results and was smiling the next day.

Both carries to Nido were hard, but I felt good: my digestive system was organized and I had recuperated some body strength. I was not suffering from any high altitude aliments. Mom, Dad and I were on Diamox, which I think helped. My idea was to start on Diamox, but to stop if I felt okay. Enrique went over medications with us one day and said, "You've been on Diamox? You stay on it until you are back down in Puente del Inca." Enrique's concern was that one of us might stop taking Diamox for a day, then get up to Nido and flip out. So, we took his advice.

I was also taking a multi-vitamin mineral supplement. I'm not a pill popper, but the combination of not feeling great and being under the weather in Puente made me want to pump myself up and get energized. I was working toward a good curve—getting to the top on a strong day— and had that mapped out pretty well.

ANIL PATEL   I had researched high-altitude sickness and had read an article about it in the *New England Journal of Medicine*. There are some precautions which can be taken to avoid acute mountain sickness, like climbing high and sleeping low. Climbing a mountain should never be a race. You have to take time to acclimate. And there are some drugs, like Diamox, that help with acclimation.

Most doctors believe that the higher one goes, reduced attmospheric pressure and lack of oxygen causes changes in blood gases. Blood vessels constrict and tissues fight for oxygen. Diamox inhibits the enzyme carbonic anhydrase, and increases the acidity of the blood by favorably excreting bicarbonate. Diamox, being a diuretic as well as an alkalizing agent, helps to counter some of the effects of carbon dioxide loss caused by rapid breathing at high altitude. It increases blood oxygen levels and helps keep breathing regular.

On Aconcagua I took Diamox everyday, starting at Plaza de Mules. If I had not taken Diamox I might have suffered severe headaches and other high-altitude sickness syndromes such as high blood pressure, or possibly developed pulmonary edema. You never know. I grew up at an elevation of 6,000 feet, had climbed Mt. Kenya seventeen times and Kilimanjaro three times. I was never bothered by altitude sickness on those climbs, although the last time I went up Kilimanjaro I took Diamox.[14]

MR. GOULD   I was making it alright. I did have trouble eating with enthusiasm because of an internal disorder which had plagued me since arriving at Puente del Inca. I was prudent in whatever I did to avoid intestinal problems; I either drank boiled water or used Halazone which helps purify the water. I think the problem is just 'el tourista'— some type of endemic organism—and you can get it no matter where you go, particularly in South America.

Diamox didn't have any effect on my digestive system one way or another. Taking Diamox was a recommendation by my physician. I had also taken Diamox on my first attempt. I had not had a problem acclimating ever, but don't really know if Diamox helped. Neither Mary nor I noticed any side effects. Mary is very healthy and seems to stay in shape, so she is lucky.

ANIL PATEL   I lost twenty pounds on Aconcagua. I don't know what caused the diarrhea—maybe unclean hands. Mr. Gould had some Lomotil, but it didn't help me at all. Diarrhea was one thing I didn't really mind.

Diamox can actually compound the problem of diarrhea in a sense because, if you are losing fluids through diarrhea and are losing fluids through diuretics, that is not a good thing.

◊△◊△◊△◊△◊△◊△◊

BILL ENGLISH   It was a funny, weird, eclectic group. I remember Anil Patel looking up at the top of the mountain we're about to climb. I forget what Anil had on from the waist down, but he was wearing his ever-present black and white flannel shirt, not tucked in and unbuttoned to the belly, with red thermal underwear underneath. That's all he had on. It had to be 25°F.—even at mid-day the temperature never got above 25°—yet we would frequently see the doctor around camp dressed in this manner. Everyone else is practically frozen, even with GoreTex jackets on and hoods secured around our

---

14 Altitude sickness, caused by decreased oxygen in the blood (hypoxia), is brought on by climbing too high too fast, and failing to acclimatize. Symptoms include 'dry' coughs, shortness of breath, severe headaches, loss of appetite, ataxia or lack of coordination, nausea and vomiting. Advanced stages of these aliments can lead to pulmonary or cerebral edema—the accumulation of fluids in the lungs or brain. The best treatment is immediate descent. If not treated edema can result in death.

Consult your physician before taking any 'quick fix' drugs, including Diamox (Acetazolamide), Dexamethasone or Nifedipine, as well as any sleeping aids, at high altitude.

faces. But Anil is standing there as though nothing is going on, without a hat or anything on his head.

There were a lot of clearly distinct mini-groups: Mark, Lewis and Borgel; Trevor and his buddy Neil, who stayed really off to themselves; the Frank brothers whom Anil ended up tenting with; Craig and myself, who had our own tent which we were thankful for; Dick; and the Gould's, who were a separate entity.

So, the group was very divided. I would never say the group was cohesive from day one, or even worse, by the last day. There were strange animosities between certain individuals which, I suppose in a group of fifteen people, are going to happen anyway. Craig and I pretty much stuck to ourselves, or stuck to our own selves. We didn't take sides or form allegiances.

I got to know the Gould's better than anyone else. I was impressed with them, and really liked their spirit and their openness. They were non-judgmental and positive all the time. They had a lot of good energy. As a family, and physically, they were a self-sufficient unit. They stuck together and took care of each other.

DICK GORDON   The cliques started from the beginning. Everybody tended to pair up with someone who had similar feelings: if two people have a problem with something, they are going to listen to each other; those people who are aggressive and fast-paced will get together; those people with great attitudes, or those who are funny, will get together.

Everybody on the expedition had a difficult chore to perform and I certainly did not want to spend time with anyone who was continuously going to complain, or not have positive thoughts, hopes and feelings. Problems were going to occur within the group, so you go and help those individuals, get the expedition back up to speed, then continue on as a team. This is why I tried to help the guides.

The Gould's left their small tent at base camp to cut down on weight, so young Kingdon took up my offer to share my tent. We had conversations about our opinions of family, sibling rivalry, and details about philosophy. We discussed the incidents which had happened with Taplin and Stasiak, various symptoms of high-altitude sickness, and, of course, we talked about the mountain and the days to come.

NUNZIE GOULD   King was pretty mellow and was gravitating away from all the noisy, young guys. He said, "Come on down," so I'd go play cards with him and Dick. We had tea in the morning or at night over at Dick's tent. That was nice. I felt like I had to give Mom and Dad some time together—and just get away from them.

King and I had some interesting chats about different trips, the outdoors, and his philosophy about raising children. Before the trip I really didn't know King that well. As kids he and I were in different age brackets; he had different experiences and interests as we were growing up. The trip gave me a chance to catch up with King.

I was feeling an affinity with Dick because he wasn't involved with all the goofy stuff. I felt he was more mature than the other guys.

Romance on Aconcagua? I wasn't into the romantic scene. I'd just come off a major relationship and was trying to get back on my feet.

Dick felt a fondness for Mom. He called my mother 'Mom' throughout the trip. That was interesting. Dick kept saying, "How we doing, Mom?" Actually, a lot of people related to her on a 'Mom' basis. No one called her 'Mary' except for Enrique and Craig.

At Nido I discussed with Mom her desire to climb the mountain. I was quite vociferous about it and said to her, "You basically threw all your gear together on the last day. What is your commitment to the mountain? You have to voice your commitment." I was irritated and wanted to pump this out of her. She had made it to Nido without going through the training. I was beginning to wonder why I had gone through all the training. Inside she was committed to go to the top, but she wasn't willing to come out and say, "I'm committed. I'll take the challenge and the pain that goes with it."

MARY GOULD   I did not want to influence any of the other members of my family. I didn't want them to feel that I was going to hold them back, and I didn't want them to feel that I was going to go on if they wanted to hold back. I went along for the fun, and I was having a good time. I wasn't waiting to see how I felt higher up at Camp 2—I was planning to summit and felt physically able. But you never know if you might be stuck in a snow storm for a week. Those things can happen, so you do take it one day at a time.

There is a challenge when you get up there, but I don't feel the challenge as strongly as my husband does. There is a change in him when he goes off on these adventures. He gets away from all his problems. When you are that far away, nobody can reach you. That's great. My husband is obsessed by anything that he has not been able to accomplish. That doesn't just mean a mountain—anything he decides he wants to do, he is very determined.

MR. GOULD   What may have stimulated my original desire to climb Aconcagua was an article about some local people who had attempted the mountain. They hadn't been properly equipped and they'd had a bad experience—'That was kind of an amateurish way to do it. I should be able to do better.'

Of course, King and I had not had our summit opportunity three years ago. Although I wanted to take another shot at Aconcagua I abandoned any thoughts about returning for awhile because I had a back operation in the spring after that first attempt. I had a very, very slow recuperation, and at one point was pretty depressed because I wasn't sure I'd be able to ever do any more backpacking, hiking or running. Nobody could figure out why I hadn't been able to make a good recovery. The doctors gave me pills for this and pills for that, and they took a tap out of my bone marrow—a whole lot of whoopla.

Finally I arrived at the extraordinary conclusion that Knox Gelatin, which physicians sometimes prescribe to people who have very brittle fingernails, might be good for disks and for cartilage, because disks and cartilage do not regenerate; that is why they wear out. So I took Knox Gelatin for eight weeks and threw away all my pills. Haven't had any pills since.

Maybe Knox Gelatin has nothing to do with enabling me to regain some flexibility. But to my way of thinking it has been the difference between night and day; I went from not being able to run, to being able to run. Isn't that bizarre? Four months before this attempt I had improved a lot. I started to get back in shape by jogging and back-packing with firewood in my pack—not the two together though.

◊△◊△◊△◊△◊△◊△◊

THOMAS BORGEL   When I'd arrived at Nido after the second carry I was in major pain from a headache and a pinched nerve in my neck. I went over to Enrique and said, "Listen, you have to give me some medicine because I can no longer put up with this." Enrique let me into his tent and massaged my neck which made the pinched nerve feel 100 percent better. I really appreciated him doing that.

Then Enrique gave me two muscle relaxants. He didn't tell me I was only supposed to take one of those suckers. He gave me two, so I took both of them and they wound me right out. I don't remember what happened. People said I started running around shooting pictures. I must have taken three rolls of film in one hour. Everyone thought I had all the energy in the world. But I still had a headache. I wrote in my diary that I was going down to base camp the next day. Mark and Craig Roland were a big help because they gave me suggestions on how to relieve those headaches, and they talked to me about the breathing method. Lewis told me to go to sleep and see how I felt in the morning. I woke up the morning of our rest day at Nido feeling unbelievable, like a new person—'Erase last night's part of the diary!'

Sunsets at Nido were beautiful. And there was an incredible thunderstorm one night; a big, big storm which looked as though it was heading our way, with huge bolts of lightning starting in these cumulus clouds, then shooting all the way to the ground. With the red light hitting the snow on the mountaintops—the alpenglow—it was just unreal. I'd never seen anything like that before.

< 16 >

PIERDA BLANCA
Expedition Day 9: To Camp 2, White Rocks

KINGDON GOULD III   The trail up the standard route, from Nido, curves around the northwest edge of the Gran Acarreo and follows a ridge to camps Berlin and White Rocks. The Gran Acarreo is that portion of the upper mountain which sweeps down into a semi-basin at camp Alaska; unconsolidated stones—a wide scree slope for the most part—with only one or two distinguishing outcroppings of rock. Enrique warned us that, during a descent from the summit or one of those high camps, it would be dangerous to avoid the trail by cutting straight down the Gran Acarreo; it is pretty exposed and there is not much shelter from storms.[15]

TREVOR BYLES   Neil and I were both acclimated from spending a rest day at Nido, and were the first to leave for Camp 2 at White Rocks. We took it steady and slow up the switchbacks, stopping for a rest at Camp Berlin {19,500-feet} with Gustavo. Above Berlin there are some steep sections with rocks you have to scramble over, but nothing too difficult. When Neil and I arrived at White Rocks, Enrique had already cleared a space for our tent.

We knew the group was going to pass Camp Berlin and continue on to White Rocks. That was planned by Enrique because he had tried to point out White Rocks from Nido—"Follow my finger. There is White Rocks where we will camp." I kept thinking, Yeah, but which white rocks is he talking about?

Passing the intermediate camps was not that big a deal; I'd made it to Nido without getting too tired, and I was in a hurry to get up the mountain because my dad had told me the weather in late February would start to deteriorate. There was no way the beautiful weather could last. Every rest day, even though it was good to rest, I wanted to climb higher because I didn't want to forfeit our summit attempt. But other people were hindered by moving up the mountain too fast. Realistically, intermediate camps or additional rest days are very necessary.

NEIL DELEHEY   After passing Berlin, Trevor and I both sped up a little. Forty feet below White Rocks I had a relapse of my base camp heart condition and I had to stop and rest. I didn't tell Trevor or anyone.

---

[15] There is a small hut, the refugio Antartida Argentina, located on the bottom slope of the Gran Acarreo near the Nido plateau. Judging, however, from the condition of other refugios on the mountain, this structure is probably only useful for emergency bivouacs.

'Acarreo' literally translates as cartage, transport, or haul.

It only lasted about fifteen minutes, then it disappeared and never came back.

MARK CORNWALL   Going high on Aconcagua is similar to going to the end of the earth, working through the rubble, with a long line of carcasses along the trail. There was even a dead horse just below Berlin at 19,000-feet. I could not figure out how that horse got so high.

MR. GOULD   My previous high on the mountain with King had been Camp Berlin. It felt good reaching at least that point again. We didn't have a celebration. Berlin is a miserable place; one of the three huts was filled with trash, and another had its roof torn off.[16]

NUNZIE GOULD   The problem with Berlin was that it grossly stank of urine. If we had camped there we would have died from urine-halation.
There was an American at Berlin, Nicholas, who had tried the summit and was resting for a second attempt. He offered us hot tea. Nicholas had been living in Argentina for a couple of years. We first saw him at Puente del Inca, where he was selling mineral samples from one of those wheel-about stands. The next thing we knew he was at base camp hiking up the mountain with some people he'd met. He had bummed gear, which was weird because climbers from other groups had gear, such as boots and crampons, stolen at Nido. Although people coming off the mountain had sold some of their equipment at Puente, I wondered, Hey, where did this guy get all his gear?

MARY GOULD   We also saw the Japanese climber, whom we'd had dinner with at Puente del Inca, at Berlin. He had gone slightly snow blind and was laying low for a couple of days until he could see. Then I understood he was going to try the summit again. I was surprised he was on his own. I don't think it is a good idea for anyone to solo Aconcagua. That is a foolhardy thing to do. It's not that you might not be able to summit, but there might be weather that socks in, or an avalanche. There might be no way to get word out. So many things could happen that are not in your control. We did not meet anyone else soloing the mountain.

KINGDON GOULD III   Above Berlin there was more snow and the colors of the rock changed. It was getting colder. You could wear a lot of clothes without getting too hot.
I felt good. It was easy for me to pace myself with my folks. One of the key factors is not to push yourself to where you are out of breath. Nunzie was in good shape. She had taken a stress test and scored very

---

[16] The three refugios at this site are named 'Plantamura', 'Libertad' and 'Berlin.' The Plantamura shelter (named after the first Argentine to climb Aconcagua) was constructed in 1946, the Libertad in 1951. The Berlin refugio was built by German climbers in memory of a companion who died there.

high, one of the highest the doctors had ever seen. And relatively, because she only weighs 103 pounds, she was probably carrying more weight than I was.

MR. GOULD   Nunzie is a good athlete. And Mary is a country person; she loves nature and likes to walk. I have two speeds: slow and stop. I guess you can't go as fast when you are older. Maybe that is why you are pacing yourself!

The four of us brought up the rear. I had no problem getting to White Rocks, and felt good when we got there. White Rocks was a surprisingly nice setup.

◊▵◊▵◊▵◊▵◊▵◊▵◊

CRAIG ROLAND   White Rocks is about 19,700-feet. I arrived in the late afternoon, probably four or five hours after leaving Nido. Again, we straggled in at our own pace, but everyone made White Rocks. It was just a matter of putting one foot in front of the other.

Although there was a scheduled stop at Berlin, going higher was a real smart idea. Attempting the summit from Berlin would have added a half-hour. Not having that extra 250 vertical feet on summit day might make a huge difference.

So, the good news was that we went to a better jumping-off spot. The bad news was that there was still more than 3000 vertical feet to the summit, with everyone struggling from altitude.

I realized that at my age—I turned fifty-four on February 20, the day we first arrived in base camp—what happens is that it is much easier to stay in shape than to get into shape. The biggest question in my mind, however, had to do with altitude rather than training and condition. Altitude can affect people regardless of conditioning.

I made a point of drinking a lot of fluids. I also did a lot of special, forced breathing which I had learned on mountains elsewhere. It's not related to yoga much, but is more over-oxygenating your body by forced exhale, which increases your inhalation. This is a way to provide your body with a lot of oxygen and help your body acclimate because, at altitude, your body is not voluntarily asking itself to do that. You simply maintain a heavier breathing rhythm than normal. You can't do this at night after you fall asleep, so nighttime is when the worst problems occur. At night I woke up a lot, but had no serious problems besides mild headaches. I didn't hear of any serious altitude problems. Nor did I hear anyone discuss who might make the summit. People were superstitious about that subject. We were just happy to be there and were looking forward to our summit attempt the next day.

Dick cached some of his gear at Nido, then joined Bill and me in our tent at White Rocks. Dick and I felt in good condition. Bill was still struggling a little. The interesting detail about Bill was that he didn't really have a pre-departure training program, but was getting stronger as the trip went on. Some of the others were getting weaker the higher we went.

_____

BILL ENGLISH   I remember asking members of the expedition how they got in shape for Aconcagua and being surprised by the number of people who basically said, "Nothing." Mike Milford was one of those people. Then again, I was in the worst shape I'd been in for five years. Compared to the rest of the group shape-wise or endurance-wise, I fit into the middle or upper-middle category.

Getting up to White Rocks was probably my best day. I got my motor running and was not far behind Craig—maybe second or third into camp. Half of it was will power. The other half was acclimation and getting in better shape.

No one improved with altitude. I remember pitching the tent. Every time you bent over and stood up you felt the altitude. If you put your head down below your waist and then stood up, your head really throbbed. You tried not to bend over. You just moved real slow, and if you regulated your breathing and could breathe a lot, that helped. Craig and I had our tent set up before anyone else arrived. By then my head was pounding with a good headache.

At White Rocks tempers were short. The ability to cope with anything difficult was almost nonexistent. I remember hearing the Goulds' snapping at each other. They were on edge, not their usual selves making sure that everybody was happy with everything that was done or said. Virtually everyone who got up there after us—everyone trying to set up their tents in the blowing wind—was having a bitch of a time. Our heads were killing us. It wasn't any fun at all. There was no levity or tolerance. Craig and I were not snapping. We knew each other, but more than that we were there and had our tent set up in a nice spot. Craig and I walked way out on one of the points and took pictures. We gathered snow for melting from a little crack above our tent and crawled back. I just remember other people setting up their tents and it was tense.

How everybody was going to do the next day, higher up on summit day, was frequently a topic of conversation. You'd hear people say, "I don't know if I can go any further. I don't know if I want to do this. I feel like shit. This is god-awful." You'd hear that all the time. Sometimes people are saying that because they want a little reinforcement. I don't know that I said to anyone they were fine because I didn't really know if they were fine or not. What I would say instead was, "Hey, the alternative is to turn around and go down, or to have never tried this mountain. No matter what, it is better to be here and have the experience even if it is negative or you feel like shit." Or I may have cajoled people by saying, "Look, you have a whole night of sleep ahead of you. You'll feel great tomorrow. You can do it. We'll do it."

Keeping psyched and focused was mostly unspoken between Craig and myself. We would enquire as to how each other was doing or how we felt. Half of the reason for doing that is just to have something to compare your own feelings against. This became very discouraging on my part because Craig always felt fine. He is impervious to altitude. I'm too damn honest and was saying I could have felt better. We didn't get into pep talks or cheerleading. We were all adults and were going to take care of ourselves.

I wasn't really taking mental bets on anyone else; it was just me, that damn mountain, wondering how I was going to function at higher altitude, anxiety about the weather, and getting up the next morning in the dark when it would be windy and minus zero degrees. I was reminding myself that it would be one foot in front of the other, that it would be a plod, but that I could do it—'You're not going to be the fastest, but you'll be ahead of some of these other people.' This was a positive psychological attitude. I was psyching myself to tough it out.

Dick was very considerate when he began tenting with Craig and me. He tried not to be anymore intrusive than possible; it was hard to have three people in those tents. Dick had strong opinions. He had an I'll-take-charge-of-the-situation attitude. Craig and I don't have that kind of attitude at all. We're pretty laid back. I need to admit that part of me, because of Dick's know-it-all attitude, wanted him not to make the summit. He never indicated at all he had any doubts he would make the top; he was always going to be on the top. The question to him in my mind was: 'How do you know that? Altitude strikes people at different times in different ways. How can you be so damn self-assured?' Part of me, maybe just to wake him up, would have been happy if he did not make the summit—whether I made it or not—just so somebody could knock him on the head and say, "Hey Dick, you don't have all the answers. Look, you didn't quite make the top."

Dick was in good shape, but he was a lone wolf.

DICK GORDON   I spend a lot of time alone. I'm good at spending time by myself. Keeping apart is more of a life style than a tactic or a strategy.

Craig and Bill are good folks. Bill surprised me and Craig impressed me. They had the wisdom of age, which doesn't have anything to do with climbing, but they had 'life' experience. They understood patience and they knew how to tolerate. They were healthy and motivated. I wasn't sure if Bill was going to make the summit, but he knew what he could or could not do. Bill was as comfortable—'comfortable' being a relative term at White Rocks—as any of the rest of us. I don't know why I use the word 'comfortable.' It has nothing to do with the way we felt. Everyone was exhausted.

By White Rocks, everyone's foresight and peripheral vision had begun to deteriorate. You really start looking after yourself. You did what you could to help when you felt able, but there wasn't much of concerning oneself over others. Dr. Patel and I chatted a little, but he seemed somewhat reserved. We had a general conversation, nothing of substance—"How are you feeling? How are you doing?"—and he might have said, "I'm a little tired, but everything is good."

The extent of camaraderie did not go much outside the tent. You certainly did not want to exert much energy. Everything feels heavy.

You just want to relax and take a hot shower. I finally took a long breather before dark. I felt pretty selfish and became very introverted. I felt better at White Rocks than how most people told me they felt. I don't consider that feeling good, but I felt better than most. I was hungry, so I was eating and drinking. Other than general discomfort, a headache and constipation, everything for me was where it needed to be.

Craig, Bill and I weren't concerned about any part of summit day until the beginning of the Canaleta, a long gully leading up that final thousand feet or so to the summit. I was reserving all doubts about personally making the summit until the Canaleta, but felt comfortable that I could make it there and start into that section. What we'd heard about the Canaleta was that you could take your worst nightmare, double it, and you would still fall short. The condition of the Canaleta would depend on the weather and the amount of precipitation which had fallen. If the weather was warm and windy, and if there wasn't much snow or ice, we knew the Canaleta section would be long and grueling. I'd been told the Canaleta started off steep and continued to get steeper all the way to the top, with rocks varying in size from golf balls to three feet in diameter, and that all these rocks shift so that you could take three steps forward and only gain one. I knew the Canaleta would be energy draining, and that it would be important to conserve energy and be prepared.[17]

◊△◊△◊△◊△◊△◊△◊

NUNZIE GOULD   When I went to get tea that evening Enrique asked, "How is it going to go with Mary? Your father mentioned she would go to Nido."

Enrique, in Mendoza, wanted to know our conditions. Dad, understanding what getting to Nido entailed, told Enrique that he felt Mom could get that far. The impression I had was that Enrique now wondered: 'Your father said your mother would only go as far as Nido. What is the story now?'

I told Enrique, "Mary is fine. If something goes wrong tomorrow during our summit attempt, we'll work out a plan, or I'll go down with her."

Enrique really wanted Dad to summit. But actually, my observation of the person not doing the best was Dad; he still had digestive problems and the altitude was getting to him.

I did not talk about the summit with either Enrique or my parents. I knew that if a person did not have the mental desire, then physically getting to the top of Aconcagua was not going to happen. In terms of weather, if nature is going to be persistent and if it is going to snow, I'm happy to step back and let nature take its course. Nature eventually

---

[17] 'Canaleta', literally translated from Argentine Spanish, means 'drain-pipe.' {Adapted from the Italian 'canaletto'—'little channel' or 'little canal'.}

perseveres. If there is a storm then that is just a little message that maybe you are not wanted. This is where I deviate a little from my father. I might say, "If there is a snow storm tomorrow, we won't have a summit attempt," while he might want to carry on.

MR. GOULD   Enrique was keeping an eye on us and asked how we felt. Relations with Pépe and Gustavo were also good. We had all the attention we needed. Mary and I were holding up okay. I was moderately psyched up. I felt a responsibility to my wife, daughter and son to make sure we left on time, had enough to eat, were well, and that we were properly equipped for our summit attempt.

I imagined getting to the summit was going to be hard for some of the people in our group who were not experienced mountaineers. I wasn't sure I could make it myself. I didn't know what the Canaleta would be like, or how I would deal with it—'Is the Canaleta something I will have to climb with my hands and knees? Will it be terribly cold? How cold will my hands get? If the wind whips down, will I lose my glasses? How much gear will I need to take?' This was part of the evaluation going through my mind.

On my first trip there was a dead Japanese fellow whom people were trying to scoop off the mountain. I think he had died up on the Canaleta.

◊∆◊∆◊∆◊∆◊∆◊

MARK CORNWALL   Borgel, Lewis and I reached White Rocks around 7 PM. We were pretty beat and laid down haphazardly in the tent across each others legs. We didn't care. All we wanted was to get through the night, then go for the summit.

GREGG LEWIS   I'd pulled a muscle in my lower back at Nido picking up rocks to use as tent anchors. It still hurt at White Rocks. Enrique actually did notice my predicament at dinner time since I was hunched over like an old man. He asked, "What's wrong with your back?"

I was a little worried he might tell me not to continue. So I made light of it—"Oh, my back is stiff. It hurts, but I'm okay."

Mark, after resting, felt fine. Borgel still had a headache and was feeling rotten.

THOMAS BORGEL   When I arrived at White Rocks I was coughing and spitting up blood—just a little blood with my saliva. Enrique kept telling me I had pulmonary edema, although he never checked my vital signs. I thought I just had a sore throat from breathing in the cold air. Once I had water I was fine.

Enrique told us to ready our gear. He said that we would get up at 5 AM if the weather looked good. If the weather did not look good, then 6 AM. Enrique told us, "You get up. I give you something to eat, and you go."

We stayed up late playing 'Crazy Eights' with Trevor and Neil. Those were the longest 'Crazy Eight' games I've ever played. People had a hard time remembering the eights were wild.

MARK CORNWALL   I really began to contemplate what this sport of expedition mountaineering is all about. It's about how much you can take after putting yourself in some of the worst conditions known to mankind: you can't breath; it's 20° below zero; you have shitty food, and you are cramped into a tiny tent. There is a real art in just getting your clothing on or off, and deciding what clothing you are going to sleep in. Then you're trying to keep all your gear organized. At this point everyone's gear was inside the tent.

Expedition mountaineering is also about putting yourself in a position that no one else can get into—unless they climb the mountain. Then your reward is these fantastic views of the world. From Nido to White Rocks, even though the mountain is still desolate with rocks, barrenness and ice-caps, one has a much better perspective of the landscape because one can look down. This comes down to a personal philosophy. For me the view from the summit is what it's all about, and nothing feels as good as the personal achievement. You cannot share that feeling.

Borgel and Lewis were good tent mates. They were best friends and had a lot of respect for each other. Lewis and I had some differences; he was a little argumentative and liked to bite off a small conflict every now and then. Borgel was more willing to just go along with the program. I thoroughly enjoyed their company and humor. Your privacy, however, in those tents is nonexistent. You are completely jam-packed and have no room to yourself, not even enough room when you move around to avoid disturbing the other two people. Even when somebody is hurting or having sinus problems you want to have compassion, but it's like— "Shut the fuck up and die on your own time! I'm trying to get some sleep."

◊△◊△◊△◊△◊△◊△◊

KINGDON GOULD III   I had trouble eating the freeze-dried dinner and popped my cookies a little bit. My stomach was going fast and was upset. I went and sat by myself and tried to meditate my way through the meal—'Alright stomach, you just have to accept this food.' Eating becomes mechanical. I was finally able to get some dinner down. Aside from that, I felt remarkably well the whole trip; I did not have to take antibiotics or Lomotil, and I did not have a headache.

Leaving Dick's tent at Nido allowed for shelter in case someone wanted to descend. Neil and Trevor were nice enough to have me in their tent. They were great fellows and pretty gung-ho. We talked about the University of Colorado because my son is considering that school as a college choice.

<u>TREVOR BYLES</u>   Neil and I had been living the good life since we had a tent to ourselves. When Kingdon asked if he could sleep in our tent we said, "No problem. We might even be warmer." We were camped on a fairly exposed ledge.

We stayed up late. Kingdon did most of the talking. Kingdon was cool; he had great stories and was fun to listen to. He told us that when he was eighteen he left his family in Maryland and hitch-hiked across the country in three days. He got one ride with a boy and girl, sixteen and seventeen years old, who were going to get married. These two kids had taken the family car and had taken all the appliances out of their parents' houses. They traded appliances for gas and food. Kingdon got to San Francisco, hung out and became a deadhead. He talked about the sixties era and some of the wild people he associated with in Haight-Ashbury.

Everyone had questions, even at base camp, about summit day. There was a lot of curiosity and speculation. Neil, Kingdon and I discussed who we thought would or would not make the summit. I felt the group was falling apart. Borgel had a big headache, although I figured both he and Lewis would summit unless the altitude got to them. Mark was in good spirits. Dr. Patel had a glazed look in his eyes and was fumbling his way around camp. I don't know why Dr. Patel kept ascending the mountain. I couldn't believe he made it to Nido, much less White Rocks. The guy was tough and had heart, I'll give him that much. Dick and Nunzie were strong hikers. I thought both Bill and Craig would summit. Kingdon said he was a little tired and not feeling well. Since Kingdon had made it to White Rocks I figured he would summit—until I saw him throw-up, then I had second thoughts. It seemed to me that Mr. and Mrs. Gould were getting past their peak. Kingdon was concerned for his parents—he said they weren't feeling so good—but he didn't seem too worried; Nunzie was with them and taking care of them.

Initially, I didn't have a good sleep that night. It was crunch time. Besides being a little worried about the weather, there was always a doubt in the back of my mind whether I'd make it or not. But there was also something telling me there was no way I would not make the summit. I knew in my heart I was going to make the summit.

<u>NEIL DELEHEY</u>   White Rocks was very cold. We weren't hanging around outside the tents. We ate dinner, then climbed into our sleeping bags.

Trevor and I were psyched for the summit all the way. The summit was always on our minds. Every minute was, "We're here to make the summit and we're ready to make the summit." We really psyched each other up: I knew what Trevor was like, he knew what I was like. This had helped our pace up the mountain. And we shared a lot of things; we didn't bring a food bowl, so we sacrificed a water bottle by cutting it in half. That's what we ate out of. It was going to be our pee bottle.

Some people talk about summits as omnipotent—as a spirit—but Trevor and I would tell each other, "The summit is up there, yeah, yeah. We're going to make this, we're going to make this." Trevor and I were certain that, since we made White Rocks and felt good, we could summit. We had noticed that the summit would stay clear until early afternoon then cloud over. We thought we could make the top and take a great summit photograph before the weather turned.

We were prepared to leave early at 6 AM and make a charge, but Enrique told us we would leave later. We asked, "Why not earlier?"

"No, no. We leave at 8 AM."

"Well, okay."

◊▲◊▲◊▲◊▲◊▲◊

__DICK GORDON__   All you really think about is trying to get sleep. Of course that's the night you want and need a lot of sleep, but sleep was rare. The cold temperature and winds didn't let any of us sleep very well. I recollect getting five or ten minutes of sleep per hour, or every other hour. Every time I would turn and roll over Bill or Craig might say, "Kind of tough to sleep, huh?"

Everything inside the tent, except what was in our sleeping bags, was frozen. It was close quarters in each person's sleeping bag because our boots are in there and we were wearing pile clothes. Then the wind would blow really hard and shake all the frozen condensation off the inside of the tent onto our faces. If it wasn't one thing like that it was another. Sometimes the wind blew so hard the whole tent was peeled down to the ground as though it was going to blow away.

(Mike Sanson)

Aerial view of Aconcagua from the southwest. Arrows mark approach hike through the Superior Horcones Valley to Plaza de Mulas base camp.

top : Chapel, hotel ruins and spa at Puente del Inca. (Tom Taplin)

middle : Hiking to Confluencia. *left to right* : Mr. Gould, Kingdon Gould & Bill English. (Tom Taplin)

bottom : The second river crossing, below Confluencia. (Tom Taplin)

top : Hiking up the Horcones Valley to base camp. The upper half of Aconcagua's South Face (and snow-capped summits) is flanked by the ridgelines of peaks Piramidal and Mirador. (Tom Taplin)

bottom : Lunch break, below Confluencia. *Left to right* : Trevor Byles, Neil Delehey, Thomas Borgel, Mark Cornwall and Gregg Lewis. (Tom Taplin)

top : The Horcones Valley—"Dragon of the prime." (Craig Roland)

middle : Mule driver unloading gear at base camp. (Tom Taplin)

bottom : Plaza de Mules base camp {13,900-feet.} Cathedral Peak, Horcones Peak and Horcones Glacier in background. Trail up standard route is visible at right.
(Craig Roland)

Anil Patel at base camp. (Tom Taplin)

Dick Gordon and ice pinnacles on the Horcones Glacier. (Craig Roland)

Taplin being rescued from the moulin. Note glacial ice beneath moraine. (Gregg Lewis)

Aconcagua's West Buttress as seen from Mulas base camp. (Tom Taplin)

Halfway up the switchbacks leading to Nido. (Mulas base camp off frame left.) Cathedral Peak and Horcones Glacier in background. (Craig Roland)

top : Mike Milford at Nido de Condores (Nest of the Condores) after the second carry. (Anil Patel)

middle : "There was always soup and a laddle full of something." Meal time at Nido. Nunzie Gould at right. (Craig Roland)

bottom : View of the Gran Acarreo (far right) and north summit from the Nido plateau, a vertical gain of nearly 5,500-feet. Note snow trail below summit leading into Canaleta. (Bill English)

top : Typical light show at Nido {17,500-feet} following an afternoon storm. (Tom Taplin)

middle : Hikers approaching camp Berlin. Horcones and South Güssfeldt Glaciers in background. (Bill English)

bottom : 'Berlin', 'Libertad' and 'Plantamura'—the three refugios at 19,500-feet. (Tom Taplin)

top : The camp at White Rocks (Pierda Blanca) on the north ridge.
(Craig Roland)

bottom : Telephoto shot of Aconcagua's north summit from Nido. 'X' marks site of Patel's accident on traverse leading into the Canaleta.
(Tom Taplin)

top : The traverse at the top of the Gran Acarreo. South Güssfeldt and Rio Vacas Glaciers in background.
(Linda and Dave Bujnicki)

middle : Taplin at the Independencia refugio, at 21,400-feet one of the highest permanent structures in the world.
(Claudio Ramirez)

below : "Take your worst nightmare and double it..."—the bottom of the dreaded Canaleta.
(Linda and Dave Bujnicki)

The top of the Canaleta, 100-feet below the north summit. Guanaco Ridge in background. (Linda and Dave Bujnicki)

Pépe and Craig Roland on the north summit of Aconcagua, top of the Americas. (Dick Gordon)

The Aconcagua region as viewed from space. Port city of Valparaiso, Chile, on the Pacific Ocean, is at upper right portion of photograph, near the Rio Aconcagua. Santiago is on a diagonal below and to the left of Valparaiso. Mendoza, Argentina is at lower right edge, below the clouds. To the right of a direct line between Mendoza and Valparaiso, in the snow-covered Andes, is Cerro Aconcagua. (NASA, Challenger 6, Mission 41 G, October, 1984)

< 17 >

COLD SHADOWS
Expedition Day 10: Summit attempt, Morning

DICK GORDON   We got up at 6 AM, not that anyone was actually sleeping. Enrique and Pépe started screaming, "Come on! Breakfast is ready! Hurry up! Move it! Let's go!"

Craig was determined. He had the kind of motivation that it takes. It's always a lousy feeling to be the first one up and the first one to get your boots on. It was good to share that with somebody, good to have that energy nearby. Someone had to start the ball rolling.

It was dark. Everyone had their headlamps on, was coping with the cold, and making sure they had their crampons in their day-packs.

CRAIG ROLAND   The temperature was 5° F. below zero, which was warmer than some of the other days. Most people had little headaches. Several people had not eaten much, if anything, the night before. They were probably feeling nauseous. Quite a few people woke up feeling nauseous—not so serious they couldn't walk, but more of an appetite killer. And there were some cases of diarrhea.

We tackled the summit on one tiny packet of powdered oatmeal and a cup of hot chocolate or coffee. That was our days ration—pretty meager portions and way undernourished. When I saw what breakfast was going to be I went back to Enrique and asked, "Hey, don't you have anything else here? We're going to have a very strenuous day." The guides fished out another packet, so I ended up with two oatmeals. I don't know how many others did that, but one packet of oatmeal was definitely insufficient for a whole day. We didn't have anything else to eat unless we had a candy bar.

We had to struggle to get water, but I was bound and determined to have two full quarts. Several people, however, did not get two full quarts and Enrique, although he should have, did not stress such a need.

NEIL DELEHEY   It took a long time to put on our clothes. I wore two pairs of expedition-weight underwear, pile pants, bibs, a down jacket, a Polarplus jacket, and a GoreTex shell over that. Maybe other people went lighter, but the temperature was butt-cold.

TREVOR BYLES   Neil and I were forcing our oatmeal down. That's hard, but we knew we had to eat something. We should have had a big meal that morning. And we should have had all the water we could have carried. There was only enough for one, or one-and-a-half water bottles apiece. Neil and I had been very conscientious about drinking enough water. We did have Taplin's packets of Gookinaid which we mixed with our water. Since we didn't have a lot of water Neil and I figured that reinforcing the salt packs in our bodies and having a little extra glucose might help. Any type of energy drink at high altitude will help.

NEIL DELEHEY   Kingdon asked how I felt. I didn't want to talk about my condition, not even with Trevor. I felt nauseous, but choked down a candy bar or two.

Trevor and I were set to go. We left White Rocks, by ourselves, at 7:45, using our headlamps. I was leading and went extremely slow since I was frightened about the altitude and not feeling well.

An hour out of camp the sun began to rise. There was a band of orange, then black. Everything was black—the world was black. We could see rock outlines on the slopes above, then look over and down on the sun coming up. There were sheets of clouds below us. I'll never forget how that looked.

When it began to get light, Trev and I left our headlamps on a rock. The trail winds up a relatively gradual incline, then comes to a plateau at the bottom of a small basin. We took turns carrying the pack which had our water and crampons. I continued to walk slowly. We both had cold feet until the sun came out. Trev had put on two pairs of socks which might have caused his circulation problems.

◊△◊△◊△◊△◊△◊△◊

KINGDON GOULD III   Neil and Trevor did not feel well, but they got up early and were the first ones out of camp. I knew they were heading up together and knew they were looking after each other. I directed my thoughts to our family and how we would manage. I was anxious to get going; we only had so much time and could only walk so fast.

NUNZIE GOULD   When I woke up the altitude got to me. It was a major effort to sit up and lace my boots. A major effort. Mom didn't understand why Dad decided to strip down and put on an extra pair of long-johns. It was so complicated and irritating to have someone fussing around in the tent. As the three of us were getting ready, I told Dad we were like a bunch of geriatrics. I said it as a joke. My mother thought it was funny and I was cracking up hysterically. But Dad did not like that comment at all; he had turned sixty-five and was going through this moral dilemma about getting old. The word 'geriatric' is not popular around him.

I reminded Mom to take Diamox. My parents seemed to be coping with the altitude, but I realized Dad was not quite there. He wanted to organize everything—roll up his sleeping bag and put it away neatly—for when he came down. That was his nature; keeping things tidy for his return. At the time, however, the purpose was to summit. Organizing everything was taking enormous energy and antagonizing me, which wasted my energy too.

Everyone else already had their tea, so I went out with Dad's cup and got tea for him. Then he wanted oatmeal. He poured the oatmeal into his tea but made too much. He wanted to throw the extra oatmeal out. I said, "Here, give it to me." He was reluctant to give me his cup because he thought I was going to dilute it with the Gatorade I was drinking. I laughed and told him, "Dad, don't worry. I will get rid of the extra oatmeal."

In the end he didn't eat his oatmeal anyway. I understood, from little paranoid things like that, why an expedition can just go haywire; how someone's brain could stop functioning rationally. You slow down. There are no two ways about it. Everything takes a big effort. You're out of breath just unzipping the tent to go for a nature call. It's ridiculous. There are so many other things to keep on track. This is where mental training comes in. Certainly being close and watching everyone is important.

◊△◊△◊△◊△◊△◊

CRAIG ROLAND   Just after 8 AM everybody else lined up. Pépe started off and I walked behind him. I was focused on making the summit. By this point I did not think I was going to have a serious altitude problem. My conditioning seemed to be holding up. I passed Trevor and Neil and was walking ahead of everybody else.

So I felt confident, except for the weather. Enrique was clearly superstitious about the weather. In fact he said to me, "Don't ask me that question. I don't want to talk about it," as though it was a verboten subject and that if he talked about the weather it might get bad. There was no question he was superstitious, so I dropped my questions about weather. On previous days clouds had been in over the mountain and the weather had become unpredictable. I knew we were only going to have one shot at the summit. Instead of the two or three days we had been told would be allotted, we would have just one day. And if we did not make the summit we would then come down off the mountain.

But that morning was just fabulous. I took a picture of the shadow of Aconcagua stretched out fifty miles on the haze towards Chile. This was a very interesting phenomenon, like an optical illusion. You could see Aconcagua, including the summit, in a pyramid shadow form stretching out all that distance, then the haze dissolved and it was crystal clear. Actually it would clear every morning like that. The air is so thin and dry that visibility is outstanding; the quality of light is great. Shortly thereafter we wrapped around the northwest ridge and were in shade.

Dick caught up with me and we continued to follow Pépe. Bill was relatively close behind us. There is another refugio—a small A-

Frame—in disrepair at Independencia.[18] We stopped there for some time. No one was camped there; too windy for anyone to be interested in camping there. I had a candy bar and within half-an-hour people came straggling in.

BILL ENGLISH   Getting started is a pretty uptight moment. It's every man for himself. Most of that anxiety dissipates once you hit the trail, then your thoughts turn to how to pace yourself. I was hiking by myself nearly the whole time. Again, you're pretty much focused on yourself and how miserable you feel.

The problem I had nearly all morning was frozen toes. They were frozen. I'm sure I'd gone to bed with my inner boots on, but those outer plastic boots were cold. What went through my mind for one hell of a long ways—even well into the snow field above the ice traverse—was: 'Should I stop? Should I try to take my boots off and warm up my toes? Is it pre-frostbite? What is going on?' So every time I took a step I'd curl my toes. My hands were cold, but not like my toes which were a real concern.

◊▲◊▲◊▲◊▲◊▲◊▲◊

E.A. FITZGERALD   Zurbriggen was going very fast; I was obliged to call to him several times, and ask him to wait for me, as I did not wish to exhaust myself by pressing the pace so early. I was surprised at his hurrying in this way, as it is generally Zurbriggen who urges me to go slowly at first. However, I soon discovered the reason for this; he was suffering bitterly from cold. Seeing that his face was very white, I asked him if he felt quite well. He answered that he felt perfectly well, but that he was so cold he had no feeling whatever in his feet; for a few moments he tried dancing about, and kicking his feet against the rocks, to get back his circulation. I began to get alarmed, for frozen feet are one of the greatest dangers one has to contend against in Alpine climbing.

The porters who had been lagging behind now came up to us; I at once told Zurbriggen to take his boots off, and we all set to work to rub his feet. To my horror I discovered that the circulation had practically stopped. We continued working hard upon him. At last we observed that his face was becoming pallid, and slowly and gradually he began to feel a little pain. We hailed this sign with joy, for it meant of course that vitality was returning to the injured parts, and we renewed our efforts; the pain now came on more and more severely; he writhed and shrieked and begged us to stop, as he was well-nigh maddened by suffering.

---

[18] The Independencia refugio was erected in 1951 by a group of Argentinean Army climbers. At 21,000-feet it is reputedly the highest permanent man-made structure in the world.
  Independencia is located on the north-northwest ridge.

Knowing, however, that this treatment was the one hope for him, we continued to rub, in spite of his cries, literally holding him down, for the pain was getting so great that he could no longer control himself, and tried to fight us off. The sun now rose over the brow of the mountain, and the air became slightly warm. We slipped on his boots without lacing them, and supporting him between the two of us, we began slowly to get him down the mountain side.

We succeeding in getting him back to our tent, where he threw himself down and begged to be allowed to go to sleep. We could not permit this, however, and taking off his boots again we continued the rubbing operations, during which he shouted in agony, cursing us volubly in some seven different languages. We then prepared some very hot soup and made him drink it, wrapping him up warmly in all the blankets we could find and letting him sleep in the sun.

In the afternoon he seemed quite right again, and was able to walk around a little, though he was very much depressed, and kept muttering to himself that now for twenty years he had been climbing mountains, and that this was the first occasion upon which his party had been compelled to turn back owing to illness on his part. I narrate this incident at length as an example of what Aconcagua does to even the most hardy and experienced of mountaineers.[19]

◊△◊△◊△◊△◊△◊△◊

MARK CORNWALL   It was Gregg Lewis who first referred to the Gould's as Swiss Family Robinson. I jumped right on that. Everyone in the Gould family hauled butt to White Rocks. They were strong all the way up, until somewhere near Independencia, when Nunzie and Mumsy went poof and were eliminated.

MARY GOULD   Our family was a little late leaving camp. We should have started up an hour earlier, even if it meant using our headlamps.

I felt okay and was comfortable except for my hands. I was wearing liners, mittens and those awful, woolen Dachsteins. Don't mention that word. That was the worst. I could not do anything with those Dachsteins on my hands; they were too big and too stiff to adjust anything, and my hands were cold in them. That was terribly frustrating. I lost time adjusting something, which I couldn't do without taking those over-mitts off. My hands kept getting colder and colder. Nunzie was nice. She waited around and was trying to help.

---

[19] Frostbite (freezing of tissue) is a cold injury, usually the result of exposure, hypothermia, or impaired circulation. Treatment should not include rubbing, which can further damage tissue and result in loss of flesh. Hospitalization and rewarming in a water bath is the perferred treatment for severe cases. In the field, keep the victim warm, prevent refreezing, and make plans to evacuate.

NUNZIE GOULD   I told Mom to make a fist. She misunderstood and took her hands out of her liners, then couldn't get the thumbs of her liners inserted into her big Dachsteins. The thumbs were tight which may be why her circulation cut off. That was the only reason why she and I fell back.

King, Dad and Enrique were walking ahead of us. We had fallen behind them by about fifteen minutes. I helped Mom get straightened out and we caught up with Enrique, who had stopped to wait for us. Enrique said to Mom, "It will take many hours to reach the summit at your pace."

MARY GOULD   Maybe Enrique did not realize I was struggling with my mittens there for awhile. I was very disappointed because I felt in good shape, but I did not want to jeopardize anyone else being able to get to the summit by holding Enrique or the other guides back. I did not argue with him. That would not be very nice for the rest of the group. When Enrique said that I should not continue for the fourth or fifth time I said, "Okay." He was the leader.

NUNZIE GOULD   Enrique did not fully understood my mother's potential. He didn't make it clear that she needed to step up her pace. The weird thing is that we just accepted verbatim what Enrique said. I didn't think to question him. I don't know why. If I had thought twice I would have tried to convince Mom to walk faster. Deep inside Mom was committed and would have summited. As Enrique started to descend with Mom, he turned to me and said, "Mary will be fine by herself at White Rocks. You should keep going."

Enrique took Mom down, then King and Dad turned around and found me. The three of us had this hour long discussion—I'm not kidding—about who would go back to White Rocks and stay with Mom. Even though I had committed to Enrique the night before, I was selfish and was into continuing up the mountain. I wanted to summit.

When I told King what Enrique had said—that Mom would be okay by herself—King flipped out. King said, "I don't care what Enrique says. Someone has to be with Mom."

KINGDON GOULD III   I'm sure my mother would have been fine at White Rocks, but my personal feeling is that when you are on a mountain like Aconcagua the buddy system is a good system. People get hurt when they don't think they're going to get hurt. I'm sure Taplin didn't think he would get hurt, but it was damn good somebody was there when his accident happened. The trail seems safe, but people can trip and fall; people can get disoriented and wander off; people can think they're too much trouble for everybody else and want to descend to the next camp. People's decision making abilities are often not very good. And then there is no food or no fire. So I was probably the one who insisted somebody go back to stay with my mother. My father said he would go back, but he is sixty-five years old and I'm forty. I'd get other attempts at the mountain and felt my father should take his shot.

NUNZIE GOULD   There was no sibling rivalry going on. King said, "I came on this trip to be with Dad and to have someone with Dad. I feel the same way about Mom. I'm going down to be with Mom."

I said to King, "I cannot believe how you have this selfless attitude."

At one point Dad started down. King and I ran after him trying to explain our points of view. Then King and I said to each other, "Wait a minute. This is absolutely ridiculous. If it weren't for Dad we wouldn't even be here. So Dad, turn around and start walking up the hill!"

And by this time Enrique had come back up from White Rocks. Enrique said to Dad, "This is your summit day."

I was pretty adamant about King not descending. King had accompanied Dad on the first trip and I felt that if anyone should make the summit it should be those two. I finally said, "King, you and Dad were the original team. Go for it." I made the decision to descend and I made it for a group reason; it was my choice.

Before King and Dad headed up, Dad said, "Your mother will never admit to it, but she'll feel like she made you turn around."

As I started down Enrique was standing there. He asked, "What are you doing?"

"I'm going back to be with Mom."

Enrique accepted my decision. He had left his hot water bottle with Mom, so I said to him, "Here's mine. Good luck."

I had tears in my eyes and was really upset. I knew it was over and I felt a lot of bitterness. I'd trained and done a lot of conditioning to prepare for the mountain. Although I went to Aconcagua with Dad, deep inside I also went for myself.

I reached a spot that I'd remembered on the walk up earlier that morning when the sun was just lifting and where I had looked down on the other peaks and the beautiful clouds. I said to myself, "This is as high as I'm going to get, so I should take a picture." I wanted to capture that moment even though I was mad about going down. Boy, did I chomp the bit as I walked back to White Rocks.

Mom was surprised, but not super surprised, to see me. She felt responsible for my return. It was a sensitive issue and I didn't want to discuss it. We crawled into our sleeping bags and dozed off for a couple of hours.

◊∆◊∆◊∆◊∆◊∆◊∆◊

TREVOR BYLES   Above Independencia is a short, steep slope. At the top is a ridge connecting to the ice traverse. Before we came to the traverse the focus was just pace. Neil and I were going really slow. We had paced ourselves slow all the way up the mountain and that had worked well. Even though Neil and I had left White Rocks first, almost everybody else caught up to us. Except for Pépe, Gustavo, Dick, Bill and Craig, the others decided to stay with Neil and me because we had a good pace. We were in a train, one behind the other.

DICK GORDON   By the time I caught up to Craig, Enrique had already gone down to help the Gould's and had come back up. He did that several times that day—fall back then catch up to us—and it killed me. I could not believe Enrique was running up and down as though ascending the mountain was a hundred-yard dash.

Craig was always ahead of me, whether it was a couple steps or a couple hundred steps, and I barely kept up with him. Craig was extremely strong. I think we wanted to pace each other, but surprisingly enough Craig's pace was stronger than my own. I needed more rest between spurts. I was looking for a consistency to the point where I could stop, rest, then catch up again. Craig would always go about 25% further than I could before he had to stop and rest. There was no sense of competition; Craig never implied the need to be first. There was a feeling of fellowship. We both understood the importance of consistency for success, so we tried to keep our paces as close together as possible, yet still be independent.

CRAIG ROLAND   Everyone stopped to put their crampons on at the ice traverse. People had difficulty with their crampons. I particularly had trouble walking on the snow and ice. I thought I'd checked my crampons out, but there was so much torque on the slope I found myself twisting out several times. I was furious because it always took a lot of energy to put those crampons back on.

The ice traverse is at the top of the Gran Acarreo, and cuts across a section that would make quite a beautiful ski slope; hard-packed snow, partially in shadow, with rocks sticking out. The line of the traverse was not steep, but the angled side hill as one approaches the Canaleta at the end of the traverse became very steep. I was never concerned about not having an ice axe. A ski pole worked fine under those conditions.

BILL ENGLISH   We were now above 21,000-feet and everything took a lot of effort. Even talking to someone was an effort; you just don't make much small talk.

I looked out across the ice traverse, wondered if crampons were really necessary, then said to myself, "What the hell," and lashed my crampons on as tight as I could. Two or three steps later I knew why I had my crampons on; crampons were vitally important because the slope was slick, steep and treacherous. The crampons did not sink in very far. My previous crampon experiences had not been on such a resistant surface.

The ice traverse was a psychological letdown in that, from Nido looking up to the summit, it seemed maybe a couple hundred yards long—not realizing that the perspective upwards is almost 6,000 vertical feet! That traverse is monstrous and never-ending, at least a thousand linear feet long. When I throw my slides up on the screen now, the traverse looks like a cake-walk, but in some places it was quite tricky. At one point I dropped my ski pole and it slid off the trail coming to rest against some exposed scree about fifteen feet below. Scrambling down to get that ski pole then coming back up about wiped me out. That was just exhausting.

NEIL DELEHEY   Trevor had the lead from Independencia until the ice traverse. He and I both had experience with crampons, but it seemed to take a long time—ten or fifteen minutes—just to put my crampons on. Trevor pointed out, two or three times, that I'd put my crampons on incorrectly. I felt punch-drunk, as though I knew I'd done some stupid thing, then I'd laugh about it.

We got across the traverse and started up a snow field, which rises on a sweeping angle into the Canaleta. Suddenly, Trevor and I picked up speed, which I couldn't understand. Maybe it was because wearing crampons felt so different, or because we could see the saddle just below the summit and we began to get excited.[20] We knew the summit was close. We began to outdistance the people behind us, or maybe the others just slowed down.

It would have been nice to use an ice-axe as a cane on that incline if nothing else. I was coping with a goddamned ski pole. I knew that if I fell and tried to self-arrest with a ski pole and crampons I'd just do a back somersault. There would be nothing to stop you. The actual slope was fifty-five or sixty degrees steep; you'd just roll forever. That was definitely on my mind.

We could see Craig and Dick ahead of us. I was panting like crazy, like a woman giving birth.

BILL ENGLISH   When Trevor and Neil went by, I could not believe it. Every other day, on the approach up the mountain, I would frequently pass them because they'd be dragging. But this day I felt good and their passing me was another psychological letdown. Something clicked with them and they started moving. I was really surprised. That caused self-doubts.

◊∆◊∆◊∆◊∆◊∆◊∆◊

GREGG LEWIS   Borgel, Mark and I were late getting out of our tent, late preparing our day packs, and the last to leave White Rocks. We were always the last. Once the sun hit you, you'd warm up to the point of feeling alive.

---

20 This saddle is called the Guanaco Ridge, and is a depressed col which links the north and south summits of Aconcagua.

We passed Dr. Patel on the slope above Independencia. He was going real, real slow. Dr. Patel reminded me of the way Stasiak looked going up to Nido. We asked Patel how he felt and he said, "Fine."

Borgel, Mark and I arrived at the ice traverse at noon, and pulled out our crampons. Someone said it was 15° below zero with the wind chill factor. When Borgel took his gloves off, his hands froze immediately.

I never correctly got my crampons on. Every fifteen minutes the damn things would twist off. I'd adjusted them to my boots in Atlanta and they seemed to fit, but to be honest, I'd never tried them out. I almost took my crampons off on the traverse. A voice in my head went, "No, no, no. Leave them on."

On one occasion—when I sat down to tighten my crampons—one of my water bottles fell out of my pack, scooted twenty-five yards down the ice and banged into a rock. I told Borgel, "Don't worry about retrieving it. It's dead weight. Leave it." The water in that bottle was frozen like a block from the night before. Even though I'd put it under my jacket it never did melt. I'd drunk all the unfrozen water in my other bottle and was eating chunks of snow. I was dying of thirst. And I was tired; all Borgel, Mark and I had for breakfast that morning was a cup of hot chocolate.

We were two-thirds of the way to the summit.

18

"SOMEONE HAS FALLEN!"

ANIL PATEL   It was a struggle to talk myself into getting up that morning; the night was very cold and no one had slept well, not with that howling wind. Everyone complained about there not being enough food for breakfast. I had a bowl of hot water. I didn't mind that.

During the hike to base camp we did well in terms of pacing and keeping together as a group, but that was not an indication of what would happen later. Climbing a mountain should always be a real steady climb to get to the summit. Not for Enrique. After base camp there was no collective pace. Instead, people were isolated in groups of two or three. Aconcagua had become a free-for-all.

As I approached the ice traverse, Mr. Gould and Kingdon were behind me. Mark had started across. Another group was way out, beyond him. I put my crampons on and took quite a few steps up the ice traverse, to the point where I could see towers which the Canaleta passes through.[21] I knew I would get to the top by the 4 PM deadline.

Then my crampons became loose. Although I have crampon experience from climbing in the Cascades, I'd watched Enrique adjust them for the bunny boots the night before; he had to bend out the metal strap clips and tighten a couple nuts. Still, they came loose.

My hands were freezing and my fingers were numb. My hands were cold when we started off from White Rocks. I didn't want to take off my gloves to fix my crampons, so I discarded the crampons. That was my mistake. The people who had traversed the slope in front of me had loosened the ice and cut steps. I thought I could get toe holds for the next fifteen or twenty feet. I thought I could take that chance. I was thinking very rationally when I made that decision. I wasn't affected by altitude and had rational thoughts all the way up. My goal was to reach the summit at all costs.

KINGDON GOULD III   There is a rock outcropping at the beginning of the ice traverse where people had stopped to put on their crampons. Beside this rock was a pack and a set of crampons. One or two hundred yards out on the traverse was Anil Patel. He was walking slowly. My father and I wondered why this other set of crampons had been left there. The pack we could understand—someone figured they didn't need their pack—but we did not know about those crampons, or to whom they belonged. We could not see if Anil was wearing his crampons.

---

21 Anil is referring to the rock steps and buttresses which flank the north and south summits.

MR. GOULD   I was trying some different mitten combinations in order to warm my hands. I have difficulty with cold hands anyway from injuries I've suffered in the past.

I wasn't psyched up by then. Just the fact that we'd had this discussion about someone going down to stay with Mary distracted our attention. I didn't feel badly about Mary because she was just along for the ride and hadn't really set her goals on the summit. Mary was a little slow, but considering she hadn't trained at all she did fine; she had gotten up to 21,000-feet and could have gone higher. I was not worried about Mary or wondering about her condition. She has a strong heart. She must have—she's survived me for forty years. But Nunzie going down upset me a lot because I felt we were preventing her from having her summit opportunity. Nunzie had worked really hard; trained for it, gotten all the gear, and made the effort. I felt terrible about Nunzie.

Not having perfected my own gear and not having figured out a nice solution for Nunzie to continue her climb were all distractions. Any distraction you have from your climbing rhythm and purpose is exacerbated by the altitude. You really have to keep your purpose in front of you and not have any distractions.

King was very patient. He was accompanying me, but he could have easily gone ahead. I felt I was being too slow for him and was sorry I was holding him up. King was doing well. He wasn't cold. He never complained about the altitude.

KINGDON GOULD III   Beyond Anil Patel, on the far side of the traverse, we could see other people climbing up to the left, toward the Canaleta. My father and I thought we could catch up to them.

I was just getting my crampons out to put them on when I looked up and saw Anil's feet slip out from under him. He started to slide down the slope on his rear end. It was one of those things that happens very quickly and very slowly at the same time. I said to my father, who was sitting beside me, "Oh my god, Anil is falling!"

We were unable to do anything—Anil was totally out of reach. It was similar to someone taking a good skiing fall, except Anil essentially was falling feet first. Every so often he would tumble over because there were rocks in the snow. The slope was hard-packed snow just less than fifty degrees steep. He did not have an ice axe. I'm sure he was somehow trying to self-arrest, but he looked out of control. I did not shout at him, nor did I hear him yelling anything.

My father and I watched in horror as Anil slid further and further. He was moving. I don't even want to guess how fast he was going. He was like a rag doll, flipping over, getting smaller and smaller and smaller.

ANIL PATEL   I knew that if I could not stop with my boots or ski pole I'd just keep sliding and end up at Nido—Nest of the Condors— three thousand feet below. It looked like a long drop. I tried to self-arrest, lost my ski pole, then tried to grab rocks. I still had my glasses. I'm blind without my glasses.

There was a point when I knew I could not stop myself. I saw a rock outcropping down slope and thought I could buttress myself on my flank, hit the outcropping and slow down. There was a loud crack—I heard it in my ears. Because of mistiming or how I was maneuvering I hit my skull, not my flank, on the rocks. Once I hit that outcropping I knew that was the end. I was frightened. I knew I was going to die. I may have been momentarily knocked out, but I kept sliding hundreds of feet further down. I was in shade for three hundred or four hundred feet, then in the sun.

It felt so good sliding that fast. I'd smashed my head and thought that maybe I was already dead. I'd lost my glasses and could no longer see; I couldn't make out any more outcroppings. The slope was really steep. I knew I'd end up in Nido. I knew I was going to die. I thought about my wife and my twin daughters—'My daughters will be alright, whatever happens.'

KINGDON GOULD III   Anil slid about four hundred yards. His slide took perhaps fifteen seconds. Finally he came to a rest where the snow ran out. It was hard to see him as he laid there; he wore a black parka and might as well have been a rock to the naked eye. I got out my binoculars and we were able to see he was alive because he was moving. But he didn't jump up and dust himself off; he sort of rolled onto his side, then got himself to a sitting position. It was clear he was pretty shaken. Neither my father nor I could tell to what extent he was hurt.

We shouted, "Anil! Anil! Are you alright?" There was no answer. He was sitting up, but slumped over.

We yelled a few more times and thought immediately about going down to him. I said to my father, "We'd better wait. We don't know if this whole slope might slide. And we don't want debris or rocks falling down on Anil. We don't want to loosen anything or get hurt ourselves. Let's call and see if we can get the guides to come back." We figured the guides could not have been much further ahead. We could not tell who was next in line on the traverse, but we could still see people spread across it.

We started yelling, "Get the guides! Anil has fallen!" We didn't know if anyone could hear us or not. I did not have a watch, but it seemed we yelled for a long time. We didn't know if we were being understood.

ANIL PATEL   My first reaction was to dig into the snow with my hands and feet because the area where I stopped was not flat; I wanted to prevent myself from sliding further. My gloves had stayed on, so I dug in quite deep while lying horizontally. Then I passed out, probably for a few minutes. When I regained consciousness Kingdon was yelling, but I could not see him.

My first thoughts were about how to get down to Nido de Condores which I could see. I was lucid enough to remember there was a tent at

Nido, and to think I could slowly slide down. But I didn't slide down because one of the Gould's yelled that help was on the way.

◊▲◊▲◊▲◊▲◊▲◊▲◊

MARK CORNWALL   Traversing toward the Canaleta is the worst goddamned trail you could ever dream up. Lewis, Borgel and I finished the traverse on a diagonal line, and had started up the snow field at the base of the Canaleta, about 900 vertical feet below the summit. We could see Enrique, Pépe, Gustavo, Dick, Craig, Trevor and Neil approaching the summit. They were at least 600 vertical feet or so above us—an hours walk at the pace we were going.

We'd stopped to take a rest, and were about twenty yards from each other when we thought we heard something. The yells were faint enough so that we had to say, "Hey, what was that?"

At first we had no idea who was yelling. There is a bend in the route, where the snow field curves into the Canaleta, which makes it impossible to see the progression of anyone coming up the ice traverse. We couldn't see the Gould's, or tell from the sound of their voices that they were the ones yelling, but we knew the Gould's and Dr. Patel were the only ones back there.

We heard more shouts: "Help! Help! Mark has fallen off the mountain!" Somebody thought it was me.

Borgel yelled down, "Mark is okay. Mark is here."

Then we heard, "Someone has fallen! Get help! Get Enrique!"

There was a lot of screaming. No one quite knew who was hearing what. Information was passed up and down several times before we, or anyone above us, knew Dr. Patel was involved.

I'd hung out with Dr. Patel in Mendoza, and had talked with him during the hike in. As he progressed up the mountain Anil was so gung-ho, but as he got higher and higher he became more introverted, almost incoherent. I had last seen him as he approached the ice traverse. He was just as exhausted as he could be. Anil was pretty much on his own. He liked to walk by himself, but he put himself in a position where he was away from the crowd. And that's where he ended up.

We were about fifteen minutes—between three hundred and five hundred yards—from the accident site. We yelled up to Bill. Bill hollered up to Neil and Trevor. We all just stopped in our tracks to wait for Enrique.

< 19 >

STORM GHOST

DICK GORDON   Craig and I tried to maintain sight of the guides. We traversed the Canaleta on a rise and were pretty close to them. Then Enrique, Pépe and Gustavo pulled ahead, but would realize they had pulled ahead and would stop. Craig would catch up to them pretty quick, putting some distance between him and myself without any problem.

Fortunately there was enough snow covering a good portion of the Canaleta on the right side so that we could wear our crampons.

CRAIG ROLAND   The snow became soft and there were already footsteps. I took my crampons off and carried them to where the snow petered out.

We heard about Dr. Patel's fall via a relay of calls which came over a terrific distance. We didn't know who it was, or where the fall had taken place. We could see a long ways down the mountain, but there was no sign of anybody in trouble. We could only see some of the crew strung out on the bottom of the Canaleta, then winding out of sight.

DICK GORDON   The messages did not seem important in the beginning, which may have been due to the tone of the messages themselves or the altitude. My first thoughts were that perhaps someone had broken a crampon or had frostbite. It sounded serious, but not detrimental. Then the message was that someone had fallen and my feelings were that maybe this person had just fallen on the trail and broken something. Finally the understanding was of an emergency— that someone had fallen down the slope and needed help. We passed along word, then Enrique came down.

CRAIG ROLAND   Enrique turned, and said to Dick and myself, "Congratulations, you've made the summit."

We asked, "What do you mean, 'made the summit'?"

Enrique said, "The summit is right there," and pointed at this rock which was just a few hundred vertical feet away. We had been so intent on climbing up step by step that we hadn't realized we were so close to the summit.

Then Enrique said, "I have to go down. Gustavo and I will go down. Pépe will take you to the actual summit." Enrique shook our hands as though we'd already made the summit, even though we still had a least an hour to make that last 300 or 400-feet.

DICK GORDON   Enrique said, "Good luck. Wish I could be with you. He was disappointed. Enrique's desire was to be with the lead group for reasons of safety or whatever. He would have liked to have been there when the first summiteers arrived, which is something, traditionally, he has been able to do on his climbs. This was one of those instances, similar to when Taplin fell, when his reaction was: 'Darn! Again!', and off Enrique goes to take care of it. I don't know how the others viewed it, but his reaction—'Just what I need, another problem'—could easily be misinterpreted. Not going to the summit caused frustration for Enrique, but he went down to take care of the emergency in a fashion I respected and admired.

On a mental level the accident was not real important. There was no room for it. The accident was forgotten pretty quickly. Maybe that is just the way I dealt with it. I'm not sure Craig reacted the same way. Focusing was very difficult; we were not enjoying a walk in the park and thinking about family or injured individuals. I could not think about Dr. Patel's situation or the time or the weather. I had such in-depth tunnel vision that all I could think about was where my foot was going to go and where my next breath was coming from.

NEIL DELEHEY   Trevor kept dropping his ski pole which is something you just don't do. Finally I said, "I'm not picking up your pole again. Here, take one of mine." Then he dropped my pole two times. There wasn't a whole lot of oxygen. Your motor skills are so effected by altitude and exhaustion. You deal with it and say to yourself, "Hey, keep going."

We'd learned, since the first calls for help, that Anil had taken a slide. In all honesty we didn't know if he was dead or alive. Trevor and I were at the start of the snow field when Enrique and Gustavo passed us.

Since I could speak pig Spanish, my communication with Enrique was better than most. And Enrique spoke a little English, so together we had Spanglish. Enrique appreciated me trying to speak Spanish. I gave it my best shot. Just trying to communicate makes anyone encourage you. Enrique said, "Congratulations. You guys make the summit in two hours."

"Great! Thanks."

Enrique also told us, "I need your help. After summit, when you come down, walk behind people."

TREVOR BYLES   Enrique told us how bummed out he was about having to go back down—"What the hell happened? This is probably the last time I'm going to climb this mountain and I really wanted to make it."

Looking back on it, there was no guide behind the group making sure people were doing the right thing. All three guides had been way up there, even ahead of Dick and Craig, going balls-out for the summit.

When Neil and I first heard about the accident I don't even know that we discussed whether to go down. It wasn't even in my mind to go back and see if Patel was alright. I wanted to keep ascending. We seemed too far up to be of much help.

BILL ENGLISH   Ten or fifteen minutes after the relay calls Enrique and Gustavo passed me. They were moving at a good clip.

The best thing Enrique did on the whole trip was right then and there. He patted me on the shoulder and said, "You are doing great. Keep going. You are only twenty minutes from the summit." Of course that was a crock of shit because even if I was Craig Roland I was more than twenty minutes from the summit. But this was a real psychological boost. I did not believe the summit was only twenty minutes away, but essentially Enrique said, "You've made it. You're practically there. Don't quit now," because I'd probably admitted to him that I was tired.

It was very, very, very slow going. During previous mountaineering trips I could count twenty-five steps or fifty or a hundred, then rest, and it is amazing how well that works. On the Canaleta I'd be lucky to get five step counts. And they weren't very big steps either!

GREGG LEWIS   I was praying to God that Dr. Patel was alive. He picked the wrong spot. In this situation we were just helpless; I felt, from our experiences before with there being no rope, that we were of no value to the poor doctor.

As we stood there waiting, Borgel said to me, "Hey man, I'm feeling pretty beat. I'm going down with Enrique and help the doctor."

Mark and I asked, "Are you sure that's what you want to do?"

Borgel said, "Yeah."

Borgel's pace was erratic. I wanted to encourage him to continue, but I didn't want him to over-extend himself. This was a fine line because he is my friend. I knew, from climbing Kilimanjaro, that a couple of guys who hadn't made the top felt bad, felt that they'd wimped out. I looked at Borgel and said, "Don't feel like you've wimped out. You've tried as hard as you can, man. If you feel you're at the point where you can't continue, it would be a good idea if you go down and help Dr. Patel."

THOMAS BORGEL   Enrique descended to Mark, Lewis and me, and said, "Well, what is it now?"

We said, "The Gould's think they need your help down below."

Enrique said, "I was close to the summit. You all can go down to help. You don't have to call me down."

I said, "What the hell do you mean, Enrique? You are supposed to be leading us and watching us, and you're not doing a damn thing!"

Enrique thought the situation was ridiculous, but none of us knew the severity of the accident—only that Patel had fallen. Apparently the Gould's couldn't see Patel's condition because he'd slid so far. Enrique started rattling on until I couldn't understand a word he was saying. He just raised hell.

Enrique told us we didn't have enough time to reach the summit. It was 1:30. He said it would take us three hours and that we'd have to turn back at 4 PM. Enrique said to me, "You, Lewis and Mark need to come down because you are going too slow."

Mark told Enrique, "You can forget that. I'm continuing."

Enrique said, "You will not make it. We need some help."

I said, "Listen, I'm pretty tired and don't feel too great. I'd be willing to go down and give you a hand. You might need help."

Lewis and Mark didn't believe time was running out. They decided to keep climbing. Mark said to me, "If you don't make the summit today you can give it another shot tomorrow."

As Enrique, Gustavo and I headed down toward the accident site, Enrique began bitching about the whole expedition and how no one listened to him. He went on and on about several people—"It goes to show you. Those two, they do not listen. I don't care. I let them do whatever they want. And Taplin. I try to tell him, but he would not listen. He just went wherever he wanted."

I said, "Listen man, that's not the way it was at all."

"See? Now you argue with me too."

I couldn't get a word in because Enrique was so defensive about everything he said. It wasn't worth arguing with him.

◊△◊△◊△◊△◊△◊△◊

KINGDON GOULD III   Once my father and I felt that our calls for help had been heard and understood, it was a relatively short time until Enrique and Gustavo arrived. They came down pretty damn quickly. Borgel was a good ways behind them.

My father and I asked ourselves if we should continue our ascent or stay to help. We realized, in this case, if help was needed we should stay. On one level we felt not all that needed since two guides were there. We asked Enrique, "Which would you like us to do? Should we go down with you to help? Should we stay here? Do you want us to continue up?"

Enrique said, "Stay here. I'll go down to the doctor. If I wave my arms this way, that means 'come'."

THOMAS BORGEL   We could see a speck halfway down the slope. Dr. Patel had tumbled a long, long way down this steep incline of rock and ice. That slope was bad news.

Enrique descended to Patel, then signalled for Gustavo, who had gone halfway, to come join him. Enrique then signalled for two more people to come down and for one person to stay in case more help might be needed. The Gould's volunteered to descend.

KINGDON GOULD III   Crampons are funny because they catch before you feel your boot is down. I almost felt I was going to trip, but I didn't want to stumble forward and fall. We also did not have ice axes.

We did have ski poles which we could plant in front. The slope was hard-packed, crusty snow; steep enough that we did not want to walk straight down. We had to zigzag as quickly as we could.

MR. GOULD

When we reached Anil he was sitting up. I was tickled to death to see him alive. I was thinking we might have to carry him down, and was trying to figure out how we could make a stretcher with ski poles and inside-out rain gear.

KINGDON GOULD III

Enrique had put a bandage on Anil's head and had gathered some of Anil's belongings. Anil was conscious, but stunned. It did not appear that he had lost a lot of blood—there were not pools of blood in the snow and his garment wasn't soaked in blood—but the whole side of his face was bloody. He'd taken a good whack and he looked miserable. We asked Anil if he was okay and he indicated he was okay. He was coherent—not saying much—but coherent.

I wouldn't have been surprised if Anil had died. When I think about his slide as a really long fall—well, we've all taken some of those on a ski slope and survived. But given the dramatic circumstances we did not know what Anil might have hit on the way down. There were obvious rocks which we could see on the slope.

ANIL PATEL

The first thing I heard from Enrique was, "We can get you a helicopter, but it will cost $4000."

I said, "Fine." For me, money was not the problem.

Then Enrique said, "Maybe the helicopters can not come right now because of the weather." The weather was awful; it was windy and had started to snow.

Enrique asked if I could walk to base camp and I said I would do that.

I didn't know my ribs were broken until I stood up. Then I knew I had a rib fracture because they were so painful. I had also dislocated my left shoulder, which was put back immediately by Gustavo. Both my hands were frostbit from being dug into the snow. I knew I had a big head gash, but was unsure if it was a concussion or a cranial fracture. I knew I did not have a broken leg, but my whole right side—pelvis, knee and hip—hurt.

There was no way a helicopter could fly up there. The only choice was to walk. I couldn't expect to be carried.

KINGDON GOULD III

We got a length of cord, put Anil on his feet, then tied this cord around his waist. Gustavo led, holding onto the cord, while Enrique held Anil from behind by the belt. I stood on the downhill side so Anil could put one hand on my shoulder for support. Anil held a ski pole in his other hand.

My dad went ahead to break trail through the snow. We traversed to a scree field on the same slope. Essentially we had to get back to the trail higher up.

We did not ask Anil a lot of questions. You don't want to do that. We wanted to help him along. We said, "You're a brave man to do this. We're going to get you out of here. Just keep going. Go slowly. If you are tired or want to stop, tell us." Anil would nod and keep going, or every so often he would want to rest.

ANIL PATEL   It was so painful. There were two or three times when I wanted to give up; I just wanted to be left on the mountain to die. Again I thought about my daughters and my wife—'Well, I have to keep going.' And there is that instinctual will to live. I knew there would be a warm bed at the end of the road—something waiting to help get me out of my misery.

THOMAS BORGEL   I walked twenty minutes down the trail, to the crest above Independencia. The rescue party had a hell of a time; it took them an hour to reach me.

The bandage wrapped around Patel's head was completely soaked in blood. His whole face was covered with dried blood and his entire right eye was crusted over. I thought, My God, how is he living?

I asked Patel some questions—his name—but all he did was just mumble. I never got him to say his name. I judged Patel to be in major shock, off in never-never land.

KINGDON GOULD III   Once Anil was brought back up to the trail my father and I again asked Enrique, "Should we continue our ascent, or should we stay and help? We'll do whatever you want, because we feel it is important to get people off safely."

Partly because of the weather Enrique said, "No more summit today. You want to pack your stuff. We go down."

I wondered where we were going—'Are we going down to Nido?' It was unclear.

THOMAS BORGEL   By this time a snow blizzard had come in. The wind had picked up to about thirty-five knots. The sun was gone. The temperature was well below zero. Enrique said, "You cannot miss the trail to White Rocks," and sent Kingdon and me out into the blizzard. It was snowing so damn hard the trail was gone.

After a bit I asked, "Well Kingdon, which way?"

"Let's go down here."

"Man, I don't think this is the right way."

Kingdon and I went in circles and had to backtrack several times. Finally we saw White Rocks.

KINGDON GOULD III   You would not want to get lost on that trail. You might not know if you take the wrong route. It's not like walking home; everything is backwards from coming up. I focused on finding the trail, and we did go the right way. We did not make any wrong turns.

About halfway down I went ahead. When I got to White Rocks I told my mother and sister, "Look, Dr. Patel has fallen. We want to pack up and go." Suddenly we had four sleeping bags that had to be stuffed. Sleeping bags don't stuff well at altitude.

Borgel was really tired. He just wanted to lie down and go to sleep which is not a good idea in the extreme cold. That's what happens to most people before they freeze to death. The first priority in that type of situation is to descend. I said to Borgel, "Look, get your gear together."

He said, "Well, I don't know that I want to go down."

Borgel went into his tent and crawled into his sleeping bag. I couldn't tell Borgel what to do. I could advise him, but it was not really my role. It was up to Enrique to talk with him. Borgel doesn't know the outdoors, or the conditions on the mountain, like Enrique. For all I knew, Enrique might well tell Borgel he could stay at White Rocks.

NUNZIE GOULD   By the time Dad arrived, which wasn't ten minutes after King, our tent was disassembled. Dad was upset that we'd already packed his gear; he didn't know how his belongings had been organized. He was tired and hot. He unzipped his jacket, took off his gloves and laid down. I tried to convince him to zip up his jacket and he really got mad at me. He said, "Please. I just want to rest." He wasn't yelling. He was just very frustrated and wanted to be left alone.

I picked up Dad's gloves which had accumulated snow at the cuffs and put them in my jacket to warm them up. After a half-hour rest Dad got up, couldn't find his gloves, and was mad about that. When I told him I had his gloves he said, "Don't you touch my gloves." He was unaware of the reasoning behind it all. He was struggling, and he was muttering things that didn't make much sense.

King did not feel well; he had a headache. Mom had it together on a mediocre level. Who knows what the hell one person, all alone, would do up there? I was glad I had come down to stay with Mom.

MR. GOULD   I was disappointed I wasn't in charge of things—not the climb—but I wasn't at peace with myself. I wasn't being manipulated by events, but things had not worked out the way I had anticipated. I was concerned that we hadn't been able to give Nunzie and King a shot at the top; that I hadn't really had a proper shot at the top myself; that I hadn't tried out my gloves so I knew exactly how they would feel and how comfortable they would be. That was stupid of me to not have perfected some technique to cope with that situation. All of this caused aggravation.

NUNZIE GOULD   Anil came into White Rocks not long after Dad. In a trauma situation you have to control yourself and do whatever has to be done. There wasn't a lot to do for Anil. His head was wrapped. The blood from his head wound had coagulated.

I was amazed Anil's clothes were relatively intact. He was wearing bibbed snow pants with a jacket over the top. His pants were ripped on the inside seam from the thigh up to the crotch, then partway down the other leg. His jacket was ripped on the shoulder.

Enrique and Gustavo occupied themselves with Anil and checked him again. Then we sat around while Enrique gathered some of Anil's personal gear. Everyone was pretty quiet.

MARY GOULD   Nunzie and I had talked earlier about a second attempt on the summit, but there was all this business about going down because the mules were waiting. Well, at that point, I could have cared less whether the mules were waiting or not. I mean, we had gotten all the way up there and we were in good shape; we could have spent another day and had another try.

The important thing, of course, was for us to get Anil Patel down as safely and as quickly as possible. There was no alternative. We couldn't tell if Anil had a concussion, or exactly what his condition was.

NUNZIE GOULD   When Mom and I were waiting at White Rocks we never discussed a second attempt. When I descended to White Rocks I had a gut feeling the climb was over. I didn't know when the mules were coming back or that Anil had gotten busted up—I didn't know any of that. I just knew it was finished.

Dad talked about a second summit attempt and the possibility that, since there were three guides, one of them might stay up on the mountain. Enrique saying, "We go down," concluded any discussion.

KINGDON GOULD III   Everyone was tired and we were facing bad weather. We did not know if the snow storm would last two hours or two days. If there was going to be a big storm we'd rather spend our time at Nido. We only had so much food and so much fuel at White Rocks. We had more supplies and water at Nido. If there was a small break in the weather, we could descend below Nido. You would not want to get socked in up at White Rocks, or try to beat your way through bad weather at 20,000-feet.

THOMAS BORGEL   When I woke up, Enrique and I had a big fight. He'd packed all my gear. I said, "What the hell are you doing? I'm staying here."

Enrique said, "No you're not. You are not going to stay. There is no food. There is no food for the others. They must come down right away."

"We should have food. We have several days left."

"No. We are out of food. Weather is bad. Turn winter. When it turns winter, you cannot go up anymore."

"Enrique, what are you talking about? What if the weather clears and we can try for the summit again?"

"No, no. There will not be another good day of weather. I've been on this mountain many times. I know when winter sets in and when winter will stay. Trip is over."

I said, "Well, if the others have to come down, we'll all go down. I'll go to Nido and that's it."

We left White Rocks mid-afternoon. It was snowing; visibility sucked. I was so frustrated and tired that I could barely stand on my feet. I was in no mood to put a sixty-five pound pack on my back. Everyone was toting full packs. We had no water. Eating snow was useless; I'd stuff my mouth full of snow and get two drops of water.

Dr. Patel was white as a ghost. He'd lost at least a pint of blood. I walked behind as Enrique and Gustavo held him up.

NUNZIE GOULD   Borgel did an amazing turn around. Being away from Mark and Lewis brought out another side to his character and his maturity. Maybe his bubble had been burst. Maybe he was depressed because he had not summited and that was showing. On the walk down to Nido Borgel had one hell of a headache and was suffering, but he was more group-oriented.

When we got to Nido I went to get water from the pond. It took awhile for Enrique, Gustavo and Anil to descend. That was a hell of a long walk for Anil just from White Rocks to Nido. He had a jolty gait from pulled muscles in his legs. He had minimal movement in his arms. His ribs hurt. He was probably slightly in shock. Anil sat on some rocks with us while we rested and collected our thoughts.

KINGDON GOULD III   It was snowing on top, there was sunshine at Nido, and below Nido was another storm. It was bizarre. I gathered the gear which we'd left in Dick's tent and stuffed it in my pack.

We didn't stay at Nido because Enrique said we should descend to base camp. We might have stayed at Nido and made another summit attempt from there, although we wanted to be prepared for different eventualities and weather changes. You don't know where you're most useful. I didn't mind going down. We could always come back up. I was hoping my folks would be okay, so I wanted to stay with them—not that they couldn't fend for themselves—but I felt we should be together.

I wondered if the rest of the expedition was okay and if anyone had made the summit because of the weather. And I wondered to myself what we would do with Dr. Patel—'How will we get him out? How far can he walk? Is he going to have to be carried? When we get to base camp will we have to make a litter and carry him down? How will we make a litter? If we carry him down what items should I take with me?' I ran through all these different scenarios trying to figure out how to deal with each one because, while the situation was a manageable emergency, it was still an emergency.

Anil was pretty amazing. He was consistent the whole way down. I really have to take my hat off to Anil. He was fairly lucid considering what he'd been through. He did not want much conversation. He was obviously stunned and hurting, but he wasn't ranting or delirious.

Borgel was a tired puppy. He was ready to lie down and sleep just about anywhere. Frankly, it was a good idea that Borgel had come down. He'd really tuckered himself out hiking that day. You can push yourself and push yourself and there comes a point when your energy leaves you. Borgel had reached that point.

THOMAS BORGEL   When we got to Nido I threw my pack off and crashed. I've never felt so exhausted in my whole life. We'd been going since 8 AM that morning with no food and no water. My body was just screaming at me.

Enrique came over and said, "Get up. Let's go."

I said, "You have got to be kidding! You all can go wherever you want, but I'm staying here and sleeping in Dick's tent."

You're not going to believe this. Do you know how Enrique got me to descend from Nido? He told the Gould's to head out, then he said to me, "We need your help getting Dr. Patel down."

My reaction was: 'Do whaatt?!' Without the Gould's I was the only other person, besides Enrique and Gustavo, to help with Dr. Patel. I was so beat I didn't think I could take another step. I'd felt bad descending from Nido to base camp after the first carry and thought *that* day would never end. Now, I was looking at hours of more walking.

We left Nido at 6 PM.

< 20 >

SUMMIT SHRINE

<u>CRAIG ROLAND</u>   Up to the point where we stopped I felt good and my breathing was fine. Essentially I had been taking a step and a breath, then another step and a breath. I had been making good time walking right behind the guides.

With a few hundred feet to go—this would have been about 22,600-feet—I experienced a noticeable increase in breathing difficulty. Dick had the same problem. It was as if we passed an invisible barrier and the oxygen supply shut off entirely. I went from one step/five breaths to one step/ten breaths, until below the top where it was one step/fifteen breaths. I was just flat out of oxygen.[22]

The footing in the Canaleta was very unstable with slippy-slidey, rolling rocks. We had to constantly focus, not just on getting up, but on finding stable rocks. The rocks, however, were never quite big enough to be stable.

Those were the toughest few hundred feet I've ever had in my life. It was a single-minded, intensive effort to concentrate on one step, breathing, then the next step. Thoughts of the summit, taking pictures, other people—all of that was completely absent. When the effort is that demanding, everything except the effort disappears from your mind.

<u>DICK GORDON</u>   Halfway up the boulder section the weather did not look good. A frontal system was coming in. I felt I needed to pick up my pace before Pépe decided to call off our summit attempt.

It could have been as early as base camp that I'd talked to Enrique about the Canaleta. Enrique had said that the Canaleta would take everybody by surprise. He seemed to think we'd get a lot of people on the Canaleta, but that not everyone would make it through. Before descending to deal with Dr. Patel, Enrique again reminded me, "Don't look at the summit. The summit will never look close. Look at short goals. Pick big rocks, pick little bends, slopes, flags, or look at the crosses where people have been buried."

You are praying for some 14,000-foot altitude on the Canaleta. The energy requirements needed to climb the Canaleta are so extensive that you can not take breaths by speaking. Numerous times Craig and I would sit down and just shake or nod our heads because we were breathing so hard. You didn't have to speak—you knew there was frustration as well as mental and physical deterioration. Breathing had to have a rhythm; Craig and I didn't want to take an extra breath for an extra word. You just could not justify the energy. Every bit of energy had

---

[22] It has been estimated that the summit of Aconcagua offers only 41% of the oxygen available at sea level.

to be directed toward climbing the mountain. Even a poorly placed step, which caused an imbalance that needed to be corrected, was a waste of energy. Every footstep, every hand placement, every movement was focused. But you are too fatigued for precision; movements are just that much more clumsy and difficult.

At this point Aconcagua is not a physical climb anymore. The individuals who had mentally put together the survival techniques, and who had hiked that far, certainly had the potential to reach the summit. Everyone was capable.

At high altitude the decisions are very basic: 'Do I take another step? Should I stop, sit down and rest? Should I turn around?' My body was completely fatigued and I had no desire to continue. There was a willingness, mentally, to continue, but it took a lot of focus to overcome the desire to stop and rest. Sitting down in the Canaleta passed through my mind. If I had sat down I would have relaxed and fallen asleep. Of course, if you fall asleep, that is where you would stay for the short period of your life's duration.

The real question was: 'What am I taking another step for? Is going for the top really what I want to do?' Several times my mind just had to refocus and answer that question. I had to take a couple of breaths, think about how I felt, where I was, and if I could quit. Nobody likes the decision to quit. Quitting was the only alternative. It was possible to rationalize quitting—'People will still respect me. I took a shot at the mountain.' But my ego goals threw out the notion of quitting relatively quickly—'Who cares what people think? Am I going to get this close, turn around and quit? Forget that...come up with a better option.' By then I'd be looking up at my next goal, which was a little higher, and I'd shoot for that—'Well, I'm taking another step for that short goal, to get over to that rock, because the next goal will be easier and then I'll make a better decision there.'

CRAIG ROLAND   Pépe moved ahead and made the summit. The steep talus slope abruptly flattens out and you're on the north summit of Aconcagua. The top is a rock-covered, flat table about forty by sixty feet. You can walk around on this platform. A ridge, at the top of the Canaleta, connects with the south summit. The other side of this ridge drops off to a solid wall of ice and snow.[23]

I remember the time exactly—1:45 PM; five and one-half hours after leaving White Rocks. Any sense of exhilaration, conquest, or achievement was obliterated by the effort and by physical exhaustion. Being so tired had a way of peeling those more subtle emotions away. As I was standing on the top with Pépe, getting my camera ready, I wasn't thinking, I've reached my goal and isn't this the most wonderful feeling in the world. That came later. Mostly I felt a sense of relief that I did not have to take another step up.

---

23 The South Face, divided by the French Spur, which drops 10,000-feet to the Inferior Horcones Glacier.

Pépe showed me where someone was buried under a mound of rocks. There are some markers and a couple of crosses. Just as we got to the summit a cloud came in. I was intending to take a lot of photographs, but it began to snow almost immediately. Visibility dropped.

Five minutes after I summited, Dick came up. He also did not really communicate any elation.

DICK GORDON   Pépe came back to the edge and was waiting for me. He reached out, we made a handshake, then kind of a pull-up grip, and I was on the summit. Craig was off on the other side of the summit plateau. As he turned around we made eye contact and we made some gesture that we both recognized as having made the summit.

Because of the weather Pépe said, "We cannot stay long."

I said, "Fine by me." The snow was going to make the descent difficult if we didn't start down soon. I went across the plateau and took a picture of the North Face and the South Face. I wanted to go to the other side and look down the Polish route, but I didn't.

I said to myself, "I've got to sit down. I'm really tired."

Another inner voice said, *No, don't do that. You really don't want to do that. That's stupid. That's how people get left up here.*

"But Craig and Pépe are up here. They won't leave me."

I sat down. Then it was my upper body that also needed some rest— "Lay down."

"Don't do that. You'll freeze. You'll be another tombstone."

"But Craig and Enrique are up here."

"All right, lie down for just a minute."

I found a rock, laid down and closed my eyes, but I was so uncomfortable on the rocks that laying down did not help. Also, it was cold; shivering kept me awake. I got back up. If I had found a place where my body could have relaxed, then I would have fallen asleep. I have no problem at all understanding how easy it would have been to fall asleep and freeze to death. That makes sense to me now.

CRAIG ROLAND   Pépe was getting very, very nervous because he wanted to get off. We were concerned about getting down since the snowstorm became worse as we stood there.

We watched Trevor and Neil crawl up the face of the mountain, 100-feet below the summit. We wanted them to make the summit. Pépe began to shout to them, "Come on! Hurry up!" Of course, there was no such thing as hurrying up.

Below Neil and Trevor, near the top of the snow field, were another group of people. This group was moving upwards, but it was clear they would need another hour or two to make the summit.

◊▲◊▲◊▲◊▲◊▲◊▲◊

NEIL DELEHEY   Everyone says the last thousand feet is just hell. I can back up their words.

The incline of the Canaleta steepens to about forty-five degrees. Every rock you stepped on slid out from under you, and we're not just talking small talus rock, but bed-sized slabs. You would take one step, start sliding back, then take four quick steps to get where you were. This was beating the hell out of both Trevor and myself. We were working and sweating like crazy.

I had a few gulps of water left, but didn't want to bother drinking. Trevor and I said to each other, "We're gonna make it. We're gonna make it, man"—all those stupid things guys say to each other.

Soon after that it started to snow. This was something I truly did not anticipate happening. Even the semi-stable rocks became slippery. Then it started snowing and blowing very hard. The summit was obscured and all I could think was, Oh my God, can this happen? Can we get this close and not make it?

TREVOR BYLES   We had been told not to go up the center of the Canaleta, but to go up the left or the right. The lead group had gone up dead center. Everything was sliding, which is why people had said to go off to either side. Even though I thought we should follow the tracks of the lead group, Neil and I traversed over to the right side. That's when Pépe yelled down from above that we were going the wrong way—"No, no! Go this way! Go over this way!" I started cussing because we had to go back to the center and face all those rocks.

The Canaleta is so horrible. Mentally you just hate the situation. You had to convince yourself to work through the pain. The Canaleta is a lesson in frustration, that's all it is. We could not get ahead; the summit never looked as though it was getting any closer. There it was—you reach, but you're sliding backwards. My chest was burning. I'd have to stop, catch another breath, then take off. It was exhausting. 'Jesus. This isn't worth it. I'm dying up here'—that went through my mind a couple of times. Then it was—'Well, I'm here. I'm this far. I've got to make it to the top.'

I stopped looking up at the summit. By not looking up I could focus on something else to keep myself going.

Psychologically, it did not help to know there were people above us. Knowing that Pépe, Dick and Craig were on the summit, and that they had gone faster, was worse. Here were Pépe and Dick yelling, "Go faster, go faster," as I'm about ready to die. No, it didn't help one bit. I was pissed off at them. Neil felt the same way. If they had been standing next to us, we would have just gone nuts and killed them. It was like— "What are you talking about? Shut up! We're going as fast as we can!"

Neil and I were both in the same frame of mind and couldn't move our little legs any faster. I cursed the summit. I started screaming and cussing out the mountain. Neil was just looking at me.

It's hard to say how my brain was functioning. My brain was in 'go up' mode. It definitely helped to have Neil as a partner. We both encouraged and helped each other. Neither of us would have made it that far without the other. We kept each other focused on the same goal. Mostly we helped each other with pacing. When one of us didn't feel like walking, we could look at each other's feet and keep going. That was the biggest factor; having someone else there to push you, to keep you going.

We knew we had to continue.

Neil and I were not really having any conversations on that last section. We were too exhausted to talk. At one point we stopped and Neil sat there and zoned for a little bit. It was just one of those things—"Hey, Neil. What are you doing over there, buddy?" He was just zoning. It was funny. He sat there long enough that it became noticeable. Neither of us were concerned about each other because we both knew we were tired. But we also knew we weren't so exhausted that we couldn't keep going. We hadn't reached the point where we were so dead tired we couldn't go on anymore. There was no way we were going to give up. We would never give up, unless our bodies shut down.

NEIL DELEHEY   Trev and I continued up. It was a struggle. The snow began to accumulate one or two inches. Everything brown had turned white. We rested all the time; we couldn't help it. I was panting constantly, as though I was running an uphill marathon on ball bearings with a bag over my head. All the rocks were sliding, causing tiny avalanches—'Am I meant to do this? Everything is falling down.'

◊△◊△◊△◊△◊△◊

DICK GORDON   The weather was shortening the amount of time we had to wait for Neil and Trevor. This was very difficult for Pépe. He finally decided, "The weather is getting bad. Forget it. Let's get down to Neil and Trevor and tell them they cannot make it up."

Well, I looked at Craig and our hearts just dropped. I know we both felt the same way; Neil and Trevor were so close to the top. I could understand Pépe's position and wondered, along with him, what the weather would do in the next couple of minutes—'Will the weather worsen to the point we won't get off the summit?'

It was tough for Pépe, with his not speaking English too well, to make this decision.

We yelled to Neil and Trevor, "Turn around. Forget it. Go on down."

I could see the disappointment in one of them—I forget if it was Neil or Trevor—but I could see his whole body relax. He hit the snow with his hand.

NEIL DELEHEY   Trev and I got within thirty-five feet of the summit and were resting. Dick yelled down, "Uh-oh, Pépe has a big decision to make. You know it's snowing and we have to get down." It was snowing pretty hard, but the wind made the storm seem worse than it was.

Trevor and I didn't have to listen to Craig or Dick, but we did have to listen to Pépe. Pépe's concern was that he had all these people strung out across the mountain and that he was responsible for them.

Pépe called to us—"Too dangerous to continue. Congratulations. That is your summit."

Trevor and I put our heads down on these rocks and said, "No, no, no..."

We were crushed. We didn't know what to say. Trevor and I had been climbing for this pinnacle. We didn't want to stop.

Then, divine intervention: suddenly the sun came out in a quick burst, the wind let up slightly, and the snow did not seem to be coming down as hard. This only lasted a couple seconds.

Trevor yelled back, "Come on! We're so close. Ten minutes! Give us ten minutes!"

We had been pretty friendly with Pépe; he was our age and I'd been speaking my pig Spanish with him. Pépe yelled, "Alright. Up and down. Ten minutes! Go!"

Well Jesus, we heard 'ten minutes' and that was like hearing the starting gun all over again. Trevor and I took off at a blazing snails pace. We were crawling to get to the damn top, jamming our hands and knees into cracks to get leverage. Trevor was right behind me.

Dick, Craig and Pépe started off the summit, and came down to a little flat area a few yards below the top. Trevor and I had made it to there.

Dick said, "Way to go, gentlemen. The summit is right around the bend. Take some quick photos and get down before the weather gets any worse." Then the three of them descended and disappeared in a cloud.

◊▲◊▲◊▲◊▲◊▲◊▲◊

TREVOR BYLES   Neil and I came over the little summit ledge, laid on our backs and tried to catch our breaths. We reached the summit at 2:15, so it had taken us six and a half hours from White Rocks.

The snow storm picked up again and was even more intense than before. Dick, Craig and Pépe had been on the summit for forty minutes; they'd been able to sit and think about the accomplishment. There Neil and I were, and we couldn't even say, "This is great!" Neil and I were happy to be on top of Aconcagua—we gave each other a big hug—but there wasn't enough time to take the accomplishment in.

NEIL DELEHEY   I was breathing even worse than before, as though I'd just done a sprint. Outrageous. I'd collapsed before even getting to the top and could not catch my breath at all. Trevor was the same way. I'm guessing it took well over two hours to make the summit from when we had spoken to Enrique.

We couldn't see anything. I couldn't see anyone in the Canaleta. I could barely see Trevor, ten or fifteen feet away, trying to take a picture!

Trevor was saying, "Come on. Picture, picture!"

I said, "Let's go! We have to get down from here!"

"No, no. We have to get pictures!"

Trevor had kept his camera in his jacket, next to his body, the entire way up. When he took his camera out the shutter froze. The batteries were fine, but the shutter would not go. In retrospect that picture would have shown that we had made the summit, but it would have been all white with two ghosts—not the classic summit photo which anyone else would have wanted to look at.

In the past, when I'd climbed to the top of 14,000-foot peaks, I didn't expect any great insight into Man. On the summit of Aconcagua I felt incredible exhilaration and a feeling of accomplishment. There was a lot of adrenaline flowing; it was a huge release. I didn't express the exhilaration and I was not jumping around, but there was a euphoric feeling. I felt privileged to be on the summit.

Trevor and I walked over to the two crosses. There was also a quasi-naturalist religious shrine: a pile of rosary beads, fake roses, and the stems of real roses which still had a faint scent.

I wanted to leave an offering—not a bumper sticker on one of the crosses saying 'Neil Was Here'—so I left a hat pin of the Irish Flag. I'm not a religious person; I'm Catholic but haven't been to church in years. I'd been given a Saint Christopher's medal which I'd also been wearing in my hat. I was going to leave that medal, then I looked at the weather and decided I might still need Saint Christopher.

Trevor and I were only on the summit for two or three minutes.

< 21 >

COVERED TRACKS

BILL ENGLISH   You want to just stand there. For half-an-hour you want to just stand there and do nothing. You don't want to lift your foot up three inches again and set it down.

Suddenly I had to make a bathroom stop really badly. I was in the middle of the Canaleta, about halfway up the snow field, which was too damn steep to try and do anything safely. Finally I got over to the edge, where there were some rocks. But even sitting on the rocks was treacherous as hell. It was such a muscular strain to get enough clothes off to the point where I could squat or kneel down. I had to do it or I would have messed my pants.

Not much goes through your mind. There just isn't much. You don't look far ahead and you rarely look up. And even less look down because it is too steep. I never had a sense of lack of balance or lack of judgement which they say comes with altitude sickness. In fact, I know my mental capacity was there because, when I sat down, I opened my eyes enough to see that it was snowing, and that it was snowing considerably hard. Everywhere I put my hand down was half an inch of fresh snow. I was very lucid about my decisions. Everything was very clear in terms of what was happening and where I was; I was at 22,500-feet.

Stopping took quite a bit of time; the people behind me were getting closer. My feet and hands had warmed up, so that wasn't a factor. Exhaustion and no oxygen were the factors.

I snapped a couple of pictures up the Canaleta. Then I put my camera away, lashed my crampons to my pack and started up the rocky part. It was a struggle to get up the rocks. I didn't go too far and finally stopped again.

GREGG LEWIS   Mark and I carried on, got off the snow field, and took off our crampons. Then we started up the boulder field. That boulder field was God's last way of making everything a bitch. I was taking eight breaths a step.

Mark's frame of mind was fine. He'd given me some of his water. Bill was fairly close to us. Bill looked tired and was having maybe a rougher time than we were. Everyone trudged on a ways.

It started to snow just after two o'clock. We all stood there for ten minutes. Initially we thought the bad weather would clear off, but the longer we stood there, the harder it snowed. Clouds were rolling up the side of the mountain. On the summit, drifting in and out of view, we could see Pépe, Craig and Dick. We were hoping to get some kind of sign from them as to whether or not to come up, but they never shouted down to us. Although the weather made it hard to judge distance, we figured we were 400 vertical feet—an hour and a half—from the top.

BILL ENGLISH   We discussed the situation and bantered back and forth—"What's happening? Should we keep going?" We were feeling each other out a bit.

Mark wanted to continue. I said, "I'm really not sure about this. Hey, we don't know what this storm might become. I've been in whiteouts before and it is not worth it. If you guys want to be macho and go for it, go ahead. But I'm getting out of here. I'm heading down."

And I didn't know there was a guide up top—'We are going to be on the mountain by ourselves, in a whiteout, without knowing the way back to White Rocks.' I knew Enrique and Gustavo had gone down. It hadn't entered my mind that Pépe was above us, or that he had been in the lead from the very beginning. One of the guides had to be bringing up the rear!

So I figured there were no guides above and none below that I could see. As far as I knew, the only people on top were Craig, Dick, Neil and Trevor. And they didn't know jack-shit about being at 23,000-feet in a whiteout, or about the mountain itself. I knew how steep the Canaleta was, and I could look down and see that our tracks were getting covered up. It was frightening.

Mark headed up. Lewis hung back.

I felt bad, but I made a judgement, right or wrong. I was real strong about my decision. Part of me was happy I'd gone that far and didn't have to go any further. Maybe in saying that, I'm saying I copped out, or latched onto bad weather coming in, and thought to myself: 'I can quit now. I can go back down because this is getting too dangerous.' I saw a way out. To some extent that may be true. I sat there for a long time and really pondered it. But I was also relieved that I did not have to make that last pitch up the Canaleta.

I never had any other moments of fear, except possibly that morning when my toes were frozen. I put my crampons back on, turned around, and went down fast. I wasn't panicked, but I was determined to get down as quickly as possible.

GREGG LEWIS   Getting to the summit by Enrique's 4 PM deadline would have been close. Bill had had enough and was not sticking around. He and I knew that in one hour we would not be able to see a damn thing. My mind flashed on losing the trail and staggering all over the mountain. It just was not worth the risk. I had also promised my wife that I would take care not to do anything stupid.

Finally I said to Mark, "I'm not going any further. It's snowing too hard."

MARK CORNWALL   Lewis said to me, "Hey Mark, give it up. To hell with it. It's all over. Let's go down."

Then I saw one clear spot in the sky, one last ray of hope. I traversed to the middle of the Canaleta, thinking the storm clouds would pass by, but no—they did not pass by. The weather became more ominous. You can die up there in weather like that.

GREGG LEWIS   As Pépe and the others began to descend from the summit they were waving and screaming, which I took as an indication not to come any higher. That was alright with me because my brain had shifted gears and I'd already made up my mind. Mark saw the others descending and said, "Well, shit." He turned around to put his crampons on.

I thought to myself, Too bad...we were so close.

Being the last to leave camp had really proved to be our downfall. Mark, Borgel and I had gotten such a damn late start. Neil and Trevor had left White Rocks a good hour before us. If we had left with them, Mark and I would have made the summit. Bill would have summited also.

MARK CORNWALL   I was extremely disappointed. I had no expectations other than to make the summit—sure, more slowly than those ahead of me, but still within the time frame allotted to us. There was nothing more frustrating than being an hour away, watching the weather close in, then realizing I could not do it. That was the first time in my life that has ever happened. Everything was geared toward making that summit and I was forced, by nature, not to be allowed that dream to come true.

◊▲◊▲◊▲◊▲◊▲◊▲◊

E.A. FITZGERALD   At a point about a thousand feet under the great peak my old symptoms of nausea gradually came on. At times I would fall down, and each time had greater difficulty in rising; black specks swam across my sight; I was like one walking in a dream, so dizzy and sick that the whole mountain seemed whirling around with me.

It was one o'clock, and though I had sat down half an hour before with success within my grasp, I now felt as if it were impossible for me to move farther on. Of my disappointment I need not write, but the object of my expedition was to conquer Aconcagua; I therefore sent Zurbriggen on to complete the ascent. He seemed in good health, and was confident that he could reach the top. He had been suffering so much at night from pain in his shoulder, that I felt it would not be right for me to keep him at this high camp much longer, and after the good work he had done for me before, I thought that it was but justice to him that he should have the proud satisfaction of the first ascent.

I shall never forget the descent that followed. I was so weak that my legs seemed to fold up under me at every step, and I kept falling forward and cutting myself on the shattered stones that covered the sides of the mountain. I do not know how long I crawled in this miserable plight, steering for a big patch of snow that lay in a sheltered spot. On reaching the snow I laid down, and finally rolled down a great portion of the mountain side. As I got lower my strength revived, and the nausea that I had been suffering from so acutely disappeared, leaving me with a splitting headache. Soon after five o'clock I reached our tent.

Zurbriggen arrived about an hour an a half later. He had succeeding in gaining the summit, and had planted an ice-axe there; but he was so weak and tired that he could scarcely talk, and lay almost stupefied by fatigue. Though naturally and justifiably elated by his triumph, at that moment he did not seem to care what happened to him. Next morning we closed up our camp and returned to the Inca.

Thus was Aconcagua conquered. "Sic vos non vobis mellificatis apes."[24]

---

[24] Translation: "Thus you yourself cannot make honey without the bee."

< 22 >

RETREAT FROM THE DEATH ZONE

CRAIG ROLAND   Coming down the Canaleta was much more dangerous than going up; the rocks were constantly moving under foot. With our big, heavy double plastic boots, Dick, Pépe and I could plant our heels and crash down through the rocks and snow.

Three or four hundred vertical feet below the summit, near the top of the snow field, we came to the others and collected ourselves. The people in this group perhaps felt they could make the summit, but it was clearly a dangerous situation. Mark and Lewis were disappointed. We waited a few minutes for Neil and Trevor to catch up with us.

NEIL DELEHEY   Trevor and I had a big internal lift—'We made the summit and we're coming down!'—but the weather!

Once we got far enough down to rest with the others we could tell the people that made the summit, although tired, were in way better shape than those who had not. Mark might have made the summit if the weather had held. Lewis did not look well. From what I heard, his water froze on him.

There is a critical point of altitude that effects most people. Climbers call it the 'death zone.'[25] Even though I realized I was much better off than some of these folks, I had a better grasp of what senility would be like. It was apparent that people improved a lot the further we descended.

CRAIG ROLAND   Pépe said, "I want everyone to stay together going down." This was the first time anyone had ever said that on the entire trip. Staying together made a lot of sense, because if people get separated accidents can happen. We all started down together. If someone got ahead Pépe would call out to them. We made it through the ice traverse and took our crampons off.

BILL ENGLISH   I waited at Independencia and kept looking up at the ridge. I was worried I'd done something wrong—afraid I'd gone the wrong way or wasn't quite sure where to go—because I was so far ahead of everybody.

Finally I saw people, and Dick hollered down, "Wait there. Pépe wants the group together. Don't move." He was barking out commands for me to stay put.

The entire group came down and we took a brief break. Everybody was worn out.

---

[25] Mountaineers use the term 'death zone' to denote the altitude, usually above 20,000-feet, at which one's physical and mental capabilities deteriorate due to oxygen deprivation.

GREGG LEWIS   I barely remember anything about getting back to White Rocks except that my sense of thirst was overwhelming. I had a chunk of snow in my mouth during the entire descent, but it was never enough. There was no water to share; everyone had used up their water. I just wanted to get down and not get hurt. Later that day I said to Mark, "I'm glad we didn't make the summit. I was too tired and too dehydrated. If I'd gone that extra hour to the summit, then had to descend that much further, I might have slipped or fallen or killed myself."

Twice coming down the traverse I helped Roland put his crampons on. When we stopped for a rest I'd close my eyes and my mind would stay blank until someone would touch me on the shoulder and say, "Come on. Let's go." I would almost fall asleep. I felt weak and was just going through the motions without any thoughts.

The trail had almost disappeared under the snow. There were still flurries as we arrived in White Rocks.

NEIL DELEHEY   Just above White Rocks, where the people who were really fatigued could just hike in, Trevor and I stopped, sat down and discussed our feelings. We hung out by ourselves for about half-an-hour. We were both really, really pumped and gave each other some high-fives. We had a little celebration and tried to figure out if we'd done anything, physically or mentally, that was harder. I couldn't compare getting to the top of Aconcagua with anything. Climbing Aconcagua was a different genre.

TREVOR BYLES   That's when the achievement hit; when Neil and I had time to enjoy the summit experience and take it in.

The Canaleta had been complete, utter frustration. There is no way to prepare for the Canaleta. The Canaleta is something that can only be experienced. It was great to break through a barrier like that and be able to say, "There is the top. I'm going to make it."

Making the summit of Aconcagua was a big deal; I was taking a year off school and had totally set my mind to do one thing. Neil and I said to each other, "The rest of our trip, no matter where we decide to go, is gravy. We accomplished what we wanted. Now we can do whatever we want."

The only time I really had a big headache was after coming back into White Rocks. I was so exhausted that I took a lot of Tylenol and immediately went to bed.

NEIL DELEHEY   Trevor and I definitely had to suppress our exhilaration; we felt good, but we didn't want to sit around with the people who hadn't made the summit and say, "Oh, yeah! Boy, it was great on top!" Some people didn't feel well and the others may have felt they had been robbed by the weather. Sure, the weather had a lot to do with it, but the group of people who had not summited were clustered. That's how I saw it.

Mark came over to me and said, "Hey Neil, congratulations. Way to go." Not everyone said that, but it felt good when people did. Trevor and I congratulated Dick and Craig.

We still didn't know if Anil was dead or alive. Being positive, we assumed he was alive. The mood around camp was pretty somber.

CRAIG ROLAND   There was no rejoicing among the people who had made the summit. There was some conversation, but the mood was very quiet and reserved. White Rocks was quite tranquil. Several people just vanished into their tents for the rest of the day.

We did not have radios, so no one knew what had happened to Enrique, Dr. Patel, Borgel, or the Gould's. There was no note, although it was obvious a portion of camp gear was gone.

BILL ENGLISH   I was pissed off at some of the rest of the group because Craig, Dick and I had climbed to the snow bank twice the previous day to get ice to melt for water. Nobody else had gathered ice. Getting to the snowbank was difficult and then it was a bitch to pry the ice out. When we returned to White Rocks Pépe needed ice and I was damned if I was going to get ice again. Mark and somebody else finally went for ice. Part of me felt sorry for them because they had to be as exhausted as I was.

Craig, Dick and I laid out on some rocks outside our tent. It was relatively cold, but we were warm from our exertion. We were laying there bundled up, although our heads and hands were exposed. We looked at the sky with clouds going over. It was snowing, but there was partial sun. Snow flurries, sun, clouds—all at the same time. It was gorgeous. We were trying to bask in this 25° weather. We were getting snowed on, yet no one had the energy to move. We dozed off.

I'm glad Dick made the summit. He sure had an attitude, but he did it. Dick deserved to summit.

DICK GORDON   People did congratulate me on making the summit. You don't know what to do with those compliments. You had to deal with people's feelings and pre-judgements—"Will he make the summit or not?" Everybody was real good about handling both the successful and unsuccessful summit attempts.

Bill was disappointed about not making the summit, but he wasn't upset. Whatever his choice had been—timing, pace, or form—he seemed comfortable that he had taken a shot. I would have been disappointed as well, but I would have realized where I was, what I was expected to do, and what I was expected to handle. There is always disappointment if you have to go home and say, "Well, I didn't make the top."

MARK CORNWALL   The judgment of who would or would not summit was left till that day. Take Dick Gordon for instance. During our ascent to White Rocks Dick, to me, had all the arrogance of someone who had been up Aconcagua fifty times—how the ascent would be and what would happen. People actually asked him, "Have you climbed this mountain before?" Corporal Dick was very matter of fact. But Dick made the summit. He was strong all the way, I'll give him that. He was in shape and had trained intensively. He stated he had not had any alcohol for three months. He was the most psyched person on the expedition, and really geared.

Craig Roland adapted to altitude as though there was no problem, as though he was just at home. I didn't think he would adapt when I first saw him at the beginning of the trip. What this goes along with is that looks have nothing to do with getting up to altitude or not. They really don't. Craig is a sensitive guy. He was the strongest person on the climb.

Trevor was the original I-don't-give-a-fuck-about-anything guy. Amazingly, he and Neil made the summit. They just kept plugging along. At one point on the ascent we were all equal, but Neil and Trevor kept up just a little faster pace.

To tell the truth I was the only person talking about a second summit attempt. I talked to everyone who hadn't made the summit and asked them all, point blank, "How about another attempt. Let's rest up. What do you say?"

Bill told me, "The way I look at it, I was an hour from the summit. That was close enough for me. I don't feel I need to try again."

Gregg Lewis said, "Oh, I think you're goddamn stupid to consider a second attempt."

Everyone asked, "What are you going to do, Mark?"

I said, "Well, I would like a second attempt, but I seem to be the only one into it." Everyone just grumbled.

I asked Pépe about it and he said, "You have to talk to Enrique. He's the boss." Well, Enrique was clear down in Plaza de Mulas.

GREGG LEWIS   Mark absolutely wanted a second attempt; he definitely wanted to stay another night and try again. The climb had worn us down so much that we needed at least one full rest day. And there was no way to even contemplate a second try unless we had more to eat; I knew we couldn't attempt the summit again on just another cup of hot chocolate. I had no strength and simply would not make it.

There wasn't much time to ponder a second attempt. Pépe dished out some hot water and rice for dinner, then he said, "Dr. Patel is hurt. Expedition is over."

After we heard 'expedition is over', Mark and I knew that was it. We'd pack our bags in the morning and go down. Mark resigned himself to the fact that the situation was hopeless: we didn't have enough guides; no one else besides Mark had expressed any interest for another try; we had no food; everyone was exhausted. The realization came through that a second summit attempt would not be safe. The only choice was to descend.

White Rocks that night was not a camp of celebration by any means.

<u>CRAIG ROLAND</u>   I don't know who thought there was going to be a second attempt. It was crystal clear there was going to be no second attempt and that we were heading off the mountain. This had been clear, to me, for the last five days. When we first started up to Nido we knew when the mules were arriving at base camp to take our gear back to Puente del Inca.

Mark did not share his desire for a second attempt with me. He probably thought there was no reason to talk to me since I'd already made the summit.

<u>DICK GORDON</u>   More people could have summited. The energy was there, but most of the group had poor or incorrect calculations of pace. The question of how to pace oneself is difficult. One could rationalize a slower pace at the beginning by wanting to conserve energy for the Canaleta, but most people did not understand the time interval they had to reach the Canaleta. And even if you summit you have to leave enough time to descend. So there was misjudgment there.

In all fairness the people who wanted a second summit attempt should have been given another opportunity. At White Rocks, however, sleep is difficult and there is no desire to eat, so one is going to deteriorate even more. The only exception might be someone who had too slow a pace on the first attempt, and who then had a better understanding of how they should pace themselves for a second attempt. My personal opinion is that the energy expended on the first attempt probably would not be retrieved enough by a nights rest at White Rocks to make a second attempt through the Canaleta.

I wish more people had made the summit. Four people is an awfully low percentage considering the success of other expeditions, as well as Enrique's previous groups. Such a small number of people making the summit from this group was the rare exception. That was not indicative of what could have occurred.

< 23 >

FUNKY SPAGHETTI

ANIL PATEL   Thomas Borgel and the Gould's were very good to me. They accompanied us down to Nido and were so helpful. I wanted to stop and spend the night in Nido, maybe get a helicopter there, but there was no way to get a message out.

What was very disturbing was that, from Nido to Plaza de Mulas, two Argentines from another group were the ones helping me down, not Enrique and Gustavo. Gustavo was way out in front. Enrique was even further down the mountain with Mr. Gould and Kingdon. My head did not hurt too much, but it was awful to walk all the time with my damaged ribs, right knee and hip. And there was no one to help. It was easier to slide down the scree rather than walk. My pants were completely ripped from sliding down the scree. The two Argentines saw me and they said, "You shouldn't do that. It will be very painful." These strangers could see I was injured and that I needed assistance.

I don't know who these two Argentines were and I don't remember their names. I'd seen them earlier at Nido, during the ascent, and had said hello to them. They would tell me to try and make it to a certain point—"You can make it, you can make it." On the steep sections I would rest a hand on one's pack, while the other man supported me.

Soon we were walking in the dark which was hard.

THOMAS BORGEL   The only Argentines helping Dr. Patel were Gustavo and Enrique. Below Nido, Enrique took off, then Gustavo and I took turns leading Patel down. Near camp Alaska the trail became less rocky. Gustavo said he could handle Dr. Patel the rest of the way, so I went ahead and overtook the Gould's at the switchbacks.

When I came into base camp Enrique said, "Come over to the mess tent." I thought, Humm, maybe he has something for me to eat. I went in and Enrique started bitching that the cook tent and dining tent had been ransacked and that there was no food. He said, "I think Mike and Stasiak steal the food. They steal all the meat. I feel something about them from the very beginning."

"Christ, Enrique. Mike and Stasiak wouldn't take everybody's food! Stasiak is a nice guy. He just isn't a mountain climber. I never heard you say you were worried about food being stolen, or that this had been a problem before. If that's a concern, well, don't you think you should have locked the food up inside these plastic containers?"

I felt like killing Enrique. There was no food to be stolen, and I knew he had manipulated me into coming down to base camp, which is something I did not want to do.

I never got on Enrique's bad side though. He had me helping him. When Dr. Patel arrived at base camp with Gustavo, I was exhausted, but Enrique made Kingdon and me get water.

NUNZIE GOULD   Mom and I arrived at base camp at 8:30 PM. King had already set up our two family tents. Anil and Gustavo came into camp in the dark, at 10:30.

Enrique took Anil into the cook tent where it was a little warmer. The cook tent was turned into an emergency room with lantern light and water. We warmed Anil up, then undid bandages. Enrique wanted to re-bandage Anil's head. Mom acted as the nurse; she washed the dried blood from his face with hot water and soap, and cleaned up his glasses.

KINGDON GOULD III   Anil was obviously going to survive, but he was a long ways from treatment. We had to elicit details from him to try and understand his condition. We wanted to know, as well as we could, what might be wrong with him in case we needed to help.

It was our feeling he might have had a fractured pelvis. He'd said he'd hurt his shoulder or his collar-bone, so we knew he had a problem there. He probably had a couple of broken ribs; it was painful for him to cough and he could only take shallow breaths. One of his legs was hurt and he walked with a limp. Although he was in a lot of pain, he did not complain at all. Anil is a stoic.

THOMAS BORGEL   Enrique gave me some crackers which was his way of making a peace offering. I said, "My god, you've been hoarding these crackers?!"

Enrique threw a bunch of tomatoes in a pot and made his tomato concoction. There was some funky spaghetti which no one ate, since it had been sitting there for four days. Dr. Patel couldn't eat it, so the Gould's made him a cup of soup and fixed him some hot chocolate. I found out from the Gould's how badly Patel's skull had split.

Patel wanted to be flown out by helicopter and said he had $3500 in his wallet. This was a delusion he stuck to until the next morning.

NUNZIE GOULD   Enrique gave Anil some codeine, which enabled him to get a few hours of sleep. We decided Anil would spend the night in our spare two-person tent. We vacated that, put in a couple of extra bed rolls, and rigged a light so he could be by himself. I don't know how smart that was, yet there was no fear of him going comatose at the time.

Mom, Dad and I slept in our other tent, while King, Tommy Borgel, Gustavo and Enrique slept in the mess tent.

That night there was rockfall way across the Horcones valley. You couldn't tell the difference between what sounded like avalanche and what sounded like rockfall, but we could see sparks. I took it as a sign that the mountain has it's own mind.

MR. GOULD   Enrique had one hell of a long day: he left from White Rocks, walked up partway; turned around to escort Mary down; went back up, passed us and got almost to the summit; turned around and went down to get Anil, and then went through the trauma of wondering if he had lost Anil. Can you imagine, as a guide, wondering if you had lost someone? You can appreciate that that was quite a day for Enrique. And he still didn't know how the rest of the group was enduring. Suppose there had been another accident? I mean there was Tom who had a broken arm and who almost died of exposure, and here was Anil who fell an incredible distance. Enrique was probably thinking: 'Now what? If only I can get the rest of these people out of here and get them home.'

< 24 >

EVACUATION
Expedition Day 11

KINGDON GOULD III   We talked to Enrique about evacuating Anil and offered whatever seemed best. Although Anil was not in any immediate danger it was clear he had to get out sooner or later. Anil wasn't going up the mountain again. We considered a helicopter evacuation, but the radio operator was gone. For Enrique the dilemma was: Should we stay and regroup, or should we leave?

I'm sure Enrique was thinking about the people still up on the mountain—some people here and some strung out there. Enrique wanted to keep people together. He did suggest waiting one day for the rest of the group, then the mules would come which might have given Anil a way to ride out.

We asked Anil. We said, "If you want to descend, we're happy to walk out with you. Don't feel you should stay here for us."

Anil wanted to leave. He could walk by himself, but we knew it was a long walk and felt he should not set off alone. Enrique felt it would be good if someone walked down with Anil. I don't know that Enrique felt everybody had to leave base camp.

Enrique told us the expedition was over. He said we were coming to the end of the summer climbing season, and that the weather would become increasingly cold and less certain. As far as I understood, that was true. The weather at base camp was pretty good, but I didn't know if the weather on top would be good for a second attempt. We relied on our guide. It is better for the guide to be safe than sorry, and, with that attitude, the guide will miss some chances. I knew from my limited, previous experience on Aconcagua that the odd storm can come in pretty goddamn fast. I don't want to be on that mountain when a storm comes in. And I think I had a better chance than some of the others to withstand a storm.

As far as the summit goes, you either make it or you don't. When you climb a mountain, making the top is only a part of the experience, not the whole experience. If you make the summit every time and do not succumb to the mountain or the weather, the mystery is gone. That's the way I look at it. I felt glad our family was safe and that Anil was relatively okay. I had a stronger feeling on this trip about being able to summit. I felt better and got closer to the top than my previous attempt, but I didn't make it. There are worse things. I felt worse for my father not making the summit than myself.

Not making the summit was not worth dwelling on. We didn't chat much about it. I wanted to guard against being bummed out. If we weren't taking another shot at the summit we didn't want to wait around base camp. We packed our gear, leaving some items in duffel bags for the mules.

I have to say that Anil took some punishment without much complaint. I admire him. He had a very good attitude. Anil needed to be a little faster on the mountain during the ascent. I didn't think he was in particularly good physical shape. He wasn't physically strong—that is what I mean when I say he should have been faster. You have to be able to get from point A to point B within a certain time frame. Mentally Anil was fine. There were people like Borgel who were physically stronger than Anil, but who weren't mentally prepared. That's my own opinion and probably unfair to say.

NUNZIE GOULD   Anil and I headed out after Gustavo, at 1 PM. Before we left, Enrique and Borgel wished us luck.

Shuffling down the switchbacks where the dead donkeys were scattered on the rocks was a hairy stretch. If someone had had a movie camera the scene would have been very surreal. Anil couldn't take big steps. Even though he had ski poles, I said, "Anil, put your hand on my shoulder and walk beside me." He was a proud man and didn't want too much help.

We took a water break at the ruins of the refugio Columbia, then Mom, Dad and King caught up to us. Mom walked with us for a bit. Sometimes Dad walked with us and talked about the geology of the canyon.

Anil and I pretty much walked together all the way to Confluencia. I tried to keep talking to Anil, basically to make time go faster and to keep him distracted from his injuries. I wanted to talk grass roots—talk about those things that people tend to remember when all else fails them. I wasn't going to ask Anil to philosophize on life. Anil was only talking the bare minimum. His parents, who are Indian, live in England, and had been over to visit him. We talked about his medical practice and his two adopted children from India. He specifically asked me to be sure that I got his backpack with his camera. I reassured him that we'd have his gear returned.

It started to get chilly. Finally I told Anil, "I'm putting your hat on your head and you will now put your gloves on."

I wanted to keep his energy up and figured every time I stopped to eat or drink something, he should damn well eat or drink also. He was concentrating most of his effort on motivating his body to perform. What you can do with your mind to distract your body is pretty amazing. It was obvious he had to get down and that he had to go through some pain. Anil had done a few Outward Bound courses which had a lot to do with his motivation and his ability to grip the situation.

MR. GOULD   During the walk from White Rocks to Mulas, Anil was okay, he had a lot of adrenaline going. But from Mulas to Confluencia he had to go at an agonizingly slow pace due to his condition. I was astounded because he was extremely uncomplaining. Nunzie was very kind and very patient with Anil.

We all took turns to try and find the best way down through what I call 'Death Valley'—that stream bed through the Horcones Valley.

KINGDON GOULD III   We didn't know when Gustavo might show up with help. I had my little binoculars and spent some time on the west side of the valley, hoping to see someone coming up. We'd spread out, rest, then walk some more. I finally pulled ahead.

Just before the knolls at Confluencia, on the western side of the valley, there was a marshy, grassy area with a clear water source that I hadn't noticed going up. It made me wonder what else I had missed. When you walk up that valley you are fixated on Aconcagua because the mountain is quite dramatic with big walls towering above; you're looking up, looking ahead, and thinking about what you are going to do. Coming down you tend to look around more.

I came to the camp site at Confluencia just as it was getting dark and started a wood fire. By the time Anil arrived we were working on some tea and cooking a freeze-dried turkey-stroganoff dinner with instant rice. Anil was wet; he couldn't hop across streams and had ended up wading through the water. We took off his boots, tried to dry them, and gave him fresh socks. Anil was a little cold, so we got him by the fire to warm him up. We had just started eating when a gaucho arrived. Gustavo stayed at the hosteria in Puente del Inca after sending the gaucho up with an extra horse.

NUNZIE GOULD   The horse man accepted dinner and hot tea. Anil wolfed all of his dinner right down. The food helped Anil. He was a little more talkative. He'd been walking for eight hours or so. He was relieved to be there. We all were.

We weren't sure Anil had ever been on a horse before, but he mentioned he'd had some experience, so we were more confident about him riding out in the dark. We gave him a leg-up onto a couple of sheepskins behind the saddle, and said, "Good luck. Have a safe trip out."

We also told him to leave us a note if there was anything we could do when we got down. That was the last we saw of Anil Patel.

We decided to camp at Confluencia and walk out to Puente del Inca the following morning. There was no rush to return.

ANIL PATEL   I'll tell you something. I can never repay the Gould family. They came down with me, and they helped me because I was injured. You should always help people out.

I remember the exact time the gaucho and I left Confluencia—9:36 PM. Riding the horse was much better than walking. The gaucho who led the horse was the best guide. I only spoke two words to him: 'bueno', because he asked if I felt okay, and 'lentamente', which means slowly.

The only thing I really thought about was what I would eat at the hosteria, but the kitchen was closed. I picked up my passport and travellers checks. The worst part was driving to Mendoza. Willy drove so crazy. It was very painful for me in the back seat with Gustavo.

Part 3

The Mountain As A Mirror

"I think I have learned other, and more important things, as well. One is that you cannot be a good mountaineer, however great your ability, unless you are cheerful and have the spirit of comradeship. Friends are as important as achievement. Another is that teamwork is the one key to success, and that selfishness only makes a man small. Still another is that no man, on a mountain or elsewhere, gets more out of anything than he puts into it...*Be great. Make others great*. That is what I have learned..."

Tenzing Norgay
Tiger of the Snows

< 25 >

AMISH BEER

MARK CORNWALL   We had a horrible night at White Rocks—not just cold, which one expects, but wind which blew like crazy. Foul weather. We'd had a rice-type dish for dinner, which was the only food we'd had all that day, and now, for the second morning in a row, there was nothing for breakfast except hot chocolate.

I awoke having given the summit some thought. For all the ecstasy there is in reaching a summit, there is not one bit of ecstasy in almost reaching a summit. Now that I've had the experience I realize this is the wrong attitude. But at the time I was frustrated in my own mind about wondering what I should do. My absolute, number one instinct was that not summiting was unfortunate, but that I'd descend, rest up and try again. A second summit attempt would be a real challenge. I wouldn't like it, but that is what I'd have to do. I resigned myself to this plan and was willing to retreat to Nido. But then, lower down, I realized trying for the summit in a day or two seemed extremely impractical. Enrique hadn't left any food at Nido, nor had he said, "If you guys need to retreat, spend a couple of days at Nido and wait the weather out." Enrique eliminated that option. I was actually going to have to accept defeat. That was a bitch. I didn't want any part of that.

The people who had not made the summit did not share my despair. Maybe they had met their match. For myself, not making the summit shattered my dreams of the entire expedition. I had great expectations of what was going to happen if I made the summit of Aconcagua. Do you know how you set things in your mind? I do.

BILL ENGLISH   The group prepared for the descent to base camp. Virtually all of Dr. Patel's extra gear had been left at White Rocks. We split everything up and packed that gear. About the only item of Patel's I took were his white bunny boots which were like lead weights.

When we came into Nido I was perturbed because we had to empty out Dick's tent—the supply tent—and divide up all that stuff. Craig, Dick and I ended up with nearly all of it. Bulk-wise my pack was pretty full; I couldn't fit much more on it.

CRAIG ROLAND   Bill and I had tremendous loads—about fifty pounds. Having such huge loads wasn't too bad walking downhill.

At camp Berlin I talked with the Japanese fellow whom we'd seen off and on since arriving on the mountain. He had had a lot of trouble, having been snow-blind for a period of time, and his crampons had been stolen. I gave him my crampons. Hopefully he put those to good use. I wrote to him after returning home and sent him a photo of himself.

Maybe I'll hear back from him and find out if he made the summit or not.

BILL ENGLISH   Craig and I arrived in base camp, tired, around 3 PM. Enrique gave everyone a cold beer which was a real plus. I staggered over, took my pack off and sat on a rock, slowly sipping that beer. I wasn't sure I wanted to drink a beer—knowing alcohol at altitude isn't the smartest—but knew I really wanted that beer at the same time. I figured I could handle one beer. Besides, dinner couldn't be far away. We'd had only a scanty breakfast and all day had gone by.

CRAIG ROLAND   The general conversation were recollections of the mountain, though people were still in a rather quiet, pensive mood. People were writing, discussing their plans. There was a little exuberance; Neil and Trevor were clowning around.

NEIL DELEHEY   I was trying to convince Trevor that we should attempt McKinley next. Trevor had no desire. He told me, "Nope. No way. I'll never do Mt. McKinley." Then, after we got home, Trevor said, "Yeah, we could do McKinley."

GREGG LEWIS   Mark and I, again, were the last to leave White Rocks. We arrived at base camp around 6 PM. Everyone was interested in the condition of Dr. Patel, the poor bastard, and what had happened to Borgel. Borgel was feeling much better.

It was nice and warm at base camp. There was a lot more back-slapping than there had been at White Rocks.

MARK CORNWALL   The scuttlebutt on Anil Patel was that he had crashed, burned, and miraculously pulled himself together enough to descend to base camp. Even more miraculously, Anil had walked himself out with the Gould family.

THOMAS BORGEL   One of the reasons Dr. Patel fell was because he pushed himself too hard. He did not know he had over-extended himself. He wanted to make that damn summit, and he was going to do anything to make that desire come true.

BILL ENGLISH   My opinion is that Anil did not have the con-sciousness of what 23,000-feet, or what serious mountaineering, was all about. I never did feel comfortable with Anil Patel. Anil came down that mountain in his own special way.

However, all three guides near the top of the mountain? That's unheard of. Talk with any mountaineer—you just don't do that. With three guides for thirteen people on summit day there is no question whatsoever that there should have been one guide leading, one in the middle, and one at the back. There definitely should have been a guide at the ice traverse making sure that people who were brain deficient due to altitude could get their crampons on correctly. Someone should have been sitting there, but no one was. Dr. Patel would not have fallen if the guides had not been negligent and that is the bottom line.

I talked to some other mountaineers at base camp who had gone up the Polish Glacier, traversed around the mountain, then come down the Normal route.[26] Someone else I encountered was a guy who knew a woman I'd met at a language school in Mexico some years earlier. So there was this interesting international community we'd heard about, even there at base camp at the end of the season, and it was great talking with them.

But the mood with our group was not good. As usual there was a lot of negativity and dissention from Mark and that crowd.

___

MARK CORNWALL   Back at base camp the group was even more fragmented. There wasn't division because some people had made the summit and some had not. There seemed a facade of group camaraderie. I didn't really notice an exhilarated feeling from the summiteers. Trevor, Neil, Craig and Dick didn't stay on the top of Aconcagua and celebrate. Each one had to worry about saving their own ass and getting down. That may have become more important than the climb. They had succeeded, but there was no, "Hey guys, we all did this together." That wasn't the spirit. The people who made the summit did so on their own by buckling up and putting their heads down. That isn't normal. There has to be individual effort, but what was missing on Aconcagua from the very beginning was team spirit. You have to be rooting for every other person. There is a psychological need for team spirit. People benefit from that. Joining in on the camaraderie, having that closeness, and doing something together is a beautiful thing.

It's funny because I heard Dick say, "One of the best things was having a good days climb, feeling good about being strong, and the teamwork that went into it." In my own mind I thought, What the hell 'teamwork' is he talking about? Dick found a lot of refuge with the guides. He hung around the cook tent and almost became an assistant guide. Dick fantasized teamwork. What we needed was a leader who could pull everyone together to get a great feeling of accomplishment.

___

DICK GORDON   Everyone should be grateful for the efforts the guides put forth. Maybe that is easy for me to say because I did spend a lot of time with the guides and got to know them. They were comfortable to hang around. The guides never seemed to eat or sleep much, they worked their tails off, and they are not well paid. I provided support for Enrique, but personally don't believe that I was treated differently than anybody else.

Some people did not realize what Enrique's responsibilities were. I'm convinced that many of the eighteen individuals on this expedition did not get what they were expecting because they thought they were at a

___

26   One variant entails bypassing the steep upper slopes of the Polish route by traversing from a high camp of 19,000-feet and connecting with the standard route at Independencia.

country club and that the guides should handle everything. I actually heard someone say, "I'm not supposed to go get water. They're our guides. They are supposed to do this shit for us." I forget who said that, but someone else agreed, so there were at least two of them. That was disappointing. Forget teamwork. That kind of attitude, in order to attain the summit, cannot be a factor. It only means that you are wasting your mental energies on something you cannot afford to waste them on. These individuals had little things on their minds which they had problems working out. You just can't reason with the little things. People got into the trivials and burned out.

There were people on the expedition who were introverted, but who were capable of holding their own within the team effort. 'Team' implies, in a survival situation, that an individual might falter, but that we could divide that individual's load. If someone had a weakness the team could bring him back to where we needed him. A lot of support can be picked up by team effort.

On the flip side, there has to be individual ability and individual independence. When making an attempt on Aconcagua, I don't believe that the whole group can summit if everybody is not capable on their own. A large number of people in our group, almost a majority, would not have been on the expedition if the company had screened their applicants better. That is my only complaint with the company. I really don't know that I should have any complaints towards the company; I wasn't originally with them. Enrique let me come along for the fun of it. I don't even think the company knew I was there. Those individuals that felt cheated probably should not have been on the trip in the first place. I don't know. The group was a good mix and I don't have anything against anybody who was there.

TREVOR BYLES   Mark asked Enrique about a second summit attempt. Enrique said, "No, we all head down." Another attempt from base camp was never an option in Enrique's eyes. He may have been worried about the weather, but the only day it stormed was our summit day. That was too bad, not only for the people who had been caught in the storm, but also for those of us who had made the summit; we didn't get the view and we couldn't sit on top.

Mark mostly kept the frustration of not having a second summit attempt to himself. He didn't try to bring us down.

THOMAS BORGEL   One has to understand that Enrique obviously knew we would not be on the mountain long enough for a second summit attempt because he had arranged for the mules to come back early. I didn't know this until we returned to base camp. Enrique had pre-planned for the mules to come back on a certain day, and he was not going to miss rendezvousing with those mules.

I found out later Enrique pulled the same thing on the expedition prior to ours, and that the company manager knew this and still let Enrique lead us as head guide. The company should have known better and sent down one of their American reps to oversee Enrique.

CRAIG ROLAND   The interesting thing about Thomas Borgel is that he went and bought all this gear, worked out in a gymnasium—he's a body builder—and walked up this mountain, which just blew his mind. If you've never done any high-altitude mountaineering, then go to Aconcagua for your first trip, it's just overwhelming. I think Borgel was psychologically defeated a long time before he turned around.

Borgel told me, "I'm never going into the mountains again." He and Lewis sold some of their gear to a couple of Spanish climbers right there at Plaza de Mulas, which is strange because people were coming up the mountain looking for boots and food for sale.

THOMAS BORGEL   I told Roland I was never going into the mountains again *under those conditions*. Every day I wrote in my journal: "This is hell. I want down off this mountain." When I reread those entries—well, the experience is not something I want to repeat. It would have been a lot easier if Enrique had just come out and said, "Listen, I'm sorry, but there has been a big mess-up and we will have to cope the best we can." I could have dealt with that.

NEIL DELEHEY   My advice to anyone who wants to climb Aconcagua is to be completely prepared, well read, and well experienced. Also, you cannot underestimate anything.

After we returned to base camp, I saw a girl getting ready to ascend with her boyfriend. They seemed to be on a picnic; they had a couple cans of ravioli. Did they think there was more food on the mountain?—'Sure! There is an Amish farm up there where you barter with the townspeople!' What were they thinking?! Trevor and I figured they might make it to Nido. Maybe.

The truth is that Aconcagua is so deceptive. You walk in twenty-six miles and it's very dry and easy going. That girl and her boyfriend did not comprehend that for every thousand feet gained, the temperature drops 3.5-degrees Fahrenheit, and that doesn't account for wind chill or bad weather. They didn't understand it gets severely cold, even if the temperature at base camp is 80°. And they wanted to buy our crampons! What were they going to do when they got higher?—buy the rest of their equipment on the mountain? I guess that says something for winging it and traveling light, but that is plain stupid. We witnessed other people: a guy who wore regular leather boots and who said his feet were very frostbitten, and his friend who had snow-blindness, but who was still wearing drugstore quality sunglasses. He was destined to burn his eyes out again.

These people had decided to attempt Aconcagua, but they obviously had no experience and were not prepared. It made me angry that someone could be that ignorant and arrogant toward the mountain, especially after seeing Taplin fall and hearing about Anil's accident. It just made me angry.

I'm no rock star. I'm a 5-foot-8 climber. I've done mountaineering on 14,000-foot peaks, but those are not comparable to a monster like

Aconcagua. I'm not pointing fingers, but there were people on our expedition as well, who did not belong, who were not qualified, and who did not know what they were getting into.

◊△◊△◊△◊△◊△◊

GREGG LEWIS   We played cards and waited for dinner. If I live to be two hundred years old I'll never forget what we had for dinner that night. We had sardines and stewed tomatoes. It was awful, but we were so incredibly hungry. I ate some sardines, man!

< 26 >

RED NOSES
Expedition Day 12: Return to Puente del Inca

CRAIG ROLAND   Our meal the previous night had been a strange, eclectic collection of leftovers. There wasn't enough, but it was a tasty meal.

On the last day, leaving base camp, there was this unbelievable scene. After breakfast we were going to have to walk out twenty-six miles. Everyone went into the dining tent. The remains of our previous dinner—scraps of food and garbage—were still on the table since no one had bothered to clear them away. Enrique walked in with a big pot, plunked it down in the middle of this mess, and said, "Here's breakfast." It was a big pot of hot water! We had coffee or hot chocolate and that was it! There was no food left at base camp. We should have had plenty of food. I don't understand why we didn't. Very puzzling. I laughed at the time, but the others didn't know whether to laugh or cry. It was a strange scene, almost surrealistic. That was breakfast. Then we packed everything up, with our stomachs not exactly full, and hiked out.

I had a great hike, I really did. The group dissipated and went at separate paces. Bill and I did not walk with anybody else. It was a beautiful day. We had a little package of nuts and raisins. We had plenty of water. We took a lot of pictures, stopped every hour, drank some water, and had a few nuts. Our legs were a little tired, but we had a delightful walk. The air was nice and thick. It took Bill and me seven-and-a-half hours to reach Puente del Inca.

Bill is really a good companion and a very upbeat person. He felt good at the end of the trip when some of the others had faded. Bill seemed in good spirits.

BILL ENGLISH   Did Craig say he enjoyed the walk out? He would. The walk out was horrible. The first eighteen miles was fine, but after that I was just dragging; I had no energy and my legs started to cramp up. Also, I was trying to keep up with Craig. I mean, Craig runs marathons. I don't do marathons.

Thank God for that packet of trail-mix. That's what got Craig and me out of there. The Gould's gave that to us. We'd carried that packet up the mountain, but had not eaten it.

When Craig and I came to Horcones Lake we took a cross-country short cut on some horse trails and came out on the road below the park entrance. At one point we stopped to take a picture because I said, "I want to see if I can record how shitty I feel." Actually the picture is pretty good and doesn't convey how I felt at all. Most of what had happened up on the mountain had not sunk in yet. It was still a struggle for survival and wishing to hell I was back at the hosteria.

TREVOR BYLES   Neil and I were ready to party. We raced down so
we could shower first, and caught a ride with a Volkswagon bus near
Horcones Lake. We just stuck out our thumbs and rode the last few
miles to Puente del Inca. We lucked out. We were so happy. We beat
people down by hours.

As Neil and I rode the bus down we turned back to look at the
mountain. That was a great feeling. And it still is a great feeling.

DICK GORDON   Since our group was the last expedition of the
season, the dining and cook tent had to come down. The guides had a lot
of work to do, so I stayed behind with Enrique and Pépe and helped
them. Everyone else had packed up their personal gear and had left.
The amount of work Enrique and Pépe did that morning surprised me.
I was fatigued before we even left base camp.

We got off quite late, maybe 1 PM. We were excited about a really fast
pace. I knew Enrique and Pépe could bring out that pace in me, so I
wanted to hike back with them. After readying the mule loads we bailed
out of Plaza de Mulas. Our pace was incredible; we passed people who
had left at 10 AM that morning. We hauled from base camp to Puente
del Inca in six hours with only two stops.

THOMAS BORGEL   Oh Lord, that was the longest walk of my life.
When Lewis, Mark and I came to the switchbacks just below base camp
we wondered how the hell Patel had made it down. That section of trail
isn't much; that's where the mules fall off.

Enrique, Pépe and Dick passed us at ninety miles-an-hour,
chomping on apples. So those apples were somewhere, just like all the
rest of the food was somewhere.

There was no one behind us. None of us remembered the river bed
being as long as it was. Endless walking—miles and miles and miles
down that river bed. The Horcones Valley is really a huge expanse.

GREGG LEWIS   I laughed when Enrique said, "No breakfast."
Then I realized he was serious. The situation was so outrageous. We
felt like American prisoners of war. I thought, Well, I have two pieces of
candy, some water—we'll make it out!

MARK CORNWALL   Naturally we were grumbling. Twenty-six
miles. It was cruel. You can see in our photographs how skinny we
were. I lost about fifteen or twenty pounds. We were grumbling
mightily.

Remember the refugio ruins below base camp? Hiking down I
completely missed those ruins. I'd noticed, on the way up, that it had a
tiled bathroom which was pretty impressive, all things considered. It
blew my mind that I walked right by that refugio. I was spaced out.

There was a gaucho with a horse who gave each of us a ride across
the last river crossing. Borgel gave him a pair of $30 gloves. Lewis gave

him his bandana. The gaucho was overjoyed because he loved that bandana.

We finally arrived at the hosteria around 7 PM.

◊△◊△◊△◊△◊△◊△◊

MR. GOULD   Camping at Confluencia was a lovely night for the four of us, under the stars. I was thinking I'd come back someday and try Aconcagua a third time. I wrote in my journal: "Perhaps next year?"

I realized I would have to be prepared to spend time for bad weather, have knowledge in the use of crampons on ice, have better solutions to gear problems, and have solutions if someone has to turn back. If you are in good shape and expect distractions, then you can handle it better. There is no advantage in climbing with people who are not in good shape. The answer seems to be to go quietly at one's own pace, as simply, and with as small a group, as possible.

The Normal route up Aconcagua isn't technical—it just takes a lot of effort. It seemed like a lot of effort not to be able to do what you set out to do. I don't know if I assigned any blame. I got a little closer to the summit. And I think maybe the others were happily pleased that Mary, Nunzie and I didn't hold them up during the ascent; we didn't make it slow for anybody.

I'm relatively tolerant of events, and try to accommodate them once it is evident you can't change them. My disappointment at not having a full shot at the summit was nullified by having been a real help to Anil Patel.

NUNZIE GOULD   There was a beautiful sunrise that morning. We sauntered along and I took pictures of the flowers I'd missed going up. We do have a picture of 'Nunzie and Dad' standing together, smiling at the camera. That was the full circle: we told each other, "I'm sorry for yelling at you. I really love you and this has been a fun trip."

The pressure was off. Dr. Patel wasn't there. Mom and I had strengthened our rapport and our relationship. Dad was happy because he was his own boss. I had mellowed out. We were our own network again; a group within a group doing a family trip together.

We never knew who made the summit until we got to Puente del Inca.

KINGDON GOULD III   Neil and Trevor were pretty happy. And I'll tell you another thing: they were smart because they left White Rocks early in the morning on summit day. They were the first out of camp. They weren't the fastest, but that is why they got to the summit. Neil and Trevor were planning on that right from the start.

Most of us had wine or beer before eating anything at the hosteria; there were a lot of red noses.

NUNZIE GOULD   It would be pretty wild to work at that lodge for a season and see the people coming through—just to see our group coming in; it has been a long day, they trash their packs, and they head directly for the bar. I made a point of congratulating everyone who had summited and said to them, "Bravo. Wish I'd been up there to say this to you then."

Everybody had lost at least ten pounds. Both Craig and Pépe were looking pretty thin. Everyone was hungry. I mentioned before that we left some food supplies in our duffel bag in the cook tent for the mules to haul out. So there was adequate food at base camp when the other members of the expedition descended. Our family came home with food we had taken down for the trip, which was ridiculous.

You could tell that the people who got to the top went through a lot of mental strain. Some people had stayed more focused. Dick was really pumped up about having made the summit. He was able to hold his own, and had maintained his proximity to the guides with a physical and mental presence. I went with Dick to the post office/telegraph office. He wanted to notify his family that he had safely gotten off the mountain.

When I first arrived at Puente del Inca, however, I was bummed. Among the first people I saw were Greg Stasiak and Mike Milford. Mike had said that he and Stasiak would come back after spending a couple days in Santiago to meet with us and find out the results of the expedition. That was impressive, and a show of the group. Mike and I shared the frustration of not having summited, but then Mike's real anger and bitterness as he critiqued Enrique turned me off so much that I could not listen to him. Mike felt he was turned away from the mountain. In my judgement Enrique made the right decision to dissuade Mike. For the whole group's well being it made sense that Mike not continue.

Did you follow the story about the paralyzed guy who climbed El Capitan in Yosemite? He did 7,000 pull-ups and was carried to the actual summit by his buddy.[27] A person does that and it is an incredible feat, but Mike Milford has his own legs! He can't be pampered the whole way up. There is a danger if you have to baby-sit someone. There are certain prerequisites every climber should have in terms of gear, physical ability, and a general awareness of mountaineering. Every climber can't expect to put those responsibilities on a guide.

Under the circumstances I felt Enrique did the best he could. He walked along at a good pace, he encouraged people, he was very positive, and he was always available for comments or suggestions. I respected the fact that he didn't try to patsy people into getting up the mountain. He disliked being around people who were not appreciative of the mountain. Enrique enjoys being outdoors and sharing that experience,

---

[27] Paraplegic Mark Wellman and partner Mike Corbett have since completed an ascent of Half Dome as well.

although the Polish Glacier or South Face is more challenging for a mountaineer. All the guides were very skilled and had very cool heads.

I could not relate to Mike's resentment or handle the bitching. Mike was the spokesman for Stasiak as well, which was interesting. The fact that Mike had asked Stasiak to come on the expedition was sort of a security blanket. Neither of them had any idea what they were getting into. King and Dad were standing there, but I walked away and did not speak to Mike again at Puente.

KINGDON GOULD III   Although Enrique did not ask my parents or myself to write a letter to the company about his guiding capabilities, we offered to, because it became apparent that Mike was really mad and that he was going to try to make trouble for Enrique. I felt such action was not warranted. I talked to Mike briefly about his grievances. I didn't try and argue with him. You rarely sway people by arguing. I just told Mike we did not agree.

My previous experience on Aconcagua was much more rough, with less consideration from the guides. On that trip my father and I had worse food and less knowledge of the mountain. On this trip not enough consideration was given to the individual abilities of each group member. There was a divergence in attitude and ability. Some people had a party attitude. I don't mind having a good time, but that is not my bag. In terms of ability, I don't know how one goes about determining that beforehand.

In retrospect, it might have been better having more guides and fewer people. We were stretching the upper limit on how many people should be on a trip to climb Aconcagua. Having so many people made logistics difficult. I'm not sure the guides initially expected that many people, but I thought the group was handled pretty well. Enrique did a good job of modulating his itinerary to people's abilities.

Enrique had to file a report at the police station in Puente regarding Anil Patel's accident. This was in the Army compound across from the hosteria. I think that when Gustavo came to send a horse up, the fact there had been an accident became known.

Just before dark Dick came to the hosteria. He'd been at the police station with Enrique. Dick said to us, "The police are giving Enrique a hard time about Dr. Patel's accident."

A few minutes later Enrique came down and told us the police needed to have another report. Dick had told the police what he had seen and Enrique had given them information. I said, "If you are having problems with the police, I'm the one who saw the accident. I saw as much as anybody. I can describe what happened and would be glad to talk with the police."

Enrique said, "Great."

Enrique, Dick and I went to the Army barracks. We go in and shake hands. There were two policemen in a little room, and a flunky who ran back and forth fetching 'mate' tea. Mate is an herbal tea that, in this case, probably had a few coca leaves in it as well. Anyway, we're in this room with a rough wooden table, a couple of bunks, a radio squawking in the corner, and these policemen asking me questions. One of the policemen sat at a typewriter in the back. They didn't speak English, so Enrique translated my answers. Of course this was ironic—a conflict of interest—because the purpose of it all was to exonerate Enrique from whatever. We were there for about half-an-hour. This guy typed away as I described the accident in as much detail as I could remember. At the end of questioning, one of the policemen handed me the statement to read, but I can't read Spanish. I gave the report to Enrique and said, "Enrique, is this what happened?" Everything I had to say showed good action on Enrique's part. Enrique read it back to me. I said, "That's fine," and signed it. And Enrique signed the statement as the translator. We shook hands with all three policemen, including the flunky, and left. A crazy scene.

There was nothing Enrique could have done about Anil's accident. The same with Taplin's accident. Enrique wasn't really a party to their accidents. Yes, he was the guide. I suppose if Enrique had guided people a little differently neither accident might have happened. Yet neither accident was really his fault. As the guide, however, Enrique was responsible.

The trip had not been terribly successful for Enrique. Only a small percentage made the summit and two people were hurt. Enrique was anxious and frustrated.

BILL ENGLISH   The story we were given, by Pépe, was that if there was blood involved then there had to be an investigation. Blood was the critical factor. The fact that Taplin broke his arm didn't matter—nobody needed to know about that. But since blood was involved with Dr. Patel's accident, that indicates there might have been foul play.

CRAIG ROLAND   Enrique was physically tired and was worried about both accidents. He's a 'worry' kind of person. When word of Anil Patel's accident reached us on summit day, Enrique became very upset. Later, he was even more upset, especially when he heard that Patel attempted the ice traverse without crampons. Enrique told us that having accidents directly affects his future as a guide. He said that if someone died he would lose his guide license and that he would not be allowed to officially guide again. Having injuries occur while he is guiding is a similarly serious problem.

DICK GORDON   Enrique said that Dr. Patel was his first near-fatal accident in forty climbs on Aconcagua. He didn't want to lose his licence, although our party was probably going to be his last expedition. I had the impression that he knew Aconcagua so well that there was no longer any thrill in it for him. He mentioned that he was tired of the mountain and wanted to look for better work. Besides his job as a patrolman at the Las Lenas ski area, Enrique was looking forward to finding another means of income rather than running up Aconcagua several times a year.

◊▲◊▲◊▲◊▲◊▲◊

<u>CRAIG ROLAND</u>   Everyone congregated for dinner at the hosteria. Everybody was there, except Gustavo, Dr. Patel and Taplin. The mood was friendly and congenial. Mike made some comments, but everyone seemed to have a nice dinner and a nice time.

<u>KINGDON GOULD III</u>   Everybody was tired, but happy. I'm sure some people thought, Goddamn, I didn't make it. But then you would congratulate the people that did summit and ask them to tell you what it was like. If someone had not summited they would try to think up the next best story that did happen to them.

<u>DICK GORDON</u>   Everybody was glad to see the expedition over and ready to get back to their lives. Nunzie ordered champagne. We toasted and raised cane till the late hours. We were ready to drink. We really trashed the place. It just went on and on.

<u>NUNZIE GOULD</u>   Enrique was not having a good evening. He was uptight about the investigation, and under a lot of duress as a result of the harassment he received from the police. I wanted to cheer him up, create a distraction from the scene with Mike, as well as honor the guys who had summited and share in their celebration.

It was strange because, as shitty as we were treated and as shitty a job Enrique was trying to be chipper. He could have given a toast. To complicate matters, when the mules arrived after dinner, Enrique discovered his gear was missing.

<u>GREGG LEWIS</u>   Dinner was unreal. We hadn't eaten anything all day. Our taste buds no longer worked. We all pigged out and got wasted.

It was strange because, as shitty as we were treated and as shitty a job Enrique did, you never would have known we didn't love him. We were slapping him on the back, joking and drinking with him. We were just glad to be out of that valley, cleaned up, and glad to have food.

The Voyage of the Damned was over.

< 27 >

THE DAYS AFTER

CRAIG ROLAND   Enrique called ahead to the Hotel Balbi and told us there were no rooms. I was thinking that we were still on this trip and that we had reservations at the Balbi for the wine festival. Quite a few of us decided to take a chance, and took a bus to Mendoza. Mendoza was jammed with people, but the Balbi found us rooms at another hotel after all, the Hotel Garibaldi. The rooms were wall-to-wall beds. Each room cost $12.

Mike ran into Enrique in the lobby of the Garibaldi. It was quite a heated argument. Mike is hot-tempered anyway; he's got a short fuse. He started in about how poorly led the trip had been and called Enrique some names. Enrique, not exactly the smoothest person himself, became very angry.

Mike is a person with a certain amount of tunnel vision, and is fairly inflexible about his ideas. He's a difficult person whom I don't think, should he try to get reimbursed by the company, has a cent coming back.

MIKE MILFORD   I felt cheated because I'd invested time to prepare for the mountain. I was so upset that I started shouting at Enrique that he was unprofessional and that he didn't know what he was doing. Enrique accused me of inviting the two Californians to stay with us in the room at Puente del Inca and that he had to pay for them—all sorts of nonsense. We shouted back and forth, then Enrique said, "Don't forget, you are in my country. I could do something, make you stay here a long time, and make it difficult for you to leave."

I realized Enrique could make false statements to the police or whatever, so I tried to smooth things out. I said, "Listen Enrique, there is no point in arguing this matter now. You give your version to the company and I'll give mine."

These things bug me—a little thief like Enrique trying to ruin everybody's life.

BILL ENGLISH   After the verbal altercation with Mike, Enrique came over to me and said, "Mike is really mad. I can't seem to calm him down. I don't understand."

Basically I said to Enrique, "I understand why there can be a problem." I felt Mike should not have been on Aconcagua, not with his attitude.

Enrique asked where I was going. I said I was heading for southern Chile. Enrique, his wife, and Pépe gave me a ride back to the border and got me squared away with customs. I'm not much for cities; I only spent one night in Santiago, then took a twenty-hour train south and explored the Lake District for several days. I wanted to climb a volcano, but there was no way I could work that out and get back to Mendoza in time for my flight. The volcano, town and lake are called Villarrica. This is an active volcano which you can climb with crampons in a day. From the summit crater you can apparently look down and see molten magma doing its thing.

I returned to Santiago, jumped on a bus, went back over the Andes, went through customs—a long, arduous procedure—and returned to Mendoza. I called Enrique, but there was no answer. I spent one night at the Balbi, then flew home.

I remember spending a good bit of the time on the mountain saying to myself, "This is okay. The experience with altitude is great, and I'm glad I'm doing it here because it's letting me know I never want to do it again. I'll go climb other mountains." Since then I've changed my tune and would like to attempt Aconcagua again. How quickly you forget the pain.

◊∆◊∆◊∆◊∆◊∆◊

NUNZIE GOULD   Dick was heading toward Chile and Peru. He asked me, "Hey, do you want to go this direction?" The timing worked really well since I needed to be on my own, away from family.

When most of the group boarded the bus to go from Puente del Inca to Mendoza, Enrique was not aware of a few people staying behind. Dick and I made a special effort to thank him. That scene could have been coordinated a little better; there was a lot of commotion at the hosteria.

Dick and I had an extra day at Puente before we left to do some sightseeing. King had told me that there was a cemetery for climbers which is about two miles down river, across the railroad tracks.[28]

There are about fifty people buried there, including several Americans and Europeans. Some plots have tombstones with names, some have crosses in the Argentine/Christian theme, others have flowers or small, unnamed stones on the ground. After awhile, their names, how old or young they were, or on which route they had fallen, did not matter. It was just a great big statement. The whole cemetery is a mound and makes a statement, physically, in the way it is laid out. I'd read about how many people have died on Aconcagua. That had made an incredible impact. I saw the results. I wandered around the cemetery, thinking, I was really lucky on this expedition. A lot of things could have gone wrong. I'm really fortunate and nature was fortunate with us.

---

[28] The Cementario del Andinistes is located east of the hosteleria, and can also be reached from the main highway.

I thought about Taplin having busted up his arm and Dr. Patel having busted up his head, and realized how bummed out I'd have been if that had happened to me.

Dick and I caught a bus down the road at Los Penitentes, went to Chile, recuperated on the beach at Vina del Mar, then continued to Santiago. From there we flew to Lima. We had fun. Dick and I shared common ground, but we've lost touch. Maybe I was a little overbearing. I have a tendency to be like that.

When I returned to Maryland I was really torn, and still am to some degree, about not making the summit. I felt some resentment toward my parents for having limited my chance to achieve a personal challenge. That was selfish. Either you make the commitment to the group or the individual.

I didn't succeed in my journey, but I came home alive. Even though there were conflicts I was able to work through them and make the best of the situation. I feel lucky and enriched. The experience has given me a new direction and, as a result, I'm on a much better track in my own life.

I also learned I'm capable of climbing a mountain like Aconcagua. I'd be very honored to attempt the mountain again with Dad. Can you relate to that? I'd go down to old Puente del Inca and hang out there for a few days.

DICK GORDON   It was fun travelling with Nunzie. She's a good kid. She's intelligent and a jet-setter. After Peru she took off on a pilgrimage. I'm not sure what she was looking for, whether it was more travel time or more 'alone' time.

I had started the trip off by myself, hooked up with the group, got down to some more personal, one-on-one type of companionship, and then went back to being alone which worked out real well.

Climbing Aconcagua is an experience I can't really share. You can share stories, but I'm confident there is no understanding. It's like if your father or your brother dies, and someone comes up to you and says, "I understand." Unless they have had a brother or a father die, they don't understand. They try and want to understand, but they can't.

Life is a merry-go-round with time as an element; you can't get off at the same place once you get on. There are certain insights in life which most people never test or get around to understanding. Aconcagua provided some insight into some inner strengths I wasn't sure I had or knew about. Now I do. I don't know that these insights make me a better person, but I feel good about the accomplishment. I also understand how easy it would have been to not come back alive from Aconcagua. If you are not 100% that mountain will take you.

◊∆◊∆◊∆◊∆◊∆◊

TREVOR BYLES			Neil and I had planned on hitting all of South America, from Bariloche to Iguazu Falls to Machu Picchu. But we were tired of travelling and tired of dealing with people. I was ready to get back to Colorado and see my girlfriend. It wasn't homesickness; we'd done what we came to do. Neil and I bailed on all our travel plans.

NEIL DELEHEY			After getting home I called the commercial company. Trevor and I had a list of concerns—mostly about the size of the group, safety equipment and the food situation. The company manager acknowledged all these grievances, but he was just going to let me talk until I was blue in the face.

I told the manager the story about Borgel's Synchilla jacket: at the end of the expedition, Enrique wanted Borgel's coat, but they hadn't agreed on a price. Trev and I were guarding gear at Puente when Enrique came over and asked if Borgel had left his jacket for him. We told Enrique no; Borgel never once had said to Enrique, "Here, I want you to have this coat." If that's not completely dishonest on Enrique's part, I don't know what is. The manager's reaction to this story was completely idiotic—"Well, Enrique is trying to save up some money to buy a pick-up truck. He may have gotten bored with the mountain."

I can't really complain. Trevor and I got along well with almost everyone. We weren't distracted by the lack of services, which may have helped us focus on the summit. I'm not sure Trevor thought so, but I had the feeling Enrique wanted us to make it. I really believe that if a climber is not focused, all of one's fears or inhibitions come out at 22,000 or 23,000-feet. I wasn't saying any prayers to Buddha, but I fought my fears and inhibitions by staying focused on the summit.

Reaching the top of Aconcagua is now under my belt and I'm very happy about that. Nothing will tarnish my memory of Aconcagua and being on the summit. Nothing will interfere with that.

TREVOR BYLES			My father was ecstatic that I'd made the summit. He was so excited and so happy. He'd been worried about me—worried as a dad, and concerned about how I would have dealt with the failure if I didn't make the summit. He knew the climb wasn't going to be easy and he knew that I'd have to work hard, so he was really proud.

When people ask about Aconcagua, I tell them, and people realize it was an impressive feat. The achievement is a big event that's changed my life. My attitude, school-wise, was horrible before. I needed a year off to set myself straight. I've come back to the university and it's crunch time; I don't miss class and I study my ass off. I've got to get through school and get up my own summit now.

◊▲◊▲◊▲◊▲◊▲◊▲◊

<u>THOMAS BORGEL</u>   Word got down the mountain, before we even returned to Mendoza, that Enrique had starved us. Also, to have an American expedition crew hire Argentine guides, and then have accidents is a big no-no, because climbing Aconcagua is a prideful deal for the people of Mendoza.

Sure, it would have been nice to write in my book that I'd climbed one big mountain. But there are plenty of other adventures: cave diving, going on a safari—maybe an African safari in conjunction with Kilimanjaro. I've heard Kilimanjaro is no big deal, no buying a lot of fancy equipment. And it is high altitude, so that would enable me to find out if I'm capable of acclimating.

<u>MARK CORNWALL</u>   When I returned home I had no desire to go out and climb any mountains. For what purpose? To run yourself into the ground and watch people get hurt? To deal with guides who sabotage your climb by taking your fuel—your food—from you? I was left with a bad taste in my mouth and could think of better adventures. That's how I felt, unfortunate as it was. I didn't unpack my bags for a year after the trip.

The saying is: 'Never let principal get in the way of doing what is right.' What is right is to negotiate a settlement with the commercial company that organized the expedition. This is not about some of us failing to reach the summit. It is about the company's failure to follow their own operational guidelines pertaining to safety and service.

Borgel, Lewis, Trevor, Neil, Mike and I have joined forces, but these guys have put the ordeal behind them and have gone on with their lives. Meanwhile, I'm carrying the torch and dealing with these lawyers who are trying to make my life miserable. Being emotionally involved makes it really hard.

We'll probably be reimbursed our trip fees. In the end it won't matter how much money is involved—only that we have the last word, bring the company to task, and make things right.

Time heals all wounds. I'm beginning to feel the passion again, and I want to see if mountaineering can be a fun challenge. But I can't imagine going back to Aconcagua in a million years. Those blisters I got were symbolic of the whole trip.

◊△◊△◊△◊△◊△◊

<u>TOM TAPLIN</u>   The day the main party descended to base camp after their summit attempt, I was undergoing repairs on my fractured right ulna. Once the bone fragments were tidied up, a titanium plate was screwed onto the realigned bone. The only other serious injury was a bruised ego.

A week after surgery I wrote a letter to Enrique, which a friend of mine translated into Spanish, thanking him for hauling me out of the moulin. I commended him for his no-nonsense attitude in evacuating me promptly from base camp. I never heard back from Enrique, despite sending several other notes requesting an interview.

I called the company manager to get Enrique's home address. The manager had not heard about my accident, which was a little strange, but he was sympathetic and offered a discount on a future trip. He said, "Let me fill you in on what happened with the expedition." That's how I heard about Anil Patel. So I called Anil, who could only have been back home two or three days, and received a somewhat coherent account of his fall. Considering his injuries, it is obvious Anil's accident was much more traumatic than my own. That Anil even survived is no small wonder.

Mark Cornwall eventually called and said he had my pack. He was afraid to open it due to a rather ominous odor emanating from within. We ceremoniously emptied the musty contents in a parking lot near the beach in Santa Barbara. The attention-grabber was my ice axe. I still use that axe, but it has a hefty dent in the shaft. It was great to hold that beautiful tool which had saved my life. Mark said, "You should frame that or put it in a display case." The only missing item of note was my purple Synchilla jacket.

I've had a lot of time to reflect on my accident. No one could have altered what happened; it was my fault. If anything, fate could have been much less forgiving that day: I might have been alone, or been knocked unconscious and drowned; the opposite wall of the moulin might have been two feet wider at the bottom, preventing me from climbing out; or I might have succumbed to hypothermia. Any number of circumstances could have been different to insure my demise.

Common sense works in strange ways. I had my ice axe and crampons, but didn't realize the scree on that slope was dangerously unstable. Maybe I was too obsessed about seeing the ice pinnacles. Maybe a pinnacle would have collapsed on top of me. Bad luck is unnerving, although—and I'm sure Anil would agree—not nearly as unnerving as a serious lapse of judgement.

If I learned anything, it is that the Horcones Glacier, like all glaciers, represents potential hazards. Anyone exploring a glacier should be prepared for the unexpected and should have training in rescue techniques. The first thing I did, the following spring, was to sign up for a seminar on Mt. Rainier to learn more about ice-climbing and crevasse rescue.

I feel a special debt of gratitude toward Mark, Neil and Tommy Borgel. Dealing with an accident, from a rescuer point of view, involves a fair amount of emotional distress. These three guys really deserve a lot of credit for keeping their heads screwed on.

We all went to Aconcagua to test ourselves, to feel more alive. I just wish, for myself, that the test could have been higher up, on summit day.

◊△◊△◊△◊△◊△◊△◊

ANIL PATEL   The police noticed me in the emergency room at the Mendoza Hospital and wanted to know what had happened. They questioned me and filed an accident report. They also questioned Gustavo. I don't know if the police were questioning Enrique. I did not see Enrique in Mendoza. The police asked me where I came from, what I was doing in Argentina, how the accident took place, and what had happened after the accident. They wanted to make sure I had not been assaulted by anybody.

I spent one and a half days in the Mendoza hospital. The X-rays and the hemoglobin test results were adequate for me. I could not sleep in the hospital, so I tried to leave. I wanted to take a taxi to the hotel. I didn't have to pay anything—the hospital was free—but when I tried to walk out there were policemen at every exit. The police stopped me and said, "You can't leave. Go back to your room and we'll try to contact the doctor." The nurses on duty told me I could not be discharged until the next morning.

I was befriended by a woman, an American medical student. She was the one who eventually got me out of the hospital. She and I had a rapport since she was part Italian, like my wife. She had a consultant review my X-rays. The consultant said, "If you stay in your hotel room, I'll let you leave the hospital."

When I went back to the Hotel Balbi, no rooms had been reserved for members of our expedition. That was so annoying. I was very polite to the manager and I told him that I was injured and in pain. The manager finally gave me a room and said to me, "This room is yours for however long you want."

Gustavo's family had come to see me in the hospital, and they had invited me to their house. We had a beautiful, huge lunch—Gustavo's grandmother is Italian—which lasted four or five hours. Gustavo said he would take me back up Aconcagua next year, without charge.

I did not call my wife to tell her about my accident. I flew home, took a taxi from the airport, then she found out. She was extremely upset. She said, "I told you not to go!" She immediately arranged for me to have a CAT-Scan and new X-rays. My head seems to be fine, but the fingers on my left hand are still very painful between the first and second joints. A hand surgeon in New York City said that, eventually, I might need flaps from my arm or waist to replace the damaged pulp in my fingers, otherwise I might have pointed fingers. For now I'll wait.

The experience of almost dying has not changed my feelings about climbing. A similar thing happened on Mt. Kenya in 1972 when I slid down a snow field and was hanging over a 500-foot cliff. That was more scary than my accident on Aconcagua; on Aconcagua I passed out. I did a stupid thing on Aconcagua. You try not do stupid things. You try to take precautions.

My wife doesn't understand my attitude about climbing. She will be upset when I go back to Aconcagua—she doesn't want our two young daughters to lose their father—but she has no choice. My daughters are too young to understand this passion for the mountains. I want to take my children camping when they are old enough. I believe in outdoor living; it builds character and prepares one for life. Look at it this way. I'm from Kenya. I now work in a strange place, almost 5,000 miles from where I grew up. I am the first Indian to come work in South Hampton, and I've been able to work here without feeling homesick. If you have outdoor experience you don't give up easily.

◊▲◊▲◊▲◊▲◊▲◊▲◊

CRAIG ROLAND   I ran into Anil Patel in Buenos Aires—only a city of 12 million people—on Florida Street. That was the first time I'd seen him since White Rocks. He looked good despite his serious injuries, and gave me the low down on his accident. He had a bandage over his gashed head, with a big patch of hair sticking out. I guess he'd had stitches put in. He said his gloves had come off in the fall and showed me his fingers. They didn't look terribly serious. I've seen worse cases of frostbite.

I liked all the members of the expedition very much and have a lot of respect for them as mountaineers. I'd made the summit and was feeling pretty good. I didn't have a lot of complaints. As time went by and I reflected on the nature of the trip, I realized, for a number of people, the trip had been shortchanged. I put my thoughts down on paper, and sent a letter to the manager of the company and the company director. This was a three or four page typewritten letter describing, for their benefit, my own personal experiences and some observations— pretty much a critique of the entire trip.

I listed a number of specific points when information was either given to us erroneously, or not given at all. Enrique had already been on Aconcagua six times that year and I think he was worn out and bored. The trip was in his hands and I believe he shortcut the trip. We were twelve days on the mountain from Puente to Puente. We should have had fifteen or sixteen days; a second summit day, and at least two additional acclimatization days at high altitude. We just bombed up from base camp way too fast, and that affected everyone on summit day. A couple of extra days at altitude would have made everyone feel more comfortable.

The manager was critical of Enrique and wrote back: "The trip was obviously shortened. We usually send someone down with Enrique, but Enrique was running the operation by himself and I can see we're not going to be able to do that again." Frankly, I took his criticism of Enrique with a grain of salt. It is the manager's company. The manager is at least as much to blame, if not more so.

In my letter I also commented for the need to have guides that are better communicators. There was an awful lot of information that was not exchanged. For example, it would have been interesting to hear about geology, the climate, weather, climbing techniques, attempts on the summit, how to walk at high altitude, and the history of Aconcagua.

There's a wealth of subjects that we could have gotten into—subjects Enrique seemed reluctant about discussing.

While we were on the mountain I watched several other groups— groups that slowly, day by day, were dealing with getting up Aconcagua. I noticed they had many safety features. For example, one group had a rubber bag that you could inflate so that if someone had serious mountain sickness they could climb into this bag and re- compress. You could zip it up airtight, then feed bottled oxygen to the person inside. It was like a mini-compression chamber, and a lot easier than walking down the mountain to lower elevation. Somebody had pulmonary edema and damned if they hadn't used this bag! This zip- bag saved a person![29] The guides for another group had two-way radios so that, if people became separated, they could talk to each other.

At any rate, there are some guided groups that take a great deal of care, spend more time on the mountain, and treat their clients as amateurs. We were all amateurs that paid a lot of money. I don't think someone should walk us to the summit—to get to the top is our job. But it is the organization's job to provide mountaineering guidance, safety, proper nourishment, information, and interest. That did not occur with this company. Having a good reputation is important because there are competing companies and people call around.

I enjoyed this trip a lot, despite some of these negative comments. I felt strong and good the whole way. I gained confidence about my ability to deal with altitude, which had been a major concern. I was pleased that I was able to do as well as I did. The scenery, spectacle, and environment of Aconcagua were outstanding. I don't want to give the impression that the guiding, communication problems, or the company's poorly handled trip-preparation in any way overcomes my generally positive recollections of the trip.

◊△◊△◊△◊△◊△◊

KINGDON GOULD III   My folks and I came into Mendoza on a Friday night and contacted the head porter at the Hotel Aconcagua. He found us rooms at the Nutibara Hotel. If you know the hotel business— well, hotels always have extra rooms. The Nutibara was kind of funky. I recommend it if you go back.

We went out and wandered around. The tempo of life in Mendoza appeals to us. The downtown area is quite pretty without much in the way of street lights. Very quiet evening streets. There was no fear of crime or pickpocketing, except perhaps at some of the tourist places. By and large that was not a concern. And the temperature is perfect; you can eat outdoors at night.

---

[29] Craig is referring to the Gamow bag—a lightweight, portable hyperbaric chamber which has been successfully tested at very high altitudes.

We had dinner at midnight in a little restaurant with a garden just off the main square. There were lots of three-generation Argentine families with small kids, parents and grandparents. When the wine festival floats paraded by, the kids were allowed to run from the restaurant garden onto the street or sidewalk. There was no apparent concern for their safety. In fact, one of the things I was struck by in Argentina was how affectionate the families were. And the children were not required to sit still like they might have been in parts of northern Europe. The kids would wander around the table, and be patted by the parents and grandparents. It was a very nice family environment. We talked with one family which had five daughters, who took a liking to my mother. The people were very friendly.

The parade went by and there was a float from each wine town. A queen from the town's wine festival would ride that particular town float. Most floats were very elaborate, made up as big wine bottles. Other floats were lit by Christmas bulbs and spot lights, pulled by old jeeps or tractors. There were barrels of wine on the floats and you could sample the wines, which were passed out in plastic cups. The queen and her princess might be sitting in the middle of one of these elaborately painted floats on some old, metal office chairs with rollers on the legs— typically South American and great fun. Each float was announced, spectators would whistle, and the princesses had buckets of grapes which they threw into the crowd. The queens would give that 'beauty queen' wave where the wave and head are synchronized. It looks like something you'd sit on your dashboard.

The gaucho parade was Saturday afternoon—the same parade with the same floats and queens, but in daylight. The gauchos were great. They would ride in groups representing certain towns. Each group had their own particular costume. Some gauchos were older, some were little kids, but they all had great panache. Gaucho boots are soft leather and very pointed; those boots almost look Persian. And their knifes or swords would be stuck in the back of their sash. The saddles have deep seats and long stirrups. They were wearing their total getup. It was wonderful. Each gaucho rode with one hand on his hip and the other nonchalantly on the reins. If it was done just right, the horse would prance. The horses in Argentina are beautiful, much nicer than those in other parts of South America.

We got in touch with Enrique and had dinner with him and his wife one evening at the Plaza Hotel. So we had a couple of nice dinners. I changed my plane reservations because I wanted to come home, and my folks wanted to go trout fishing near Las Lenas.

Ending the trip in Mendoza during the wine festival was great. I stayed up late, slept three hours, scooted out to the airport at 4 AM, hopped on a plane, and returned to the States.

< Epilogue >

Ten months after the Stone Sentinel expedition, Mr. Gould and Kingdon returned to Mendoza for their third attempt on Aconcagua. They hired Enrique as head guide and Enrique's brother, Willy {Guillermo}, as an assistant. On the day they set off from Puente del Inca, King came down with a mysterious stomach aliment. King made it to Confluencia, then bowed out. Mr. Gould and another son, Frank, continued on to Mulas base camp. The following comments are excerpts from our conversation, shortly after Mr. Gould returned home.

"In December the Horcones glacier was further advanced; there was much more ice than existed before. During one of our rest days {at Mulas base camp} Enrique took us out and showed us ice-climbing techniques. We did some climbing and then some rappelling. That was interesting, and a great opportunity.

"Frank, Enrique, Guillermo and I got along just fine. We went along calmly with just one purpose—to get to the top of the mountain. We didn't have any problems or distractions, except getting our stoves to work the first night which we solved rather ingeniously. Everything else moved along nicely.

"A couple of times I said to myself, I must be totally losing my memory because I can't imagine why I am here. The wind was causing the dust and trash to whirl around—'Really, what am I doing here? Do I need this?'

"Enrique was extremely patient, helpful and encouraging. He did give advice about the Canaleta and he talked about staying focused in order to make the summit, which is the way to proceed through life.

"We left White Rocks at 8:30 AM. Strangely enough there was far less snow above White Rocks on this trip. It was very dry. I got to the bottom of the Canaleta in relatively good shape, then I asked Frank and Guillermo to go ahead because I didn't want to hold them up. I tagged along with Enrique. Frank and Guillermo were nice and would wait periodically.

"Then we all went together to the summit. We got to the top at 5:30 PM. We had a lot of luck with the weather, although it was windy as sin; the wind nearly tore us off the mountain. You have to have everything working just right—like the hole in the sky for the shuttle launch. We spent about half an hour on top. I went over and looked down the South Face. That was something! Enrique was holding onto me. He said, 'Don't get any closer than that!' I hadn't paid him yet. He didn't want to lose me at that stage.

"Somebody once said—maybe I said it—that climbing Aconcagua is a major experience in my life, that I'm delighted I did it, and that you couldn't pay me enough money to try it again.

"Life works differently for different people. Success comes earlier and more easy for some people by some great coup or financial effort. In my case it's by hanging on and persevering. I'm a pretty good survivor by nature. If you hang on, everything seems to work itself out."

◊Δ◊Δ◊Δ◊Δ◊Δ◊Δ◊

Two years of working on this manuscript—and obsessing about the mountain—finally began to take a toll. My post-accident mountaineering experiences on Mt. Rainier, and on an unclimbed peak in Alaska's Wrangell-St. Elias range, had been very satisfying, but it was time to confront the challenge head on and reclaim that part of my soul which Aconcagua had so unremorsefully stolen. Besides, I still owed Victor, the gaucho who evacuated me, a whiskey.

A target date was set and I tried to put together a small team. (Several months before departure I visited Anil Patel. Unfortunately I made the mistake of asking Anil, in front of his wife, if he would care to join me. Her reaction was: "Over my dead body.") Although several other members of the original expedition were asked, no one, unfortunately, was able to commit.

I decided to solo Aconcagua's 'ruta normal'—close acquaintances thought this scheme unwise—and, with the help of a computer, came up with a comprehensive blizzard of paperwork dealing with any logistical curve balls Aconcagua might throw at the last minute. The master compendium was a day-by-day, meal-by-meal schedule, as well as an extensive equipment and clothing list, including such items as emergency bivouac gear. As psychological insurance I left open the possibility of meeting another person or group already on the mountain, and joining forces for a summit push.

Everything went according to plan until I arrived in Mendoza to find that two key pieces of luggage (containing all my food and high-altitude gear) had been lost in transit from Buenos Aires. The missing bags turned up the next morning, quickly dispelling all visions of a disastrous start.

I acclimated in Puente del Inca for three days and went on several rigorous hikes. Weather reports were not encouraging: snow flurries as low as Confluencia; raging dust storms in the Horcones Valley; thirty tents flattened by wet, heavy snow at Mulas base camp. Conditions higher on the mountain were left to perverse speculation. I had troubled dreams of crawling through a white-out, battling high winds, unable to find a food cache, my eyes becoming slowly encrusted with icicles.

The mood at Puente del Inca was a mixture of foreboding and quiet exuberance: while talk at the bar centered around three Canadians who had not been heard from in over a week, famed Yugoslavian climber Tomo Cesen sat alone and undisturbed in the dining room, writing postcards after his successful fifteen hour speed-climb of the South

Face. (Rumors about the missing Canadians, and reports of their demise in the local press, later proved unfounded; they turned out to be Australians impeded by bad weather.)

At the hosteria one night I had a chance encounter with Enrique. We had a conversation over dinner about the Stone Sentinel expedition and briefly discussed some of the issues raised in this manuscript. Enrique did not understand the hard feelings, specifically Mark's and Mike's criticisms, and how those mushroomed into legal action against the company. When I suggested that, for starters, there were simply too many people, Enrique complained that he had no control over the size of the group, leading me to believe there was serious miscommunication between Enrique and the home office. Regarding the issue of food, I commented that it was interesting the expedition food might have been stolen, but not the beer. (Climber's priorities are usually the other way around.) That is all that was discussed. Neither Enrique nor myself wished to dwell on the past. The unspoken sentiment was that there will always be a disparity between guide and client points of view. (A rival guide told me Enrique had been fired by the commercial company. While it is true that Enrique no longer guides on Aconcagua—the Gould's were his last clients—he does hustle work as an expedition outfitter, and continues to guide for the commercial company on McKinley.)

Enrique was very encouraging regarding my solo attempt and wished me luck. He also wrote a note to his contact at Mulas, ensuring I would have a safe place to stash my gear. Fernando Grajalas, the local outfitter Dick Gordon had spoken so highly of, convinced me to repack my equipment so that his mules could go directly to base camp. This meant carrying a heavy pack (with food, stove, sleeping bag and cameras) the twenty-six miles to Mulas, when I'd planned on just a light day-pack with the mules trailing behind. I indulged this masochism by rationalizing a justifiable need to be in better shape.

Two days later I stumbled into Plaza de Mulas with a sore back and an overwhelming sense of déjà vu. Base camp was jammed with forty tents and 75 or so people of all nationalities. I hardly recognized the place since trash bags were piled everywhere, the result of the recent Pan American Ecological Expedition. The clean-up was a major improvement, although new refuse was beginning to rapidly accumulate. Three days were spent at Mulas, during which time I shot video, explored the sculptured ice pinnacles, and took an excursion cross-valley to a new hotel under construction. The hotel, a pet project of the Mendoza provincial governor, was the site one afternoon of a publicity concert by the Los Nubes Musical Expedition, whose goal was to get four musicians to the summit. Their concert (amplified by hotel generators) was truly a surreal event as climbers, trekkers, hotel workers, sound engineers and park rangers danced to South American folk songs with the Horcones Glacier and the craggy terraces of Aconcagua's west buttress as a stunning backdrop.

Conditions on the glacier were much more treacherous than two years ago, with meltwater causing numerous rock slides and mud flows. While exploring the moraine I observed, from a safe distance, a deep moulin, possibly the same one I'd slid into. The water flowing down the bottom of this canyon disappeared beneath the glacier, confirming my suspicions that if I had tried to float out after my accident I would not be writing this. Listening to the water churning underground was a humbling experience.

My progress up the mountain was slow and steady. Three progressive camps were established at Canada (a beautiful site by the way), Nido de Condores and Berlin, with two carries each to camps 1 and 2. I kept reminding myself that going solo was perfectly feasible if one didn't mind humping enough supplies for a minimum of ten days.

The spell of warm temperatures and good weather enjoyed at base camp was not indicative of conditions encountered higher on the mountain. A pattern began to emerge of clear mornings, afternoon snow storms (sometimes with white-out conditions) and frigid, windy nights. A fourth camp situated at Píerda Blanca (White Rocks) was ruled out because of high winds.

While not known as one of the world's most beautiful mountains, it is quite amazing how snow-dustings improve Aconcagua's landscape by hiding all the rubble. I felt as though I was climbing a completely different peak than the one encountered by the Stone Sentinel expedition. Though it was a wonderful feeling to be above Mulas, in virgin territory, it was also necessary to melt ice and snow for water—a time-consuming yet vital task. I never suffered headaches or any other ill-effects from altitude (I was not taking Diamox), nor did I have any digestive problems. The ability to both acclimate nicely and enjoy good health can be attributed to several factors: a consistent hiking pace, employing 'pressure breathing' and 'rest step' techniques, plenty of rest days, constant rehydration, and eating three full meals a day. Badly chapped lips were the only real malady.

At Nido de Condores I had the good fortune to make the acquaintance of Claudio, Chino and Fernando, three youthful Argentines more or less on the same timetable as myself. Over lunch one tent-bound, stormy afternoon, we debated combining our mutual resources to form one team. This was a difficult decision for me. On one hand I relished my dream of attempting to solo Aconcagua; on the other, I didn't wish to seem inhospitable. We reached a compromise whereas the Argentines and myself would remain autonomous entities, providing resources to one another in any emergency situation.

Shortly after arriving at camp Berlin, Chino developed severe altitude sickness and began vomiting. He and Fernando immediately descended to Nido, leaving Claudio with little food and no tent. I invited Claudio to share my provisions, and to join me for a summit attempt. Not having much choice, Claudio wholeheartedly accepted. We cooked dinner and anxiously awaited another party to return from their summit bid. It was bitterly cold. Darkness fell, and at 10:30 that evening Claudio and I set off to look for the American guide and his four clients. Had there been an accident? Were they lost? Macabre scenarios raced through my mind. Half-an-hour later we encountered them, stumbling down the trail. They had summited, but were paying the price in terms of dehydration and sheer lassitude. Claudio and I escorted them back to camp Berlin, where they immediately crawled into their sleeping bags and passed out.

Bad weather forced Claudio and I to delay our summit bid the next day—a blessing in disguise, since a rest day enabled us to refocus for the challenge at hand and to further acclimatize.

The morning of Feb. 16 dawned windless and cloudless. Claudio and I left camp Berlin at 8:30—a late start despite setting the alarm for 6 AM. As usual, it took forever to dress and melt water. I held the lead until Independencia, then Claudio took over. At 21,000-feet the altitude finally kicked in. Claudio moved ahead while I put on crampons. Not until I caught up with him, on the ice-traverse, did I realize he had no crampons, so I cut steps across the steeper sections. It was easy to understand how Anil Patel slid such an incredible distance.

Physically I was depleted before we even got to the traverse, stopping every ten minutes for a rest. The trek at this point was marked by deteriorating weather and an avid increase in mind games; constant rationalization about why to keep on going, then ignoring my body which rebelled furiously at each new step.

At the top of the snow field, about a third of the way up the right side of the Canaleta, Claudio and I found a client from another expedition sleeping in a snow bank. He was dehydrated—wasted actually—although he said he was just taking a brief rest. (Another client from this expedition, which had traversed over from the Polish Glacier, was still crawling along the ice traverse.) I was shocked neither of the two guides leading this group, both of whom I happened to know, were bringing up the rear, thinking at the time that such negligent behavior, for some reason, seems to be the status quo on this mountain. In hindsight my feelings about this have become more ambivalent: it seems perhaps unfair to pass judgement without knowing the full circumstances or knowing to what degree these guides had communicated with their clients. The ethics and responsibilities involving climbing partners is no less ambiguous.

The dreaded Canaleta is horrific enough to not only completely negate the relatively good trail conditions and scenery which proceed it, but push one to the brink of mental defeat as well. To tell the truth, if Claudio had said, "This is good enough. We've gone as far as we can. Let's just rest here, then descend," I would have given it serious consideration. Luckily for me, Claudio remained a calm beacon in the swirling mist; never too far ahead, always gesturing for movement upward, even if that gesture meant only raising his arm halfway while he stopped for a breather. We were both on the edge of absolute, utter exhaustion, yet the will to continue, to take just one more step then another, would roar like some uncontrollable impulse from the back of our brains. Perhaps what kept us going, against the grain of all reasonable odds, was the knowledge that attempting the summit again, even after a day's rest at camp Berlin, was out of the question. I finally just told myself I didn't care if I died in the process—that I was continuing until I dropped.

There was no view from the summit plateau. And as the world above and below the crest of the Andes brewed with the fury of a meteorological maelstrom, so too did the exhaustive effort of our struggle momentarily obscure any coherent notions of accomplishment. Claudio stood, zombie-like, sucking the last drops of liquid from his water pouch. However, when I turned on the video camera, set it on a rock and walked over to hug Claudio, he was overcome with emotion. I wrapped a Nepali ceremonial scarf around one of the tube crosses which marks a summit grave, then pulled out a purposely scrambled up M.C. Escher puzzle. I wanted to say (to the camera), "We're going to try to put this puzzle back together, to see how badly *oxygen deprived* we really are," but said instead, '*altitude deprived* ', which only proved the point all too well.

We spent fifteen minutes on the summit—fifteen minutes as the highest people in the Western Hemisphere.

Chino and Fernando had come back up from Nido, and were waiting for us at camp Berlin. No words can express the poignancy of that moment when they congratulated us and tearfully embraced Claudio. That night the Viento Blanco—the white wind—battered the tent. I'd never felt so depleted in all my life. The next day, Chino and Fernando, along with the Los Nubes Musical Expedition, made a bid, but all, except for the Los Nubes cameraman, were denied a summit opportunity.

At the southeastern end of the river bed in the Horcones Valley, just above the knolls of Confluencia, there is a place resembling a desolate, chaotic version of a Zen rock garden; large boulder-blocks split open and scattered across the trail—not-so-inanimate sentinels guarding the arduous passageway ahead. It was at this spot, while walking out from base camp, that I paused to rest on a flat slab. All the numbed psychological layers slowly began to peel away, and the achievement of making the summit, previously buried under a daze caused by extreme physical and mental exertion, finally hit home. There was a profound realization that Aconcagua was one of the best experiences of my life, not just because I made the summit (that, in itself, was both redemption and a logistical victory), but also because of all the people, sights and sounds encountered. I just wanted to sit there, watch the cloud shadows and shout with joy, which I did, until a dust storm chased me down to the promise of a hot shower and a cold beer. FitzGerald might not have envisioned a group of Inca chieftains sitting around the hot springs at Puente del Inca, soaking their weary bones after a hard days' march across the Andes, but I could.

◊△◊△◊△◊△◊△◊

Mountaineering is a horrible affliction, a feverish, uncontrollable urge. It boggles the imagination to realize that, in order to consummate this urge, one is willingly going to have to push one's physiological resources to the limit, assess the frightening reality of objective dangers, not to mention deal with the oftentimes emotionally destabilizing effects of expeditionary lifestyles. (Petty bickering, exacerbated at high-altitude by cramped living conditions, debased personal hygiene and hypoxia-induced states of irritability, have sabotaged many forays into the hills.) The effort wouldn't be worth the trouble, of course, unless there emerged some uncanny reaffirmation of self, the elation of having stood upon a summit, and the opportunity to celebrate these passions with new-found friends. Claudio and I were lucky; we had gambled and survived.

Someone once defined climbing as the "balance between restraint and resourcefulness." Mountaineering is a mental discipline that requires being extremely cognizant of every physical move. It is thinking with your body. You push yourself to the edge, then make the decision whether to cross the line or step back. One has to confront his or her own fears and limitations.

What is the appropriate balance between risk and safety? If you have a desire to go into the mountains, to push the survival envelope, it is extremely important, for your self-preservation, to develop a sixth sense about the risk factor; in other words to intuitively realize you may be going past the point of no return. Determining what is risky depends on previous experience. One wrong step, a brief lapse of judgement—that's all it takes. The line between crashing and burning, and flying like a condor, is a very fine line indeed. If anything is for certain, it is that Aconcagua is no place for the unfit, inexperienced, or ill-prepared.

◊△◊△◊△◊△◊△◊

A dedicated person or team will find it relatively easy to organize an expedition almost anywhere in the world. My desire to solo Aconcagua was rooted in a determination to see if I could be successful on my own terms. No one could have convinced me this was a possibility before my first attempt, two years earlier. Yet the biggest dilemma for aspiring mountaineers, and adventure-travelers in general, is whether or not to utilize the services of a commercial company. Resolving this issue depends on one's expectations and personal ethics. The flawed planning encountered on the Stone Sentinel expedition is certainly the exception rather than the rule. By no means should the reader interpret the aberrations of one company as a blanket indictment against all others. Commercial outfitters do have their place; though expensive, a majority provide realistic itineraries, nutritious food, capable and competent guides, a relative degree of security, and, in this age of 'eco-tourism', expertise in the form of naturalists, for instance, who can satisfy one's scientific or cultural curiosities. Obviously, the greater one's knowledge of a region, the greater one's appreciation. The best companies are really dream brokers, catering to small, manageable groups of clients who have compatible interests and similar physical abilities.

◊△◊△◊△◊△◊△◊△◊

We take much for granted on our journeys. We are seduced by slide shows and glossy brochures, we assume we'll be enlightened, we throw aside the possibility of not being granted safe passage, and we sometimes scoff at the probability of encountering cultural and communicative barriers. Whether we travel alone, with friends, or under the auspices of a reputable commercial company, attempting a peak like Aconcagua tends to become a sheer endurance event. Even the best-organized mountaineer or expedition has problems, owing to the vagaries of logistics, communication, and human nature itself. The tensions and conflicts which arise are but a microcosm of those present in everyday life. Endurance becomes an issue of patience and diplomacy. Our ability to enjoy the splendors of nature is ultimately defined not so much by a struggle against elements within nature, but a struggle against elements within ourselves. The mountain truly is a mirror; one's perception of the mountain reflects one's own self-perceptions. This may be the most important argument for climbing and mountaineering as an appropriate rite of passage, for it is the journey which molds our future aspirations, and which enables a more passionate outlook on life.

◊△◊△◊△◊△◊△◊△◊

Neil Delehey and Trevor Byles currently work at the Telluride Ski Resort. Neil, a Hemingway fan, would like to visit east Africa and attempt Kilimanjaro. Trevor graduated from the University of Colorado, is applying to teach at the National Outdoor Leadership School, and would like to return to the Himalayas. They continue to partner on climbs in the Rocky Mountains.

Dick Gordon is considering an expedition to Mt. McKinley.

Greg Stasiak is not interested in going on another mountaineering expedition and making the same mistake twice.

Mike Milford recently completed an ascent of the Matterhorn in Switzerland and, with *Mark Cornwall*, Charlottes's Dome, a rock climb in Kings Canyon, California. Mike plans on returning to Aconcagua with Milton, the Australian guide he met at base camp.

Besides Charlottes's Dome, *Mark Cornwall* has also climbed the East Nose of Mt. Whitney, the Exum route on the Grand Teton, as well as completed several ascents in the Balkan Mountains of Bulgaria. He plans on climbing Kilimanjaro when he's sixty years old.

If *Gregg Lewis* thought he could get away with a future attempt on Aconcagua, without being killed by his wife, he would. He and *Thomas Borgel* recently took a rafting trip down the Colorado River.

Recovered from his injuries, *Anil Patel* plans to resume climbing in the Cascades with Outward Bound.

Before selling his interest in Riley Street Art Supplies and moving to Chiapas, Mexico, *Bill English* climbed two volcanos: Orizaba {18,850-feet} and Popocatepetl {17,880-feet}, the third and fourth highest peaks in North America. Bill would like to make an ascent of Chimborazo in Ecuador.

Craig Roland and his wife, Edie, have twice returned to Nepal, trekking into the Dolpo District, the region featured in Peter Matthiessen's *The Snow Leopard*, as well as the Rolwaling Himal, where Craig ascended Ramdung Peak {19,500.} Craig continues to backpack into various ranges in North America.

Encouraged to try snow expeditions, *Nunzie Gould* has completed two seminars on Mount Rainier. Nunzie currently lives in central Oregon and is an instructor with the Mt. Bachelor Ski School.

Mr. Gould and his wife, *Mary*, visited the South Pacific, where they hiked up Mt. Kosciusko in Australia. They also climbed Gunung Agung, the highest peak in Bali.

Matthias Zurbriggen, sent to Mendoza for a few days of well-deserved rest and relaxation, dutifully dispatched news of his 'first' ascent of Aconcagua to the world media. The New York Times, reporting the feat, stated there were "only eight other mountains in the world that exceed it in altitude."[30] Zurbriggen, basking in the glory of victory, made even more friends by mischievously selling 'summit rocks.' He also managed a brisk trade in Chile, although many of his mineral samples were allegedly "gathered by the wayside."[31]

Following the second successful ascent of Aconcagua, *E. A. FitzGerald* and his team regrouped at Punta de la Vacas, setting their

---

[30] Mostly because Zurbriggen, in his dispatches, inexplicably noted the elevation of Aconcagua as 2,000-feet higher than was generally accepted. New York Times, 18 January, 1897, page 7.

[31] Letter from Philip Gosse to the Editor of *The Times* (London), reprinted in the Alpine Journal, Vol. 50, 1938, pg. 330.

sights on 21,000-foot Tupungato, an unclimbed giant located thirty-five miles to the south on the Chilean border. The first ascent of Tupungato was accomplished by Zurbriggen and Stuart Vines in April of 1897. FitzGerald and Vines, both stricken with typhoid fever, would not return to England until January of 1898.

FitzGerald authored *The Highest Andes*, an account of the Aconcagua and Tupungato expeditions, and, while he himself never stood upon either summit, regarded these expeditions as the culmination of his climbing exploits. He did not participate in any other significant mountaineering enterprises, although he subsequently became a Fellow of the Royal Geographic Society. FitzGerald then enlisted in the British Army for the Boer War. At the time of his death in 1931, FitzGerald was a retired Major of the Sixth Inniskilling Dragoon Guards.

The first European ascent of Aconcagua was an impressive accomplishment, and FitzGerald naturally garnered much fame for his role as 'leader'. The key to his expedition's success, however, belongs to Zurbriggen, whose route-finding and guiding abilities were already well-respected throughout the European and New Zealand Alps. There is little doubt FitzGerald's team on Aconcagua would have persevered without Zurbriggen.

Released from his contract with FitzGerald, Zurbriggen returned to the Himalayas, where he led several clients to first ascents in the Askole region of the Karakoram. A native of the Saas Fee region of Switzerland, Zurbriggen eventually settled in Chamonix, where he continued to guide. He passed away in relative anonymity in 1918.

Altitudes, elevation sources, and water availability
along Aconcagua's Ruta Normal

Mendoza, Argentina: 2412-feet / 735-meters above sea level.

Puente del Inca: 8950-feet / 2728-meters. Tap and bottled water available.

Laguna Horcones (Horcones Lake): 9515-feet / 2900-meters re Rudy Parra. Drinking lake water not advisable.

Confluencia: 10,496-feet / 3200-meters re Parra; 11,050-feet / 3368-meters re Jerzy Wala. Stream water at various locations. Horcones river filled with glacial particulates.

Plaza de Mulas (base camp): 13,776-feet / 4,200-meters re Parra; 13,879-feet / 4230-meters re Wala; 14,100-feet / 4297-meters re Voynick. Lake and stream water available; should be filtered or treated.

Camp Canada: 16,000-feet / 4877-meters (common estimate.) Stream (sometimes frozen) located 70 meters north of site.

Camp Alaska aka Nido Inferior: 17,000-feet / 5181-meters (common estimate.) No water.

Nido de Condores: 17,500-feet / 5334-meters (common estimate); 17,700-feet / 5395-meters re Voynick. Pond water unreliable and usually frozen.

Camp Berlin {aka Plantamura}: 19,100-feet / 5821-meters (common estimate); 19,300-feet / 5882-meters re Voynick; 19,522-feet / 5950-meters re Wala. Melt ice or snow.

White Rocks: 19,700-feet / 6004-meters (common estimate.) Melt ice or snow.

Camp Independencia: 21,320-feet / 6,500-meters re Parra; 21,477-feet / 6546-meters re Wala. Melt ice or snow.

Summit peaks: Discrepancies still exist as to the actual height of Aconcagua. Estimations of the north summit peak range from the generally accepted 22,834-feet / 6959-meters (Polish cartographer Jerzy Wala) to 23,036-feet / 7021-meters (based on a recent Argentine survey.)
  A team of Italian scientists, supported by the Argentine Institute of Glaciology and Nivology, made a new measurement of Aconcagua in February of 1989. Employing a Global Positioning System, which utilizes satellites and portable receivers, the surveyors determined a height of 22,841-feet or 6,962 meters.
  The south summit peak is about 200-feet, or 60-meters, lower.

one meter = 3.281 feet

Training & Conditioning:
     (excerpts from the summiteers)

_____

Trevor Byles (age 20*): "Prior to the trip I really wasn't conscientious at all about getting to a certain level in my training. I'd dislocated my shoulder four months before the trip, went through rehabilitation for that, then ran almost every day up until the time we left. I would jog down dirt roads and over cow fields for forty-five minutes to an hour, or until I was tired.

I also did a lot of bicycling on a Wind Trainer. I didn't train with a loaded-up pack. I figured I could carry a forty-pound pack on Aconcagua.

Neil Delehey (age 21): "For training I alternated running eight miles every other day, then two-hundred push-ups with a pack on every other day."

Dick Gordon (age 32): "My conditioning for the climb was more mental than physical. I knew altitude would effect me more than fatigue. I had read a couple medical books on high-altitude ailments and associated lack-of-oxygen symptoms. I was mainly concerned with getting my mind and body prepared for the internal problems which were going to occur. I was interested in determining what caused some of these high-altitude ailments, and wanted some insight so that these ailments would not be a surprise. I interviewed some doctors who had high-altitude experience. These doctors said there was no physical conditioning to prepare for high-altitude. You could have incredible endurance; you could have great stamina; you could be a clean, efficient hiker—all these qualities will help against fatigue. But when it comes to altitude, there has been no evidence that physical strength helps. Everybody will be effected by altitude, some harder than others.

I talked about drugs with these doctors but we decided it would be best not to get into them, although some of these drugs perhaps provide an advantage."

Craig Roland (age 54): "I've been doing a fair amount of running for the last twenty years of my life and have run a lot of marathons; one a year, some of them in pretty good times. To get back up to that condition, between marathons, was getting tougher and tougher every year. I have simply maintained a pace of running and other kinds of exercise like swimming for years, and have never let myself get in poor condition.

For Aconcagua I began running on hills and worked out on the stairs at the local stadium; two stairs at a time in sets of thirty, forty and fifty. This helped supplement my uphill muscles."

* Ages at time of expedition.

Day to Day Schedule Comparison

	Suggested itinerary as stated in the pre-departure company brochure.	**Actual itinerary of Stone Sentinel expedition.**
FEB. 16-17:	Leave the U.S. and arrive in Mendoza.	Same.
FEB. 18:	Drive to Puente del Inca.	Same
FEB. 19:	Rest day at Puente del Inca.	Trek to Confluencia.
FEB. 20:	Trek to Confluencia.	Trek to Plaza de Mules base camp.
FEB. 21:	Trek to Plaza de Mules base camp.	Rest day at base camp. (Taplin evacuated.)
FEB. 22:	Rest day at base camp.	Rest day at base camp.
FEB. 23:	First carry to camp Canada. {17,000-feet.}	First carry to Nido de Condores {17,700-feet.} Return to Mulas base camp. (Stasiak evacuated to base camp.)
FEB. 24:	Rest day at base camp.	Rest day at base camp.
FEB. 25:	Second carry to camp Canada.	Second carry to Nido de Condores. (Milford to base camp.)
FEB. 26:	Rest day at camp Canada	Rest day at Nido. (Milford and Stasiak leave expedition.)
FEB. 27:	Ascend to Nido de Condores. {17,700-feet.}	Ascend to White Rocks. {19,700-feet.}
FEB. 28:	Rest day at Nido de Condores.	Summit attempt. (Dr. Patel evacuated to base camp.)
MARCH 1:	Ascend to camp Berlin. {19,300-feet}	Dr. Patel & Gould's to Confluencia. Remainder of expedition descend to base camp.
MARCH 2:	Summit attempt.	Expedition gathers at Puente del Inca.
MARCH 3:	Second summit attempt (weather permitting.)	
MARCH 4 & 5:	Descend to base camp & Puente del Inca.	

The solo mountaineer, psyched from months of pre-trip training and meticulous logistical preparation, will probably still want to spend more than one afternoon in scenic Mendoza. Take a leisurely day to buy a bus ticket, reserve a room at the hosteria Puente del Inca and secure a climbing permit. Visit the Club Andinista Mendoza and shop for any additional, non-perishable food stuffs. (Items such as fruit, bread and cheese are available on a limited basis at Puente del Inca.) Enjoy Mendoza's restaurants and marvelous cafe scene. Don't complicate your jet lag by racing around and stressing yourself out. Aconcagua will still be there, waiting for you.

One problem with both schedules on the previous page is that they do not allow enough days at Puente del Inca. Spending 3 nights and 2 full days at Puente (allow a half-day travelling by bus from Mendoza) is just as important as the rest days you will need higher on the mountain. Arrange mule transport to base camp through an outfitter such as Rudi Parra in Mendoza, Fernando Grajales in Puente, or Ricarrdo Jabid, who is based back down the road at the Los Penitentes ski area. You can try negotiating for mules and drivers (arrieros), but most prices are fixed. In 1991 Grajales was charging $20 per day per mule and $20 per day per arriero, allowing 5 days total or $200: 2 days to base camp, 1 day out; 1 day going back up to base camp to fetch your gear, 1 day out, returning to Puente. (If you do hook up with another party, remember the mules carry no more than 250 lbs. each.)

Take some time at Puente and go on two or three day-hikes. Visit the climber's cemetery and definitely take a lunch to Horcones Lake. The sight of Aconcagua up-valley should help to put into perspective any cocky residue left over from that boisterous scene in the hosteria bar the evening before.

The hike from Puente to the various camp sites located near Confluencia is an easy half-day. Don't get started too late; score a decent site, enjoy the sunset and have a leisurely dinner. Spare the vegetation and fire up your stove. Smell the flowers—it's your last chance. If you are planning to spend an extra day at Confluencia in order to take an excursion to the South Face, don't cross the foot-bridge in the canyon; stay on the east side and find a site closer to the Inferior Horcones Valley. Stash your gear and food before leaving on any excursions.

Try to get an early start for the hike to Plaza de Mulas base camp; the early morning light is magical and the streams more easily negotiable. Pace yourself and look around. The Horcones Valley is full of subtle textural surprises. A good place for lunch is past the bend, at the end of the river bed. Base camp from here is 3 hours.

Plaza de Mulas is obviously the best place to get up-to-date information, either from other climbers or the rangers, regarding conditions higher on the mountain. The bigger commercial companies, such as Aconcagua Trek, have radios and walkie-talkies, enabling them to communicate both with CB operators in Puente and with their guides up at the high camps. Don't be fooled by the weather: You might be sunbathing at Mulas while a blizzard rages up top. Conversely, just because a storm has cycled through doesn't mean a window of opportunity for the next four or five days. The weather is unpredictable, though it does have weird patterns. Ascertain if storms have pinned other people down at the high camps. If so, those camps will be crowded and good sites will be hard to find.

Spend 3 nights / 2 days at Mulas. You'll need the time to organize for carries, and you will want to take an excursion out onto the glacier. Don't miss seeing the ice pinnacles up close. Mulas is a rollicking international scene. You'll meet lots of new friends, most of whom will be scrounging for food and gear. Befriend one of the commercial company base camp managers and arrange to stash your extra equipment and food stuffs with them, in one of their big tents, in order to have enough supplies coming off the mountain. It will be more secure. Lock and ID all bags or containers.

A collapsible five-gallon water container comes in very handy at base camp because the good water sources are 15-20 minutes away. Be on the safe side: boil or filter all water.

Pack a lunch, take one carry to camp Canada, hide your cache under some rocks, then return to Mulas. Make a second carry the next day and spend the night at Canada. Do a carry to Nido de Condores the day after, then return to Canada. Move everything up to Nido the next day in a second carry. Spend two nights at Nido and take a rest day.

With this schedule you've just taken four days to move all necessary gear and food 3,500 vertical feet. Why? Simple: Acclimatization = oxygenation. And oxygenation is ensured by slow ascent. Four carries helps avoid strenuous exercise and enables your body to adapt. In the course of these four carries, you will hopefully find a hiking rhythm, as well as uncover any acclimatization problems. If acclimating is a concern, try spending an extra rest day at base camp after the first carry to Canada. Obviously, if at any time symptoms of acute altitude sickness persist, descend immediately.

After a full rest day at Nido de Condores, assess your health and state of mind. Hide a small stash of emergency rations at Nido, then move all remaining food and gear stuffs up to Berlin in one carry. (Score a clean site a short distance above the refugios.)

Time permitting, allow for a rest day at Berlin, as well as an extra day for a second summit attempt. Many people shortchange themselves at the high camps by not bringing enough food to wait out storms. The worst cast scenario is that you are either forced to attempt the summit in a weak state or have to descend all the way back to base camp in order to resupply.

Stoke up your body with a big dinner and breakfast before your summit attempt. The earlier the start the better. Allow enough time to melt water. Don't underestimate the amount of fluid intake you will need during the day: 2 quarts minimum. It's always a good idea to take bivouac gear on your summit attempt—not necessarily a sleeping bag but at least a bivy sack. That, combined with a down parka, pile pants and other additional under-layers will improve your odds of survival.

Aconcagua is known for its extremely erratic and harsh conditions. Having the best food and gear will certainly make a difference—but make no mistake: your ability to survive will depend less on state-of-the-art technology than on psychological preparedness.

Keep your bearings by familiarizing yourself with various points of reference; if you do get caught in nasty weather, which direction you go will determine whether you live or die. One woman, caught in the vicious storms which plagued the early part of the '89-'90 season, survived a four-day bivouac at Independencia.

As you have read, the Canaleta will exact the highest physical and emotional toll. Once past that barrier, you are more or less home free. Allow 2-3 hours for descent from the summit.

If the summit is not within reach by 5 or 6 PM, think long and hard about continuing. Will you be caught in the darkness or in a whiteout. Both? Did you even remember to bring your headlamp and snow goggles? Assess whether descending, resting for a day at Berlin, then trying again is a viable option. It may not be. If so, you can always come back next year.

Glossary

Acantilado	Cliff.
Acclimatization	The gradual, physiological process of adapting to the thin air encountered at high altitude.
Altiplano	High plateau.
Altura	Altitude.
Andinista	Mountaineer.
Arriero	Mule driver.
Belay	Protective measure by which a climber is attached by rope to a stationary member of the team, who in turn is securely anchored to the rock, ice or snow.
Bivouac	Any temporary shelter or encampment (without the benefit of a tent.) Usually forced by storm or darkness.
Botas	Climbing boots.
Buttress	Section of a mountain, a cliff or rock-band, separate from the main body.
Carabiner	Oval snaplink with a spring-loaded gate. Used to attach or connect components of climbing gear, such as rope to anchors.
Carpa	Tent.
Cirque	Bowl at the head of a valley, carved out by erosion and bounded by steep walls.
Col	A pass, or depression in a ridge.
Cordillera	Mountain range.
Couloir	Gully.
Crampons	Metal frames with protruding spikes used, when attached to boots, for walking on steep, hard snow, or for ice-climbing.
Cuerda	Rope.
Cuerno	Horn.
Cumbre	Summit.
Escalar	Climbing.
Este	East.
Frio	Cold.
Harness	Waist or chest belt made of synthetic webbing onto which equipment and rope is attached.
Hielo	Ice or frost.
Hypoxia	Oxygen starvation.
Ice-axe	Metal shaft with an adze (blade) and pick tool on the head. Used as an anchor, to cut steps, and to arrest falls.
Ice-cap	Thick layer of ice sloping at the edges.
Lago	Lake (also Laguna.)
Manso	Meek, gentle, or tame.
Mapa	Map.

Glossary (cont.)

Moraine	Rock debris on glaciers.
Morena	Moraine.
Moulin	Glacial channel or gorge formed by meltwater.
Mula	Mule.
Nieve	Snow.
Nieve Penitentes	Snow pinnacles.
Norte	North.
Oeste	West.
Piolet	Ice axe.
Puente	Bridge.
Quebrada	Ravine.
Rappel	Means by which climbers use a rope to control their descent on snow, rock or ice.
Refugio	Climbers' hut.
Río	River.
Roca	Rock.
Ruta	Route.
Sendero	Trail.
Serac	Large ice walls or towers on glaciers.
Soroche	Altitude Sickness.
Sur	South.
Valle	Valley.
Vivac	Bivouac.

Notable attempts, ascents & descents on Aconcagua

Year	Route	Expedition Leader	Summit Team	Date of Ascent	Location of Camps	Misc. Information
1883	Northwest Ridge	Paul Güssfeldt	--	Feb. 20-21	Peritente Valley I - 3581 meters (11,750 feet)	Güssfeldt, a geology professor from the University of Ber.in, makes the first generally accepted European attempt from Chile. Tentless and accompanied by one arriero, Güssfeld climbed through the night, but was repulsed by storms 400 meters below the summit.
1897	Normal	E. A. FitzGerald	Matthias Zurbriggen	14-Jan	I - 14,000 feet II - 16,000 feet III - 17,000 feet IV - 18,700 feet	FitzGerald's team initially explored an approach from the Rio Vacas Valley before crossing over to the Horcones. The 'first' ascent, accomplished only after several abortive attempts, was made by the Swiss guide, Zurbriggen, alone. FitzGerald reached a high point of 6800-meters before being turned back by altitude sickness.
1897	Northwest Ridge	Emil & Robert Conrad	--	18-Jan	--	This German-Chilean group (the summit party included G. Brant and the miner Albino) abandoned their attempt on Güssfeldt's route at 6500 meters due to bad weather.
1897	Normal	E. A. FitzGerald	Nicola Lanti Stuart Vines	13-Feb	--	Second ascent made by the other members of FitzGerald's expedition. Lanti, a porter, was a miner from Italy. Vines was FitzGerald's climbing partner and a trained surveyor.

Year	Route	Expedition Leader	Summit Team	Date of Ascent	Location of Camps	Misc. Information
1898	Normal	Martin Conway	Martin Conway Antoine Maquignaz Luigi Pellissuer	7-Dec	--	This team actually stopped 100-meters below the top so as not to harm the prestige of FitzGerald's book, The Highest Andes, which had not yet been published (Conway, explaining later, that he had accomplished in a week what had taken FitzGerald's party nearly two months.)
1906	Normal	Robert Hebling Frederick Reichert	Robert Hebling	31-Jan	--	(Swiss) The third ascent.
1915	Normal	Eilert Sundt (Norwegian)	T. Bache O. L. Holm E. Sundt	28-Sep	--	First winter attempt of the normal route. Team abandoned skis in the Horcones valley due to lack of snow, but was blocked a few meters from the summit by an impassable snow cornice.
1925	Normal	(British)	J. Cochrane C.W.R. MacDonald M.F. Ryan	14-Feb	--	Fourth ascent by the normal route. This British team managed to get their mules to a high camp of 19,000-feet.
1926	Normal	--	Miguel Gossler Juan Stepanek	--	--	Death of Stepanek marks the first fatality. (His remains would not be recovered for twenty years.)
1928	Normal	--	Edward de la Motte J. Ramsey Ullman	5-Mar	--	First ascent by an American (Ullman, the noted writer) and the fifth ascent, overall, on the normal route.

Year	Route	Expedition Leader	Summit Team	Date of Ascent	Location of Camps	Misc. Information
1928	Normal	Captain B. Marden	--	July	Upper Horcones	Despite unsuitable weather, Marden left Puente del Inca on a solo winter attempt. His body was found at 4000-meters the following December. Marden was the second fatality, probably the victim of an avalanche.
1932	Normal	(German)	Philip Borchers / Mass / E. Schneider	4-Nov	5500 meters (high camp)	The sixth ascent by the normal route, although possibly the first expedition to have their Argentine porters go on strike.
1934	Polish Glacier	Konstanty Narkievicz-Jodko (Polish)	Stefan Daszynski / K. Narkievicz-Jodko / Stefan Osiecki / Wiktor Ostroski	8-Mar	I - 5500 meters / II - 5900 meters / III - 6350 meters / IV - 6800 meters	This team established the standard route from the east. A 37 kilometer hike from Punta de Vacas brings one to Plaza Argentina and the Los Relinchos (or Ameghino) Glacier. The left ridge accesses the Polish Glacier, and leads to the summit.
1934	Normal	(Italy)	Esteban Ceresa / Pablo Ceresa / Renato Chabod / Piero Ghiglione / Mario Pasten / Nicola Plantamura	8-Mar	I - 4200 meters / II - 5750 meters / III - 6500 meters	Plantamura becomes the first Argentine to climb Aconcagua. The summit party took along two dogs, establishing a canine altitude record. (The eighth ascent overall.)

Year	Route	Expedition Leader	Summit Team	Date of Ascent	Location of Camps	Misc. Information
1935	Normal	--	Carlos Anselmi Mario Pasten Federico Strasser	1-Mar	--	Ninth ascent of the normal route.
1936	Normal	--	--	--	--	Newell Bert dies of exposure, becoming the first victim from the United States.
1940	Normal	--	Etura Pablo Frank Adriana Bance Link J.J. Link Lopez Semper	7-Mar	--	One member of this expedition, J. Kastelic (a priest) died, becoming the mountain's seventh victim. Adriana Link is first woman to make an ascent of Aconcagua. (She would perish in another attempt on the mountain in 1944.)
1942	Normal	(Argentina)	Carlos Grasetti Emiliano Huerta Roberto Páez	11-Mar	I - 5900 meters II - 6400 meters III - 6700 meters	First all-Argentine ascent. Expedition composed of military personnel.
1943	--	(Chile)	--	Feb	--	Chilean scientific expedition.
1944	Normal	(Chile)	Alejandro Fergadiott	12-Jan	I - 6850 meters	First Chilean ascent. Fergadiott reached the north summit in 25 hours, 30 minutes from Plaza de Mulas.

Appendix E : Historical Data — page 222

Year	Route	Expedition Leader	Summit Team	Date of Ascent	Location of Camps	Misc. Information
1947	Normal	--	Thomas Kopp Lothar Herold	7-Jan	--	Kopp and Herold celebrate the fiftieth anniversary of Zurbriggen's 'first' ascent by making the first ascent of the south summit. Carcass of guanaco is found below ridge connecting the north and south summits, hence the name Guanaco Ridge. Ironically, this find leads to speculation that the guanaco was carried up, for sacrafice by the Incas.
1947	Normal	--	José Colli Maria Canals Frau	11-Feb	--	Frau becomes the third female (the first of Spanish nationality) to reach the north summit. She fell and died on the descent. Her teammate, Juan Maas, died in the Canaleta before reaching the summit.
1949	Normal	--	Victor Bringa Samuel Esteban Lucas Serrano Manuel Svars Jose Mirelis	15-Jan	--	Team left a statuette of General San Martin on the summit.
1951	Northwest Ridge	--	W. Foerster L. Krahl E. Maier	--	--	First complete ascent from the north, following Güssfeldt's route of 1883. (This route joins the normal route below Camp Berlin.)
1952	Normal	--	--	--	--	Two priests carried up a statue of Our Lady of Carmel and placed it on the summit.

Year	Route	Expedition Leader	Summit Team	Date of Ascent	Location of Camps	Misc. Information
1952	Normal	--	Juan Córdoba Federico Siegrist	14-Jan	--	Second ascent of the south summit.
1953	Southwest Ridge	Frédéric Marmillod	Fernando Grajales Francisco Ibáñez Doris Marmillod Frédéric Marmillod	23-Jan	I - 5300 meters II - 5700 meters III - 6400 meters	A slab route accessing the south ridge by traverses and gullies from the west side. Also called the Ibáñez-Marmillod route (possibly the longest on Aconcagua.) This was the third ascent of the south summit, and the first by a female. It was Ibáñez's sixth ascent overall. The team was unable to complete a traverse to the north summit. Variations of this route attained in 1979 & 1982.
1953	Normal	--	F.A. Godoy Emiliano Huerta H. Vasalla	15-Aug	--	First winter ascent of the normal route (see 1915.)
1954	South Face	René Ferlet (French)	Lucien Bernardini Adrein Dagory Edmond Denis Pierre Lasueur Guy Poulet	25-Feb	I - 4900 meters II - 5800 meters III - 6400 meters IV - 6700 meters	This team established the French Route by ascending the 10,000-foot central spur, an awesome feat which took a month to complete. All but one climber suffered severe frostbite. Still considered one the most challenging and hazardous climbs in the Andes.
1965	South Face	(Argentina)	--	--	--	Argentine expedition which abandoned attempt on South Face due to heavy snowfall.

Appendix E : Historical Data — page 224

Year	Route	Expedition Leader	Summit Team	Date of Ascent	Location of Camps	Misc. Information
1965	West Ridge	Gene Mason (American)	Ralph Mackey Gene Mason Richard Hill	January	5181 meters (high camp)	A direct route from Mulas base camp through much rotton rock, connecting with the normal route at 5800-meters. (Six days climbing overall.) Variant achieved by Alessio and Rodriquez in 1988.
1966	South Face	Willy Noll	Jorge Aikes Omar Pellegrini	2-Feb	I - 4800 meters II - 5400 meters III - 6000 meters IV - 6400 meters	Also known as the Argentina or Pasic Route. An easier, but longer traverse of the whole South Face from right to left.
1966	South Face	Fritz Moravec	José Luis Fonrouge Hans Schönberger	9-Feb	I - 6290 meters II - 6400 meters III - 5800 meters	A central-South Face route ascending the couloir to the right of the French spur. Very hazardous rock and icefall.
1968	Normal	(Japan)	Naomi Uemura	5-Feb	4300 meters (base camp)	Uemura first had to climb Mt. Plata in order to prove his mountaineering abilities to doubting officials. Permit in hand, Uemura acclimated at Mulas base camp for 4-5 days, then hiked to the summit in 15 hours, 15 minutes. (He slept briefly on the way up at the Berlin hut at 5800 meters.) After his descent, Uemura reported to Army officials, who felt such a fast time to be impossible. Uemura angrily blurted out, "If you don't believe me ask the climbers without permits." This resulted in the arrest of one group of unauthorized climbers. Uemura felt terrible, writing later that the incident took away the joy of his feat.

Year	Route	Expedition Leader	Summit Team	Date of Ascent	Location of Camps	Misc. Information
1974	South Face	Reinhold Messner	Reinhold Messner	23-Jan	I - 5200 meters II - 6000 meters	This direttissima variant (it has a different beginning and ending) is considered safer and faster than the French route. Also known as the South Tyrolean or Messner Direct route.
1978	East Face	Guillermo Vieiro	Jorge Jasson Edgar Porcellana Guillermo Vieiro	27-Jan	Six camps	First direct climb of the East Glacier, joining the Polish Glacier route below the summit.
1979	South Face	--	Xabier Erro Juan Hugas Martin Zabaleta	2-Jan	--	First repeat of the established French route. Also first traverse between north and south summits.
1980	South Face	Edward Connor	Guy Andrews Chuck Bludworth Edward Connor	6-Jan	I - 4660 meters II - 5180 meters III - 6250 meters (all bivouacs)	First alpine-style ascent of the French route. Andrews and Bludworth disappeared near the summit after the team was pinned down in a storm for two days. Connor retreated down the normal route.
1980	South Face	--	Brian Berg Mike French Hugh Grandfield	14-Mar	--	First alpine-styled ascent of Messner's route. Grandfield sustained a fatal fall at 6800-meters during a change of lead.
1981	South Face	(Japan)	Hironobu Kamuro Masayoshi Yamamoto	29-Jan	I - 5200 meters II - 6100 meters	Japanese variant, which exits by the right wall of the French Spur.

Year	Route	Expedition Leader	Summit Team	Date of Ascent	Location of Camps	Misc. Information
1981	Polish Glacier	--	Roger Marshall Patrick Morrow Dave Read Gordon Smith	9-Feb	I - 5029 meters II - 5791 meters III - 6218 meters	Morrow's second of his "seven summits." (see Bass & Wells, 1983)
1982	--	(French)	--	3-Feb	--	Hang glider descents from the north summit by Jean-Marc Boivin and Dominique Marchal.
1982	South Face	--	Zlatko Ganter Pavel Podgornik Peter Podgornik Ivan Rejc	--	--	A demanding route established by the Slovenes, ascending the entire south spur of the South Face.
1982	South Face	Tsuneo Hasegawa	Tsuneo Hasegawa	17-Aug	3 camps, 2 bivouacs	First winter ascent of the South Face. Combination of French route and Messner variant.
1983	Normal	--	Dick Bass Yvon Chouinard Steve Marts Gary Neptune Rick Ridgeway Frank Welles	--	I - 4870 meters II - 5330 meters III - 5820 meters	Bass and Wells' first summit as a team on their "Seven Summits" venture. (Bass had previously climbed Aconcagua in 1981 via the Polish Glacier.)

Year	Route	Expedition Leader	Summit Team	Date of Ascent	Location of Camps	Misc. Information
1983	Normal	J. Meza (Chile)	M. Campos J. Meza R. Monsalves L. Rojas N. Worth	8-Feb	--	First all-woman ascent of the normal route. (Team comprised entirely of Chilean mountaineers.)
1983	Polish Glacier	Ema Osorio (Chile)	Claudia Bastres Ivette Carrera Karen Eitel Gabriela Maass Ema Osorio Elizabeth Rencoret Patricia Sepúlveda	17-Feb	--	First all-woman ascent of the Polish Glacier route. (Team comprised entirely of Chilean mountaineers.)
1983	--	--	--	23-Apr	--	The Mendoza state legislature creates the Parque Provincial Aconcagua.
1985	South Face	(French)	Jean Paul Chassagne Pierre Raveneau	--	--	The French Direct of the South Face, connecting the south spur with the Argentine (Pasic) route.
1985	Southwest Ridge	--	--	January	5181 meters (high camp)	Climbers discover Inca archaeological site (and 500-year old mummy) at 5300 meters.
1985	South Face	--	John Bouchard Titoune Bouchard	January	--	First female ascent of the South Face. (French route, using the Messner finish.)

Appendix E : Historical Data — page 228

Year	Route	Expedition Leader	Summit Team	Date of Ascent	Location of Camps	Misc. Information
1985	--	(French)	Alain Estéve	10-Jan	--	First parapente descent from the north summit.
1985	Normal	Ron Garrett	--	14-Feb	I - 4870 meters II - 5340 meters III - 5820 meters	Richard Garrett, 14 years old, becomes youngest person to reach summit by the normal route. (2 acclimation nights at each camp.)
1985	Normal	(Chile)	Gastón Oyarzún J. Rivera	21-Sep	5340 meters (high camp)	First Chilean winter ascent of the Normal route. Team used skis from 3200 meters to 6800 meters (the base of the Canaleta.)
1985	Normal	(French)	Yves Astier	24-Nov	--	Speed ascent of the normal route (base camp to the north summit) in seven hours. The previous day Astier, and teammate Eric Soulié, made a ski descent of the normal route after a failed attempt to ski down the Polish Glacier.
1986	--	--	Gabriel Cabrera	Feb. 17-27	--	Gabrera, a Mendoza guide, traverses Aconcagua by climbing the southwest ridge (the Piramidal buttress), south summit ridge and north summit. He descended via the Polish Glacier, then traversed around the northwest side of the mountain, back to Puente del Inca.

Year	Route	Expedition Leader	Summit Team	Date of Ascent	Location of Camps	Misc. Information
1986	Normal	--	--	--	--	Clean-up operation, from Confluencia to the summit, by members of the Club Universitario de Andinismo, Mendoza. Imposition of permit fees for future removal of rubbish.
1989	South Face	--	Carolina Coda Haracio Coda	1-Feb	(5 days)	Carolina Coda becomes first Argentine woman to climb the Messner route.
1991	Normal	--	--	January	--	Pan American Ecological Expedition (140 volunteers), sponsored by the Unión Panamericana de Asociaciones de Montaña.
1991	Normal	--	--	3-Jan	--	Fourteen year-old Nerea Ariz becomes the youngest female to climb Aconcagua, matching the male record set by Richard Garret (see 1985.)

1983-1984 Season :
- 92 expeditions registered : 350 climbers (90% foreigners; mostly Americans, Japanese, Italians, Germans, French & British.)

1984-1985 Season :
- 600 climbers (60% Normal route.)

1988-1989 Season :
- 211 expeditions registered : 52 from the United States, 33 from Argentina, 21 from Germany, 20 from Spain, 16 from France, 11 from Japan. (The remaining expeditions or parties were from other Latin American and European countries.)
- Routes : Normal (159 groups); Polish (41 groups); South Face (9 groups).
- 72 out of 792 climbers were women.

1989-1990 Season :
- 353 expeditions registered : 81 from Argentina, 77 from the United States, 39 from Germany, 30 from Spain, 24 from Japan, 23 from France, 11 from Switzerland. (Remaining parties from Brazil, Bulgaria, Canada, Chile, Italy and Mexico.)
- Routes : Normal (255 groups); Polish (69 groups); South Face (16 groups).
- 121 out of 1244 climbers were women.

"Notable Attempts, Ascents & Descents on Aconcagua"
Sources : Alpine Journal (London); American Alpine Journal (New York); Servei General d'Informació de Muntanya (Barcelona); Luis Alberto Parra (Club Andinista Mendoza); Mario Fantin (Club Alpino Italiano-Bologna Section); Evelio Echevarría; Ugarte, Punzi and de Biasey (Historia del Aconcagua, Chronologia Heroica del Ardinismo.)

Further Reading & Map Sources

Books :

Bass, D. and Wells, F. with Ridgeway, R., *Seven Summits*, Warner Books, New York, 1986.
  Bass and Wells' quest to be the first to stand atop the highest peaks of each continent. Two chapters deal with Aconcagua. Very generalized accounts of both the Normal and Polish Glacier routes.

Bernbaum, E., *Sacred Mountains of the World*, Sierra Club Books, San Francisco, 1990.
  A fascinating and authoritative study on the historical, mythological, and religious significance of many sacred peaks. Excellent section on the Andes and Inca archaeological sites.

Cameron, I., *Kingdom of the Sun God*, Century, London, 1990.
  Geological and cultural study of the Andes and its people. Good chapter on mountaineering, a portion of which details FitzGerald's expedition to Aconcagua and Zurbriggen's ascent, utilizing verbatim passages from *The Highest Andes* (see below.)

Clark, R.W., *Men, Myths and Mountains*, Crowell, New York, 1976.
  Interesting overview of mountaineering history, from 1492 onward. Brief section on Aconcagua. Photographs of FitzGerald and Zurbriggen.

FitzGerald, E.A., *The Highest Andes*, Scribner & Sons, New York, 1899.
  While FitzGerald sometimes writes in grandiose, patronizing flourishes, his tone is rarely dispassionate. One genuinely sympathizes with his failure to acclimate and complete the first ascent with Zurbriggen. On the other hand, one does wish that FitzGerald had acknowledged his inability to be effective as a climbing leader, and that he, in some modest capacity, given more credit to his porters and guides. FitzGerald's attitude toward his teammates, however, reflects a different era, and is indicative of his Edwardian values.
  The expeditions to Aconcagua and Tupungato were as much scientific ventures as mountaineering exploits and, in this sense, it cannot be denied that FitzGerald's efforts contributed greatly to the knowledge of this region in the Andes.

Kerasote, T., *Navigations*, Vintage, Pennsylvania, 1986.
  One chapter deals with Kerasote's ascent of Aconcagua's Normal route. A revealing, personal narrative of a neophyte dealing with high-altitude, complete with childhood flashbacks.

Further Reading & Map Sources (cont.)

Mason, G.W., *Minus Three*, Prentice-Hall, New Jersey, 1970.
Account of Mason's climbs of Aconcagua, McKinley and Kilimanjaro.
Mason's team pioneered a route on Aconcagua's West Ridge in 1965, using
Plaza de Mulas as a base camp.

Newby, E., *Great Ascents*, Viking, New York, 1977.
   Another historical overview of mountaineering. Slightly more in-depth
account of Aconcagua and FitzGerald's expedition than Clark's book.

Post, A. & LaChapelle, E., *Glacier Ice*, Mountaineers & The University of
Washington Press, Seattle, 1971.
   Engaging study of all aspects of glaciology, utilizing superb aerial
photography.

Wilkerson, J.A., *Medicine For Mountaineering*, Mountaineers, Seattle, 1985.
   Consult this very valuable book for a more through understanding of
mountain sickness, edema, and Diamox. Also recommended is *Everest, The
Testing Place* by John B. West, M.D.

Zurbriggen, M., *From the Alps to the Andes: The Autobiography of a Mountain
Guide*, T. Fisher Unwin, London, 1899.
   This text, dealing mostly with Zurbriggen's early years, suffers from a
lackluster writing style and poor translation. The chapter dealing with his
first ascent of Aconcagua is, for the most part, frustratingly uninformative.
Only valuable, perhaps, if one compares Zurbriggen's perceptions of certain
events with those of his 'patron', FitzGerald.

Periodicals :

Martin Conway's eulogy to FitzGerald appears in the "In Memoriam" section of
the Alpine Journal, London, 1931.

Aconcagua's Normal Route, by Dan Leeth. Summit, July-August, 1985, pp. 2-7.

Magazine Articles :

Getting High On Aconcagua, by Stephen M. Voynick. v 40. Americas,
January-February, 1988, p. 20.

Pushing the Mid-life Envelope, by William Broyles, Jr. v 107. Esquire, June,
1987, p. 72.

Further Reading & Map Sources (cont.)

Mountain Sickness, by Charles S. Houston. Scientific American, October, 1992, p. 58.

Guidebooks :

Parra, Luis Alberto, *Practical Guide and Routes of Ascension to Mount Aconcagua*. (2ed Edition.)
        Contact :   Rudy Parra
                      Guiraldes 246
                      5519 Dorrego
                      Mendoza
                      Republica Argentina
                      phone : 54-61-242003
                      fax : 54-61-380321

Climbing History :

Historia del Aconcagua, Chronologia Heroica del Andinismo, Ugarte, Punzi and de Biasey. (In Spanish.) Buenos Aires, 1953.

Maps :

1:50,000 Aconcagua region. 500-meter contour intervals. A cartographic study (with descriptions of routes) drafted by Jerzy Wala and Xavi Llongueras based on materials from the Polish expeditions of 1934 and 1985, as well as the Servei General d'Informacío de Muntanya in Barcelona. Available from the American Alpine Club, New York City, 212 722-1628.

1:100,000 Aconcagua region. 50-meter intervals. An older but somewhat useful topographic map put out by the IGMA (Instituto Geografico Militar Argentino.)
&
1:50,000 Aconcagua region. 50-meter intervals. A much more pertinent topo-relief map, also put out by the IGMA.
Photocopies of four map sets available from Michael Chessler Books, Kittridge, Colorado, 800 654-8502.

Design, Map & Photography Credits

Cover design by Marika Van Adelsberg.
Jacket photograph of Aconcagua from the Horcones Valley by Tom Taplin.
Inset photograph of author by Prasna Rai.

Frontispiece regional and topographic maps scanned and modified from the 1:50,000 IGMA series.

Insert drawing of South America by Victor Kotowitz.

Photographs
1. Aerial shot of Aconcagua from the southwest. (© Mike Sanson)
2. Chapel, hotel ruins and spa at Puente del Inca. (© Tom Taplin)
3. Hiking to Confluencia. (© Tom Taplin)
4. The second river crossing, below Confluencia. (© Tom Taplin)
5. Lunch break, Expedition Day 1. (© Tom Taplin)
6. Hiking up the Horcones Valley to base camp. (© Tom Taplin)
7. The Horcones Valley—"Dragon of the prime." (© Craig Roland)
8. Mule driver unloading gear at base camp. (© Tom Taplin)
9. Plaza de Mulas base camp. (© Craig Roland)
10. Anil Patel at base camp. (© Tom Taplin)
11. Dick Gordon and ice pinnacles on the Horcones Glacier. (© Craig Roland)
12. Taplin being rescued from the moulin. (© Gregg Lewis)
13. Aconcagua's West Buttress as seen from base camp. (© Tom Taplin)
14. Halfway up the switch-backs leading to Nido. (© Craig Roland)
15. Mike Milford at Nido de Condores. (© Anil Patel)
16. "There was always soup and a ladle full of something." (© Craig Roland)
17. View of the Gran Acarreo and the north summit. (© Bill English)
18. Typical lightshow at Nido following an afternoon storm. (© Tom Taplin)
19. Hikers approaching camp Berlin. (© Bill English)
20. The three refugios at 19,500-feet. (© Tom Taplin)
21. The camp at White Rocks. (© Craig Roland)
22. Telephoto shot of Aconcagua's north summit from Nido. (© Tom Taplin)
23. The traverse at the top of the Gran Acarreo. (© Linda and Dave Bujnicki)
24. Taplin at the refugio Independencia. (© Tom Taplin)
25. "Take your worst nightmare and double it..." (© Linda and Dave Bujnicki)
26. The top of the Canaleta. (© Linda and Dave Bujnicki)
27. Craig Roland & Pépe on the north summit. (© Craig Roland)
28. The Aconcagua region from space. (© NASA)

If your bookstore does not stock our publications, they may be purchased by mail. To obtain information, please phone or fax:
(310) 399-4869

To obtain additional copies of *Aconcagua - The Stone Sentinel*, send a check or money order to:

Eli Ely Publishing
P.O.Box 5245
Santa Monica, California 90409-5245

Perfect bound (Softcover) copies are $17.95
Case bound (Hardcover) copies, with dust jackets, are $29.95

Sales tax:
Please add 6.5% for books shipped to California addresses.

Shipping & Handling:
Book rate: $2.00 for the first book and 75 cents for
each additional book.
(Surface shipping may take three to four weeks.)

Air mail: $3.50 per book.

No Cash or CODs please.